Shuart Farmhouse, artist Peter Curling

LucyAnn Curling

Curling Wisps &
Whispers of History

Vol. 1: Thanet to Tasmania

Ōzaru
Books

Curling Wisps & Whispers of History – Vol. 1: Thanet to Tasmania
by LucyAnn Curling

Published by Ōzaru Books, an imprint of BJ Translations Ltd
Street Acre, St Nicholas-at-Wade, Birchington, CT7 0NG, UK
http://ozaru.net/ozarubooks

This edition published 7 August 2022
ISBN: 978-1-915174-02-4

Contents

Author's note

In material quoted directly from original manuscripts the spellings follow the originals and may vary from current use.

Readers should also note that appendices are numbered according to the chapters they relate to, for example Chapter 6 has two related appendices which are numbered 6a and 6b, but as Chapter 7 has no appendices the appendix numbering sequence goes from 6b to 8a.

List of illustrations

i

Acknowledgements

For about fifteen years, my brother Peter Curling and my two children Ruth and Samuel Palmer have been much more than merely tolerant of my family history obsessions and have supported me in practical ways, for which I am hugely grateful. Peter generously contributed the wonderful front cover painting of Shuart Farmhouse. They, along with friends and fellow researchers, so often heard me say 'I'm writing a book' that they must have thought indulgently 'There's a pipe of dreams that's never going to be smoked.' Even so they have been unstinting in their patience, generosity and reading of the manuscript in its various incarnations. A heartfelt thank you, too, to Tim Albert, who having volunteered as mentor endured my wilfully ignoring his advice with exactly the right amount of dry wit and teasing, which egged me on in the project. You were of course right ultimately, Tim; in the end I had to put the research to one side and 'just write the book'.

Through the kindness of strangers I have stepped over thresholds and stood in the kitchens of ancestral homes, and those strangers have become friends. On the Family History internet networks I have met 'new cousins' and made new friends in corners of the globe remote from me as well as in the UK. Research has led me to cousins not met since childhood, while friends of more than fifty years as well as those met later have often said 'You must write a book.' Without exception these wonderful supporters have variously cheered or gently goaded me to persevere. This book would not be in your hands now if it were not for that chorus.

This series is an account of the lives of three generations of our Curling ancestors, and their friends and families, but it also inevitably reveals some of my sleuthing adventures and lucky breaks. I have used the facilities of over twenty archives, many providing opportunities for awaydays or weekend breaks as well as longer holidays from my residential working environments, visiting archives in England, Ireland, Kefalonia and Malta. I also benefitted via the internet from the expertise of archivists in the Netherlands, Tasmania, mainland Australia and the United States. Archivists are a special breed, with a combination of breathtakingly detailed knowledge and inexhaustible wells of helpfulness.

How fortunate I am too with my publication team. Editor Caroline Petherick, The Wordsmith, and publisher Ben Jones of Ōzaru Books are truly my writing guardian angels! Caroline's lightning-fast turnaround and super-efficient editing puts my own plodding efforts to shame, and I have been flabbergasted by Ben's breadth of knowledge, attention to detail and determination to reach the goal of an end product of the highest possible standards in all areas.

Any errors and omissions which you find are mine, and I would be grateful to know about them.

Archives

Below is a list of archives I have used in researching this book, together with reference abbreviations used in the text. It is not exhaustive. Visiting archives is generally speaking a pleasure: the vast majority of archivists are enthusiastic about the treasures they hold in their own archives, and many about those held elsewhere, too. Often you can get the information you need by emailing them. If you want to view documents you can usually order digital copies, but if you need to make a personal visit to view documents, you are strongly advised to check out the Contact and Visit Us pages of their websites: although larger archives are open to the public during normal business hours the smaller ones are not staffed full time.

BL   **British Library**
(BL Add MS = 'additional manuscript', denoting original handwritten material)
  96 Euston Road, LONDON, NW1 2DB
  +44 330 333 1144   www.bl.uk/about-us/contact-us

BMAG   **Birmingham Museum & Art Gallery**
  Chamberlain Square, BIRMINGHAM, B3 3DH
  +44 121 348 8000   www.birminghammuseums.org.uk/contact

BodL   **Bodleian Libraries**, University of Oxford
  Bodleian Libraries, Broad Street, OXFORD, OX1 3BG
  +44 1865 277162   www.bodleian.ox.ac.uk/about/contact

CLNMM   **Caird Library** (archives of the National Maritime Museum)
  Romney Road, LONDON, SE10 9NF
  +44 20 8312 6516   library@rmg.co.uk
www.rmg.co.uk/research-collections/caird-library

DRO   **Derbyshire Record Office**
  c/o County Hall, MATLOCK, DE4 3AG
  +44 1629 538347   record.office@derbyshire.gov.uk
  http://bit.ly/ArchivesDerbyshireRO

DHC   **Devon Heritage Centre**
  Great Moor House, Bittern Road, EXETER, EX2 7NL
  +44 1392 888700   devonarchives@swheritage.org.uk
  swheritage.org.uk/devon-archives/visit/devon-heritage-centre/

KHLC   **Kent History and Library Centre**
  James Whatman Way, MAIDSTONE, ME14 1LQ
  +44 3000 413131   archives@kent.gov.uk
  www.kentarchives.org.uk/

LBA   **Lloyds Banking Group Archives**. Visits by appointment only.
  archives@lloydsbanking.com
  http://bit.ly/ArchivesLloydsBG

v

LLMF **London Library and Museum of Freemasonry**
Freemasons' Hall, 60 Great Queen Street, LONDON, WC2B 5AZ
+44 20 7395 9257 museumfreemasonry.org.uk/family-history

LPA **The London Picture Library** *(holds images from the London Metropolitan Archives & the Guildhall Art Gallery Picture Library)*
Museum of London, 150 London Wall, LONDON, EC2Y 5HN
picturelib@museumoflondon.org.uk
www.museumoflondonimages.com/

TAHO **Tasmanian Archives and Heritage Office**
91 Murray Street, Hobart, TAS 7000, Australia
+61 1800 808 303 libraries.tas@education.tas.gov.au
https://libraries.tas.gov.au/enterprise-help/Pages/archive-search.aspx

TNA **The National Archives**
Kew, RICHMOND, TW9 4DU
contactcentre@nationalarchives.gov.uk
discovery.nationalarchives.gov.uk/

SLNSW **State Library of New South Wales**
1 Shakespeare Place, Sydney, NSW 2000, Australia
+61 2 9273 1414
www.sl.nsw.gov.au/research-and-collections/ask-librarian

SR **Stadsarchief Rotterdam** (Rotterdam Archives)
Hofdijk 651, 3032 CG Rotterdam, The Netherlands
+31 10 267 5555 stadsarchief.rotterdam.nl/contact/

UCJA University of Cambridge **St John's College Archives**
Visits by appointment only.
+44 1223 338631 archivist@joh.cam.ac.uk
www.joh.cam.ac.uk/archives

UCTHA University of Cambridge **Trinity Hall Archives**.
Trinity Lane, CAMBRIDGE, CB2 1TJ
+44 1223 332500 info@trinhall.ac.uk
www.trinhall.cam.ac.uk/libraries/archives/

WSAA **Worshipful Society of Apothecaries Archives**
Apothecaries' Hall, Black Friars Lane, LONDON, EC4V 6EJ
+44 20 7236 1189 archives@apothecaries.org
www.apothecaries.org/history/our-collection-and-access/

V&A **Victoria and Albert Museum**
Cromwell Road, LONDON, SW7 2RL
+44 20 7942 2000 hello@vam.ac.uk
www.vam.ac.uk/

Dedication

This series of books is dedicated

* to the memory of the three generations of Curling ancestors pictured within, and their kinsman by marriage, and benefactor:
Charles James Napier
with gratitude for the paper trails they left

* to the descendants of the Limerick line of the Curling family:
my father Edward Curling, his sister Kate Curling and her family,
and my brother Peter Michael Napier Curling

* and especially to the generations already treading on our heels:
Peter's children:
Hannah Greer Curling
Samuel Edward Curling
Rebecca Anne Curling
Peter's grandchildren:
Isabella Rose Curling
Evie Theresa Curling
Charlotte Edith Murphy
Esther Juno Murphy
Guy Peter Murphy
My children
Ruth Fiona Palmer
Samuel Palmer
My grandson
Giacomo Raffaello Napier Giannecchini Palmer

* To my Curling cousins, sisters Mary Allanah Revell Morrison Scott
and Siobhán Randall Morrison,
and Allanah's sons Thomas Liam Scott and Michael Peter Scott

* To the descendants of the Curlings of the Isle of Thanet whom I have met in online research:
Carey Bayliss (Australia), Anthony Curling (Ireland), Helen Curling (America), Stephen Curling (UK), Christopher McLeod (formerly Curling, France), Anne Poluzzi Moran (America), Colleen Ada Taylor (Australia), Peter Wilkinson (Australia), and others yet to be discovered.

And last, but absolutely not least,

* To my Family History research collaborator, cousin 7× removed and dear friend Clive Boyce. Together we have worked on the early Curlings:
https://curlingofthanet.wordpress.com/

Introduction

This book reveals the lives of three generations of our[1] branch of the Curling family, whose senior male line members were Thomas Curling I (1756–1819), his son Thomas Oakley Curling (Thomas Curling II) (1782–1825) and grandson Thomas Curling III (1805–1858). Thomas III largely relinquished his interest in the family quite early on, and his next brother Edward (1804–1874) took on the role of the eldest of the remaining eight siblings. Edward was our great-great- (hereafter abbreviated to 2× great) grandfather. To clarify, Fig. 1 gives a slice of the family tree showing the Curlings who belong in this story:

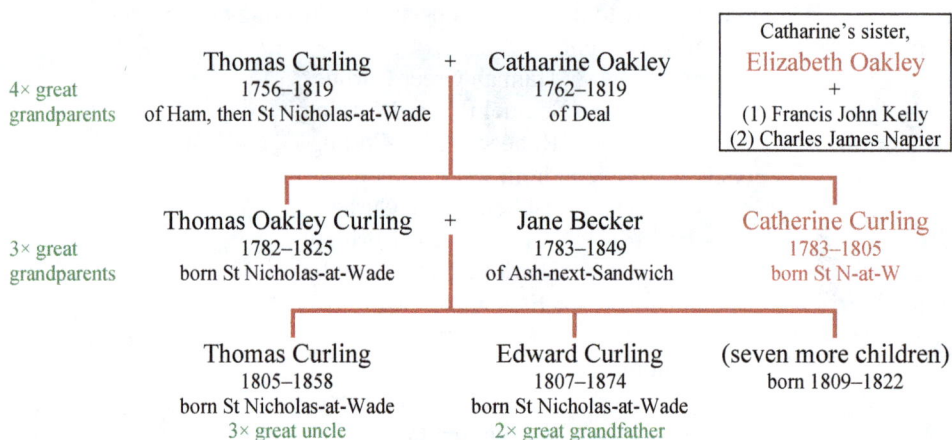

| | | Catharine's sister,
Elizabeth Oakley
+
(1) Francis John Kelly
(2) Charles James Napier |
|---|---|---|

| 4× great grandparents | Thomas Curling
1756–1819
of Ham, then St Nicholas-at-Wade | + | Catharine Oakley
1762–1819
of Deal |
|---|---|---|---|

| 3× great grandparents | Thomas Oakley Curling
1782–1825
born St Nicholas-at-Wade | + | Jane Becker
1783–1849
of Ash-next-Sandwich | Catherine Curling
1783–1805
born St N-at-W |
|---|---|---|---|---|

| Thomas Curling
1805–1858
born St Nicholas-at-Wade
3× great uncle | Edward Curling
1807–1874
born St Nicholas-at-Wade
2× great grandfather | (seven more children)
born 1809–1822 |
|---|---|---|

Fig. 1. **Three generations of Curlings, 1756–1874**

How the research began

Our father had an unusually long string of given names: Edward Raymond Joseph Napier Charles. All these except Joseph are the names of known ancestors, and his friends called him Ted or Teddy. When he was only seven years old his father Charles Edward William Curling died. His mother remarried when he was aged thirteen, and Ted grew up knowing nothing of his paternal history. In his early adulthood he began to wonder about his family, and found his way to Mrs Lucy Dorothy Hedges, whose maiden name was Curling. She was a half-sister of Ted's father. She was known to family and friends as Dodie or Tooty; and to me and my brother Peter Curling she was always Aunty Tooty.

---

[1]   Throughout the work, 'we/us/our' refers to me, the author, Dorothy LucyAnn Curling, and my brother Peter Michael Napier Curling. The abbreviation 'LAC' also refers to me.

1

She was delighted that Ted had found her. Her brother Richbell had died a bachelor, she herself was childless, and her sister Katherine had two daughters but no sons to carry on, as she saw it, the family name. One of the reasons Tooty was so excited to discover Ted was that she had a unique family heirloom to pass on to him.

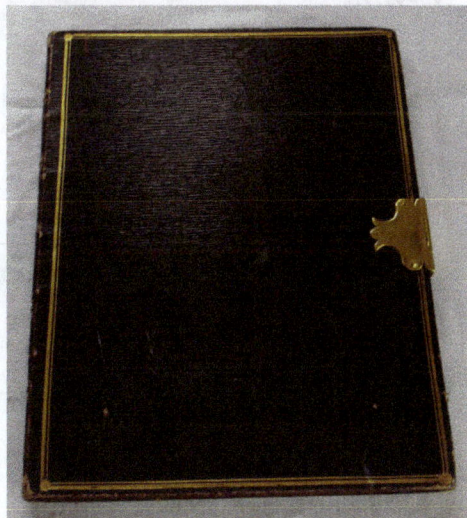

Fig. 2. **The Mildenhall Document, cover**

It was a leather-bound manuscript book, with gold tooling, gilt-edged pages and a gold hasp. I have called this the Mildenhall Document. Ted gave it to me when I was in my early twenties, because he thought that I would be the more likely of his two children to develop an interest in researching the family, but with the ultimate aim of handing it on to my brother Peter Curling and his family.

At the time it did not merit, in my eyes, more than a marginally interested glance; family history research is not generally an occupation of young people.

What was in the Mildenhall Document? It was a record, written in 1848, of the subscribers to a leaving present for our 2× great-grandpa Edward Curling. Its dedication page (Fig. 3) says:

The following List
Contains the Names of
The Inhabitants of Mildenhall
and its Neighbourhood,
Who have raised, by Subscription, the Sum of £165.13.11
for the purpose of presenting
Mr Edward Curling,
Agent to Sir Henry Edward Bunbury Bart.
for 16 years,
With a Testimonial of their Esteem and Regard and of the sense which
is entertained of the Integrity of his private character, as well as of his
numerous valuable, and disinterested exertions, as Guardian of the Parish
and otherwise during so long a period for the benefit of the Public.

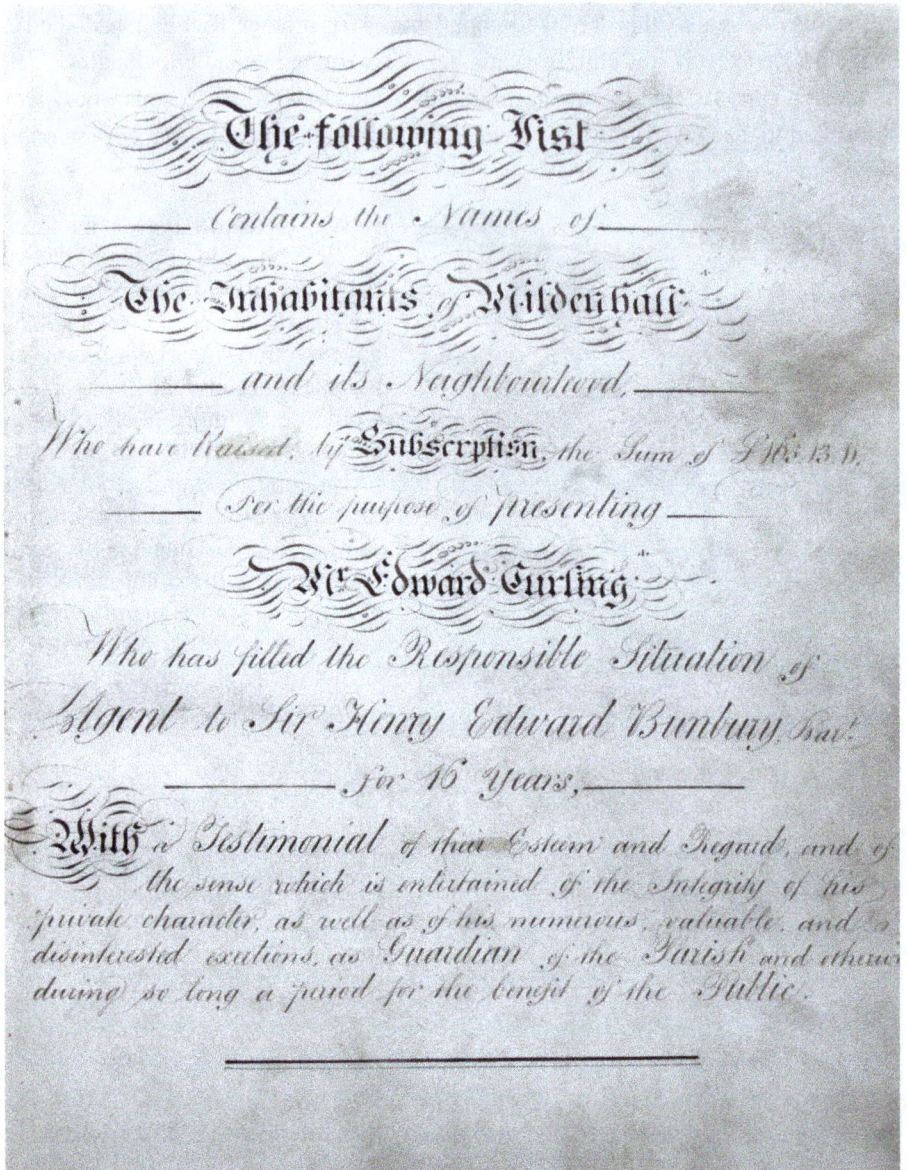

Fig. 3. **The Mildenhall Document, dedication**

Edward was moving from Mildenhall in Suffolk to Newcastle West, County Limerick. He had worked for sixteen years as the land agent to Sir Henry Bunbury on his estates in Mildenhall and Great Barton, and was about to take on a similar role on the Earl of Devon's Irish estate in Newcastle West.

To purchase an appropriate gift from the Mildenhall community, a collection was made, which yielded a total of £165.13.11. Out of this sum £30 was used to buy a gold watch and chain for Edward, and the rest was presented to him as a 'purse'. All the donors and their occupations are named, and the donations range from a single penny from labourers to £5 from 'gentlemen' and professionals such as doctors and lawyers of the district.

At the end of this leather-bound book were several blank pages, and in them one of our ancestors had begun to list family birthdays – real treasure for a novice family historian. But perhaps the most intriguing inscription was on the front flyleaf, in Aunty Tooty's handwriting: see Fig. 4. Below the image there is a transcription:

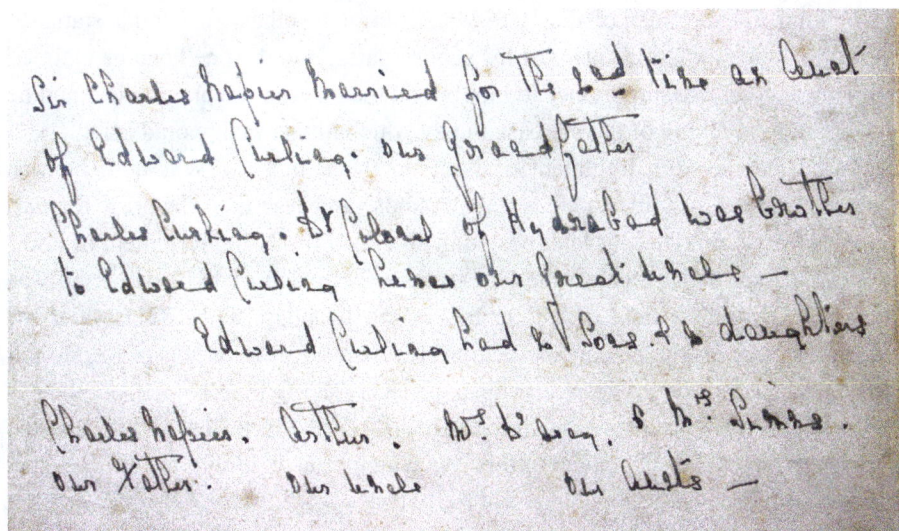

Fig. 4. **The Mildenhall Document, flyleaf**

*Sir Charles Napier married for the 2nd time an Aunt
of Edward Curling, our Grandfather.
Charles Curling, D^t Colonel[2] of Hydrabad was brother
to Edward Curling he was our great uncle –
Edward Curling had 2 sons & 2 daughters*

Charles Napier.	*Arthur.*	*M^{rs} D'Arcy. & Mrs Simms.*
Our Father.	*Our Uncle*	*Our Aunts –*

General Sir Charles James Napier (1782–1853) was one of the most famous and controversial military men of his day, primarily known for his conquest of the

---

[2]   Tooty must have transcribed these details from a note in someone else's handwriting. Her uncle Charles was not a military man but a civil servant in Hyderabad, Sindh, whose job title was deputy collector. The original might have read something like 'D^t Col.'

province of Sindh,[3] then subsumed into northern India, now part of Pakistan. However, Napier did not go to India until he was in his fifty-ninth year. His previous life had been spent in comparative anonymity; his military record remarkable but unnoticed by authority – at least in his own perception, insofar as prompt promotion and medal decorations for services rendered were concerned, something about which he retained a chip on his shoulder for many years, both after the 1809 Battle of A Coruña, when he was not promoted to lieutenant-colonel until 1811, and later, in 1838. At that point, he complained in writing to Sir Fitzroy Somerset that he had had to ask repeatedly for promotion to full colonel and that his ranking in the Order of the Bath was inferior to others of similar status to himself and even inferior to two of his subordinates.[4] On the one hand he claimed that rank was of little importance to him but on the other, more pragmatic, hand he was probably thinking of the increase in pay which higher rank would bring.

He had led the 50th Regiment of Foot[5] in the Peninsular War until he was captured, having sustained five severe wounds, and was then detained for two months at A Coruña; he was later posted in charge of the 102nd Regiment of Foot[6] to Bermuda and from there to the Chesapeake Campaign of 1813–1814; he was appointed inspecting field officer in the Ionian Islands (1819–1821) under Sir Thomas Maitland who then appointed him Resident (local governor) of Kefalonia[7] (1821–1831). After eight years on half-pay (1831–1839), he became Commander of the Northern District in England (1839–1841) at the outset of the Chartist uprising. It was his management of this role which brought him to the notice of his seniors, who decided he should be sent to India.

Discovering the identity of Napier's first wife, our blood relative, took me a couple of years. Aunty Tooty had not given any details, probably because she did not know any more. As a novice genealogist, I was slow to realize that prior to her marriage to Napier, she, as Edward Curling's aunt, need not necessarily have borne the maiden name Curling. To add to the puzzle, it transpired that our 5× great-aunt Elizabeth Oakley was Napier's first wife – not his second, as Tooty had written – and that Napier was her second husband, so at the time of their marriage her

---

3   Spellings of Sindh vary, even in the twenty-first century. The three most common spellings are the Victorian one used by Napier, 'Scinde'; the simple, 'Sind', phonically obvious to Westerners; and the now conventional 'Sindh', which gives a clue to how it is pronounced by its residents.

4   *The Life and Opinions of General Sir Charles James Napier*, William FP Napier, pub. John Murray, London, 1857; vol. 1, pp. 471–473.

5   Later to be renamed the West Kent, then Duke of Clarence's, then Queen's Own.

6   Later to be renamed the 100th, then disbanded after two years.

7   The modern spelling for the island's name is Kefalonia but in Napier's time the spelling was either Cefalonia or Cephalonia. The latter was more common among the British, and is still used by some residents today.

surname was Kelly. Perhaps, for reasons of Victorian decorum, Tooty had not been told that the mother of Napier's two daughters was Anastasia, a Greek rebel known only by her given name, who was his mistress while he was serving in Kefalonia prior to his marriage. He had no further children.

As if the Mildenhall Document were not family history treasure enough, arising from the clues in it a series of lucky breaks led me to follow the fortunes of three Curling generations in ever greater depth. Despite my feeling of an inevitable and constant connection with the women in our story, the material which surfaced initially was on the face of it telling the story from the men's perspective: two sets of Edward Curling's financial accounts for the Earl of Devon's Irish estate (1859 and 1869);[8] letters written by his father about farming issues, and the spine-tingling British Library Napier Papers letters, of which only two were from a female ancestor (3× great-grandma Jane née Becker).

Charles Napier had filed and kept many incoming letters, keeping personal mail separate from his official work correspondence. His descendants gave these personal letter collections to two archives, the British and Bodleian Libraries. There are over eighty letters from the Curling brothers to Napier in the British Library's Napier Papers, and two letters from their mother to Napier in the same collection. Separately, a contemporaneous transcription of one letter from our 3× great-grandpa Thomas II is in the Liverpool Papers[9] in the British Library. In the Bodleian Library there is also a clutch of letters from Mrs Elizabeth Kelly (she who was to become Napier's first wife), most of them written to his mother, Lady Sarah Lennox Napier

The final letter treasure came from an unexpected source. In June 2009, I was introduced, via the wonderful network of Family Historians whom I met online, to a descendant of Thomas Curling III, Carey Bayliss, who lives in Australia. In the course of our correspondence Carey told me about a set of three original letters she holds, all written in the autumn of 1819. She very kindly sent me transcripts of all three, and digital images of the original of one of them.

So closely involved was Napier in the Curling family's story that he must be considered an honorary member of the family. There is a wealth of material on Napier's life available to the researcher, much of it primary source manuscript, and there have been several biographical accounts of Napier's life since his death, most recently Edward Beasley's very thorough work, *The Chartist General – Charles James Napier, the conquest of Sind, and imperial liberalism*,[10] but Napier's place

---

8   These accounts for the Earl of Devon's Irish estate are now held in the Devon Heritage Centre in Exeter, catalogue reference numbers: 1508M/1/T/I/6/20 and 1508M/1/T/I/6/21.

9   BL Add MS 32899 ff 67.

10   Routledge, 2016.

as a major benefactor in the Curling annals reveals a uniquely personal aspect of this complex personality. The extracts from his writing which I have included in this work often illustrate his commitment to family – his womenfolk: mother, sisters, mistress, wives, and especially his daughters – as well as his brothers. All of them were the recipients of generously long and frequent letters. In remembrance of his beloved first wife Elizabeth, our ancestor, he also kept the Curlings close to his heart from the time he first knew Edward until he, Napier, died in 1853.

Progress in the research threw the family net wider, although not unmanageably so – the story introduces a few friends and relations of both Curlings and Napiers, friendships of granite strength, including Captain John Pitt-Kennedy and Dimitros Cambici, both of whom wrote letters to Napier and after his death maintained their friendship with Edward Curling.

Note on names

For simplicity I prefer to use the given names where possible. The only exception to this is in writing about Charles James Napier, whose surname alone I use in referring to him throughout the book unless one of his brothers is also mentioned in close proximity. Additionally, the convention, descending for centuries, of naming children after their parents, grandparents, uncles and aunts often makes for tricky identification issues, for example, distinguishing 4× great-grandpa Thomas Curling from his son Thomas Oakley Curling and his grandson Thomas Curling. I found that writing 3× great-grandpa as Thomas Oakley Curling every time I wanted him to appear in a sentence became cumbersome and so I resorted to Roman numerals: Thomas Curling I, or Thomas I refers to our 4× great-grandpa; Thomas II refers to Thomas Oakley Curling (3× great-grandpa); and Thomas III refers to Thomas junior, brother of our 2× great-grandpa Edward. The Roman numerals to indicate generations hold good, too, for the Thomases in the chapter on the Oakley family. (Even though there were six Thomases in our family history in this period alone – three Curlings and three Oakleys – the Curling and Oakley chapters are separate, so there should not be any confusion.)

The nature of this account

The story of this group of our ancestors is remarkable. The Curlings had been anchored in the Isle of Thanet, Kent, the south-easterly tip of England, from at least the mid-fifteenth century. They ventured a few miles further north or west, but until the early nineteenth century our branch of the Curling family stayed in east Kent. The detail of their lives is traced not only in parish records but in their personal writing. As I have aimed for a historically accurate account it has been important to record the sources, so there are copious footnotes. You can always choose to skip them and focus your reading on the story. The appendices are more extended than footnotes. They are intended to give as complete a picture as possible of the lives and their social contexts, sometimes in the form of additional text and sometimes with additional illustrations. Two of the appendices contain complete transcripts of four of the longer letters. The vast majority of the references are to primary source material, but there are two major secondary sources. The first is the body of biographical writing, six volumes, by William Napier on the life of his brother Charles James Napier. Secondly, the work of Priscilla Napier, née Hayter, was a remarkable early gateway for me to the Napier family's story. She was a prolific author in both prose and poetry, and much of her scholarly output was devoted to the family of her husband Trevelyan Napier. There are four volumes relating to Charles James Napier and his family. She wrote in a uniquely engaging style, principally to tell the story, and her work is clearly based on sound research. But unfortunately in the first two volumes – the most relevant – she did not reference her sources at all, other than in a general preliminary acknowledgement. I have used quotations from her work sparingly, particularly her second volume *Revolution and the Napier Brothers* (1973), which covers Charles James Napier's period in Kefalonia. It was because of Priscilla Napier's connection with Oxford University that I eventually thought of consulting the Bodleian Library catalogue to see whether there were any Napier documents held there, and discovered the group of letters written by Elizabeth Kelly, née Oakley, to Napier's mother, and a wonderful sketchbook which includes pen-and-ink drawings and watercolour sketches by Napier. Another of his sketchbooks exists in the British Library.

It should be noted that there are many instances in the story which invite speculation. I have endeavoured to avoid building fictional scenarios, but that does not mean I do not have theories about these situations. From time to time, the actors in the story inevitably made poor decisions. The reasons were peculiar to each situation, and would have included inexperience, inadequate information, personality flaws, the frustrations of particular circumstances. The historian's role is to record facts as impartially as possible, without making judgements, although events occasionally call for a passing comment.

It has taken over a decade to assemble the material for this story and collate it into an orderly format. The first manuscript discoveries I made were written by Curling men, so, as mentioned earlier, it seemed that the story would have a largely male slant. But as links were made with other Curling researchers and more of the background unfolded, the women emerged. Two of them, sisters Elizabeth and Catharine Oakley, the latter our 4× great-grandmother, eventually took their turns centre-stage, through their own letters. The story begins with them.

8

Chapter 1 – Deal and the Oakleys 1760–1780

By the time Catharine Oakley was born in 1762, her father, shipping agent[11] Thomas Oakley II, had married three times, seen off two major lawsuits, and been Mayor of Deal twice.[12] Her mother was Catharine Smith of St Nicholas parish in Deptford.[13] Thomas was almost certainly in the habit of visiting the dockyards at Deptford on business. The owners or operators of some of the behemoth vessels (Fig. 5) built there could have been amongst the clients of his Deal shipping agency. Catharine Smith and Thomas Oakley II married on 5 July 1760.

Fig. 5. The *Royal George* at Deptford, showing the launch of the *Cambridge* [14]

---

[11] For an excellent brief presentation of the shipping agent's role and its history, see *The Ship Agent*, a publication by the Federation of National Associations of Ship Brokers and Agents, UK [FONASBA] available online: http://bit.ly/Ch1ShipAgentFONASBA.

[12] For background on the family, see **Appendix 1 – The Oakley family, Mayors of Deal, Kent** (p. 124).

[13] Deptford was from the time of Henry VIII the principal dockyard of the Royal Navy. There is a comprehensive history of the town and yard here: http://bit.ly/Ch1DeptfordHistory.

[14] © National Maritime Museum, Greenwich, London – BHC3602, 1757. The artist, John Cleveley the elder, was a shipwright at Deptford. The Caird Library online catalogue entry includes background information on the artist and the vessels in the painting, http://bit.ly/Ch1RMMRoyalGeorge.

As well as his shipping agency, Thomas Oakley II had several other fingers in the Deal business pie, offering a banking service and various products connected with alcohol – hops for his own and other brewhouses and, through his public house in Queen Street, wine imported from France, as well as beer. He was also part-owner of at least one privateer, the *Culloden* – and he was a freemason, a member of the Royal Navy Lodge in Deal.[15]

From his earlier marriages Thomas had six children; the eldest, Thomas Oakley III, grew up to become an extrovert and active local politician, breaking trading cartels amongst the millers and butchers to the benefit of the poorer members of the Deal community.[16] Aged 30 when Catharine was born, Thomas III might have felt his father was a bit rash to have embarked on a third marriage, but as he was himself well established in the town by then he probably didn't think too much about it. Thomas II and Catharine had two further children: Elizabeth, born in 1765, and Hampden, who died in 1772 aged three. As Catharine and Elizabeth were so much younger than their half-siblings the two girls naturally grew very close during their childhood and remained so throughout their lives.

The privateer in which Thomas Oakley II had a stake was the *Culloden*. In 1749, the year in which he married his second wife, Mary Schunzar, the crew of the *Culloden* had sued Thomas II and his co-owner, Thomas Fuller, for failure to pay prize money.[17] The practice of allowing private individuals to act on behalf of the government in capturing enemy vessels was subject to detailed regulation. Calculation of the proportion of prize to which each crew member was entitled took into account: the value of the commercial and other goods aboard the ship at the time of capture; the possessions of the crew taken prisoner; and the sale value of the captured vessel itself. These proportions were all set out in the contract drawn up between the privateer owners and crew members before each new venture. There were additional complexities concerning the validity of individual captures, set out in law and regulated by the navy. On this occasion, the crew claimed that they had not received prize money for several of the vessels which they had captured, and the owners' defence was that the captured vessels had not been legitimate prizes.

Throughout the girls' childhood and well into the nineteenth century the town of Deal played a vital role in the maritime life of the nation. Three geographical features combined to give this small coastal town its unique status. First, in both

---

[15] LLMF HC 3/E/1, letter and membership returns for 1770 written by Thomas's son John Oakley (b. 1732) for the Royal Navy Lodge, Deal.

[16] *The History of Deal and its Neighbourhood*, Stephen Pritchard, pub. Edward Hayward, Deal, 1864. http://bit.ly/DealhistoryPritchard.

[17] TNA C 11/1635/31 Court Rolls cases for the plaintiffs and defendants – no judgment. 'A *privateer* was a private person or ship (sometimes called a corsair or buccaneer) authorized by government in letters of marque to attack foreign vessels during wartime, and take them as prizes.' (Wikipedia)

war and peace, local sailors were kept busy by Deal's proximity to the coast of France (Fig. 6).

Fig. 6. **Deal in relation to the French coast**[18]

It facilitated trade and passenger transport, legal and illegal, between the two countries as well as being a strategic defence hotspot at a time when maritime battles were often a major form of warfare between seafaring nations.

Its other two features are interconnected: the Goodwin Sands and the anchorage of the Downs, immediately off the town of Deal. The treacherous nature of the Goodwins is offset by the shelter they offer to the Downs, but expert local knowledge is required to negotiate the Channel at this point.[19] In ports large and small across the globe, experienced local sailors, pilots, have from time immemorial provided navigation services to large vessels negotiating coastal waters, where submerged rocks and other obstacles threaten the integrity of large hulls.[20] Local knowledge and specialist navigation skills were and still are essential, particularly for large vessels, to negotiate the Goodwins safely, a service offered in the eighteenth century by pilots in the coastal towns from the North Foreland to Dover, but particularly at Deal. Artist J M W Turner sketched a game of cricket

---

[18] © Dániel Fehér, https://www.freeworldmaps.net/
[19] There is an excellent article with cross-sections through the South Sands on this webpage: http://bit.ly/Ch1Goodwins (pp. 9 and 10).
[20] The work functions of the pilot go back to Ancient Greek and Roman times, when locally experienced harbour captains, mainly local fishermen, were employed by incoming ships' captains to bring their trading vessels into port safely. See this Wikipedia page: http://bit.ly/Ch1Pilot.

being played on the Goodwin Sands,[21] an event which still happens occasionally, Fig. 7.

Fig. 7. **Cricket on the Goodwin Sands, J M W Turner c.1828–1830** [22]

As well as ships of the line (such as the *Royal George* – that is, warships heavily armed with cannon for broadsides in the line of battle) and other naval vessels, the many merchant vessels which sailed these busiest of sea roads also required a whole range of services facilitated by shipping agents, especially salvage or repairs following storms. Bad weather could mean brisk business for agents, as they arranged not just pilots to nurse the damaged vessels to sheltered moorings in the Downs and elsewhere, but also onshore craftsmen to effect repairs for ships, and the agents also found lodgings, victuals and drink for officers, crewmen and passengers stranded ashore while repairs were carried out.

Lieutenant Gabriel Bray (1750–1823), a young naval officer whose family home was in Deal, gives us tantalizing glimpses of life in the town in some of his

---

[21] The original sketch is held by the Yale Center, but is referenced online in the Tate Collection, with the reference number TW1182 Wilton 916.

[22] Photograph: Yale Center for British Art, Paul Mellon Collection.

watercolour sketches, in an album compiled mostly in the year 1774–5,[23] when Catharine and Elizabeth were still little girls. In Fig. 8, two men are working on a small boat of the type that might have been ordered by the navy. It looks as though they are caulking the interior; one man, holding a bucket of tar in one hand, is painting it onto the base of the boat with a small brush. The other man is approaching the boat with a long-handled implement which could be a brush, or possibly a torch to heat the tar and seal the bottom.

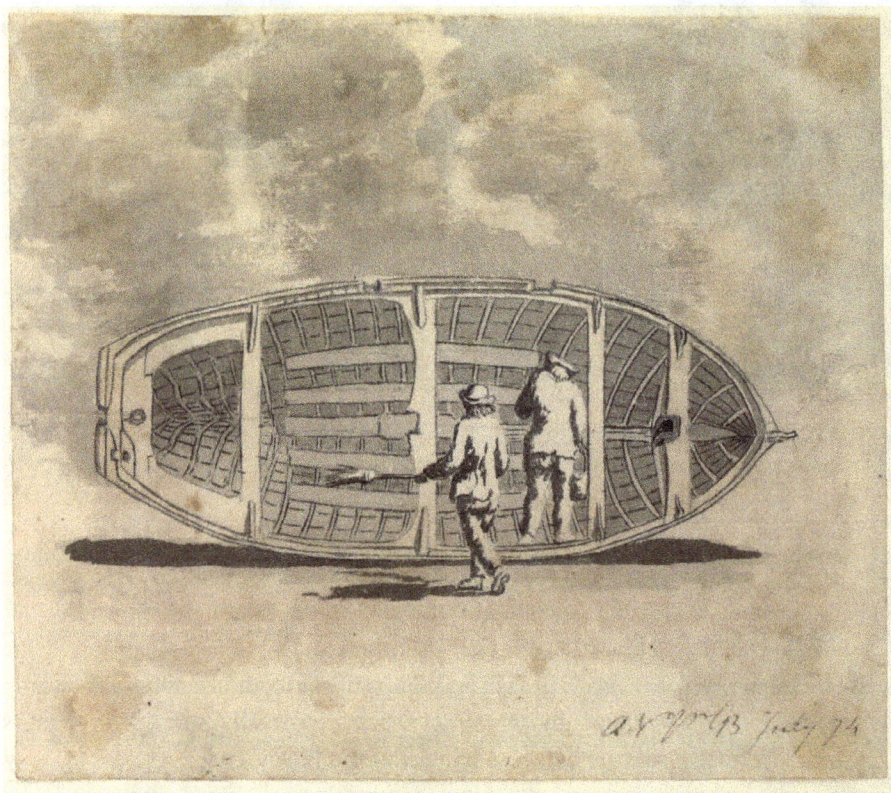

Fig. 8. **Two men working on a jolly boat, Gabriel Bray (1750–1823)**[24]

From 1703, Deal had a small naval dockyard where appropriately skilled local men specialized in building small vessels to put aboard the men-of-war as they were required. These huge ships were built and launched in the larger yards of Deptford, Woolwich, Chatham and Sheerness, and also further west, in Portsmouth and

---

[23]   *Bray Album*, Caird Library and Archives at the National Maritime Museum, Greenwich, London. The images in the album have been separated and catalogued individually.

[24]   © National Maritime Museum, Greenwich, London, PAJ1984.

Plymouth.[25] If launched from the Thames dockyards, they sailed round the North Foreland and would often have to anchor in the Downs off Deal for significant periods of time to await favourable winds, to congregate either as a naval fleet or as convoys of merchant ships, particularly in times of war when they would sail under naval protection. While they were waiting, they topped up food supplies and equipment, men being sent in small boats ashore to Deal, to commission their purchases through a shipping agent. The supplies were then rowed out to the merchant or naval ships. In the dockyard, carpenters and smiths completed commissions for small vessels to be carried by the men-of-war. Initially each builder used his own designs, but in the later nineteenth century the navy issued templates for the completion of these boats.[26] A Jarvis Curling (1732–1796) was one of the Deal boatbuilders.

Administrative paperwork could also be attended to, with letters carrying important instructions or news ferried to and from the anchored ships. Passengers too were rowed out to their vessels to commence long journeys.

Susan Burney, author Fanny's sister, bestowed the epithet 'sad smuggling town'[27] on Deal, but in fact it was far from being an uncultured place. As Thomas Oakley II was a gentleman,[28] shipping agent[29] and banker,[30] Elizabeth and Catharine must have had a comfortable Georgian upbringing, and his children's education was not neglected. Both girls grew to be articulate letter-writers in their native language, using the formal style of the time familiar to readers of Jane Austen. Their half-brother Thomas III spoke fluent Dutch[31] and Elizabeth spoke French, although curiously Catharine, the elder girl, did not. (If either of their parents had been fluent both girls would have spoken French, but in later years Catharine wrote that she had 'never acquired any knowledge of French'.[32])

---

[25] See this guide to the historic Royal Naval Dockyards: https://bit.ly/2RYkcqx

[26] From a talk given for Eastry Local Interest Group by Ian Williams of Addleham History Research Group on 26/11/2014 at the Church Hall, Eastry, Kent.

[27] Susan Burney, quoted in a letter of September 1778, in *The Early Diary of Fanny Burney, 1768–1778:* http://bit.ly/Ch1BurneyDiary.

[28] His will, dated 1783, opens 'This is the Last Will and Testament of me Thomas Oakley of the Town and Borough of Deal in the County of Kent, Gentleman'.

[29] KHLC 5CPW/AP1762/1 Case against Na. Sna. Maij de Homems; Letter from Thomas Oakley II as agent to the Dutch East India Company to his employers, SR http://bit.ly/Ch1ThOakleyDutchLetter
Letter from Mr Benjamin, Naval Officer at Deal, mentioning 'Thomas Oakley, agent to the Dutch East India Company', NMM reference: ADM 354/183/28.

[30] Bailey's Directory 1784.

[31] Collection City Archive Rotterdam / Coopstad & Rochussen, inv. 63 original letter from Thomas Oakley written in Dutch.

[32] See transcript of Catharine Curling's letter to her grandson Thomas, p. 190 in **Appendix 6a – The letters of Catharine and Thomas Curling**.

Deal's eighteenth-century feminist and blue-stocking, Elizabeth Carter,[33] was a family friend who had nine languages at her tongue-tip. We know that Elizabeth Oakley lived with Miss Carter for a time.[34] By the time Elizabeth Oakley was old enough to learn French, Carter would have been in her fifties, and she may have offered to teach French to Elizabeth, including her in the lessons she might have given her two nieces who are mentioned by Napier in a letter to his mother, written when he was aged twenty-five:

> *I have not made much havoc here with petticoat acquaintances yet, but have been invited to catlap,[35] by the amiable and accomplished Misses Carter, nieces to the mighty old maid of that name: they are excessively entertaining.[36]*

Miss Carter had various nieces and nephews, some of whom visited her or lived with her for extended periods.[37]

Fig. 9. **Elizabeth Carter's House in Deal** [38]

Miss Carter's substantial Deal house still stands on the corner where South Street meets Middle Street, Fig. 9. The board displayed between the pair of first-floor windows reads

---

[33] For details of the remarkable Elizabeth Carter see http://bit.ly/Ch1ECarterWikipedia.
[34] Napier's much later letter of 13 September 1833. BL Add MS 49109 ff 106-7.
[35] Wiktionary gives: Noun 'catlap': (uncountable) (slang, derogatory) A watery or thin drink (especially tea or milk); a non-alcoholic drink.
[36] *Life & Opinions*, vol. 1, p. 76.
[37] See *A Series of Letters Between Mrs. Elizabeth Carter and Miss Catherine Talbot from the year 1741 to 1770*, ed. Montagu Pennington (Carter's nephew), available online on archive.org. http://bit.ly/Ch1CartertoFriends.
[38] Photograph and insert, Ray Woods.

Mrs Elizabeth Carter 1717–1806.
The celebrated Scholar and Authoress
lived in this House from 1762 until her death.
Royalty and Society were her friend
and visited her here.
She died at Clarges Street, Piccadilly,
19ᵗʰ February 1806.

Thomas Oakley II was one of the listed subscribers to Carter's major work, the first English translation of *The Moral Discourses of Epictetus*.[39] Miss Carter's father had been the rector of Ham and Woodchurch[40] and minister of Deal. He educated his children himself, teaching Elizabeth Latin and Greek, although he also arranged for his daughter to spend a year living with a French family in London. She later taught herself seven other languages.[41]

If the sisters were taken as little girls for walks or carriage rides in the town of Deal or along the promenade, they would surely have been delighted by the bustle and excitement of the thriving seaport, or the vista from the beach, sometimes with hundreds of majestic vessels sailing the sea roads bounded by England's shore and the coastline of France, just visible on clear days; ships beginning or ending long journeys to or from exotic, far-flung lands, carrying all manner of goods such as silk, chintz, tea and, surprisingly, rhubarb from China, Persian rugs, spices from the tiny islands of Java, sugar from the West Indies – and slaves. It is not impossible that amongst the men working on the seafront the girls would have seen slaves attached to Kent families. Certainly we know that a branch of the Thanet Curlings, Jesse, Robert and John Curling, based in London, were involved in the slave trade in this period.[42]

Along with many other Deal citizens, men of the Oakley family leased several properties on Beach Street from the Archbishop of Canterbury,[43] so it is possible that Thomas II and his family lived just across the road from the shingle beach; but it is more likely that it was his workplace near the beach, so that mariners in need of his professional services as shipping agent could easily find him, and that the family home was elsewhere in Deal. Other Oakley premises in the town included

---

[39] *Epictetus* online copy, http://bit.ly/Ch1Epictetus.
[40] *Gentleman's Magazine* vol. 14, p. 221a, and Rectors of Woodchurch from *Woodchurch Notes*, Canon Scott Robertson, 1882. http://bit.ly/Ch1WoodchurchRectors Nicholas Carter would have baptized all 12 of the Curling children of Ham Manor.
[41] *Universal Biographical Dictionary*, John Watkins 1823 p. 334.
[42] See this page of the web-based University College London project Legacies of British Slave Ownership https://www.ucl.ac.uk/lbs/person/view/2146652683
[43] Records in Lambeth Palace archives.

brewhouses and pubs, as well as dwellings possibly let to families or as commercial properties.

Thomas II was the appointed shipping agent in Deal for the Dutch East India Company (known from its Dutch title, Vereenigde Oostindische Compagnie, as the VOC). This agency did not preclude providing services to other shipping – but he was not the only shipping agent in Deal; his main business rivals were father and son John and Edward Iggulden, who were agents for the British East India Company (the EIC).[44]

Judging from Elizabeth's book *The Nursery Governess*,[45] written towards the end of her life, her own upbringing would not have permitted any frivolous interests. Her mother would have sent and received invitations to visit friends' houses for afternoon tea and discussion of 'polite topics of conversation such as the arts, theatre and music',[46] but Elizabeth would not have been taken out much, except for staid walks; the lively social life enjoyed by children of the twenty-first century would have shocked our ancestors. She and Catharine, once they had learned to sit still, would have listened silently to their mother's conversations with her friends over tea. Discussions would have focused on news of the day such as the controversial Massachusetts Government Act passed in May 1774 in response to the Boston Tea Party episode. The Act attempted to reduce the independence of the colony by giving greater control to Parliament in London. This and other rumblings of discontent in the American colonies were the beginnings of what became the American War of Independence, extending from April 1775 to September 1783, the year in which Catharine and Elizabeth's father died. Another, very controversial, topic was the Reverend Wesley's paper on the iniquities of slavery,[47] fresh off the printing press in 1774. Several prominent members of the Deal community had business interests, either directly in the purchase and sale of African people or indirectly by facilitating the commerce of slavery, for example through shipping agencies.[48]

Both Oakley girls married young. Catharine at the age of eighteen wed Thomas Curling I, the second son of John Curling, a gentleman and farmer at Ham, 3 miles

---

[44] *British East India Company shipping agents John and Edward Iggulden,* LucyAnn Curling, unpublished paper for inclusion in Addleham Local History Research Group exhibition, September 2015.

[45] Elizabeth's book is available as a facsimile on Amazon: http://bit.ly/Ch1NurseryGovernessNapier.

[46] http://bit.ly/Ch1TeaDrinking.

[47] *Thoughts on Slavery*, John Wesley, 1774. A digital facsimile is available.

[48] 'Of all Kentish towns, Deal perhaps had most direct involvement in the slave trade.' *Kent and the Abolition of the Slave Trade – a County Study, 1760s–1807*, David Killingray http://bit.ly/Ch1KentSlaveTrade.

from Deal. Elizabeth had not turned seventeen when she married Captain Francis John Kelly.

Thomas Oakley II had endeavoured to make good matches for both his daughters. The Curlings had been well established in east Kent certainly from the fifteenth century[49] and probably earlier. Thomas's mother Jane Curling I, née Bunce, bore all twelve of her children at the family home, Ham Manor. Although Ham was – and still is – a tiny community of fewer than ten houses, 6 miles from Deal, the Manor is a large property, with its beginnings in Tudor times and with extensions added, particularly during the eighteenth century when the Curlings were in residence.[50]

Francis John Kelly probably did not tell his fiancée Elizabeth's father, Thomas Oakley II, that he had fallen out with his Kelly family to the extent that he had been disowned by them.[51] He had had sufficient funds to buy himself an ensigncy in the army and in due course purchased promotions, first to lieutenant and then captain with the 18th Regiment of Foot. His family's recorded pedigree went back even further than that of the Curlings, the Kelly family having lived in the village of Kelly in Devon 'from time immemorial'[52] and more specifically, according to Burke's Landed Gentry, to 'a time before the Conquest'.

Around the time of his marriage, Francis's regiment, the 18th Regiment of Foot, also known as the Royal Irish, may have been encamped on Barham Down or Shorncliffe; these were holding grounds for regiments awaiting orders to embark on one of the many voyages which the army undertook each year to keep order in far-flung regions of the vast and still growing territories of the British Empire. Prior to his marriage Francis had regularly been assigned to recruiting expeditions in various localities in Kent.[53] He had been in America with the regiment between October 1774 and December 1775, and posted to Dover between August 1776 and November 1777, then to Warley Camp with the grenadiers in July 1779, and to Woburn in March 1780. Promotion from lieutenant to captain happened in November 1780. In November 1782, seven months after his marriage to Elizabeth,

---

[49] The principal stronghold of the Curling family from the fifteenth century was Chilton Farm in the parish of St Lawrence, Isle of Thanet, see http://bit.ly/Ch1CurlingThanet.

[50] Information from the present owner, Mrs Clodagh Clogg.

[51] See notes on the Kelly family A Genealogical and Heraldic Dictionary of the Landed Gentry of Great Britain and Ireland, Bernard Burke, pub. Harrison, 1863. See also **Appendix 3a – Francis John Kelly, a brief biographical note** (p. 160).

[52] http://bit.ly/KellyDevon The Kelly family has lived in the village of Kelly in Devon, in an unbroken line, for 900 years, and they are still there.

[53] TNA WO 17/120 18 Foot. Stephen M Baule's excellent book, Protecting the Empire's Frontiers, Ohio University Press, 2014, gives a biography of each of the officers of the 18th Royal Irish Regiment, including Francis John Kelly (Kindle edition loc 2313), in which Baule gives a full account of Kelly's movements up to his retirement from active service by the sale of his commission in 1790.

he took command of a company in the 18th Regiment, then stationed in the Channel Islands, returning to England via Portsmouth in mid-1783, listed at Hilsea Barracks in August 1783. From February 1784 until July 1790, when he sold his commission and retired from active service, Kelly was with his regiment in Gibraltar.

The trajectory of Elizabeth's ensuing life meant that of the two sisters, hers had the far greater material influence on the course of the lives of the descendants of her sister Catharine, so although Elizabeth did not marry a Curling she plays a very significant role in this story.

Fig. 10. **Deal in a Storm, J M W Turner, 1825** [54]

---

[54] The full title of this work is 'Deal in a Storm, Deal boatmen readying a boat for launching with wreck floating nearby'. Watercolour, Joseph Mallord William Turner, 1825 (Mayor's parlour, Deal Town Hall).

Chapter 2 – An Excellent Grazier

The wedding of Catharine Oakley and Thomas Curling took place on 28 September 1780,[55] at the parish church of St Leonard in Upper Deal, where Catharine's family had lived for at least three generations. Only close family would have attended,[56] but if all the siblings of both parties had been there it would have been a goodly number. We can imagine that after the guests had gathered for the wedding breakfast at the Oakley home in Deal, the bride and groom climbed into their carriage and, maybe with a following family entourage, made the 17-mile journey to Shuart Farm which was to be their new home.

Thomas had been living at Shuart for about six months before the marriage, having paid his 'poor rates'[57] for the first time on 31 May 1780. That month Thomas I signed the overseers' accounts, along with all the other members of the vestry[58] of the parish of St Nicholas-at-Wade. He was taking on a site with a long history.[59]

By the time of the wedding, he would already have had the new home organized and got to grips with the essentials of the farm's management, so that a warm and orderly welcome awaited Catharine.[60] Thomas was renting the farm from Eliab Breton,[61] a wealthy absentee landowner.

---

[55] Deal parish records, CCA U3-95-1-19 p. 88

[56] Michael Rendell, author of *The Journal of a Georgian Gentleman*, wrote in response to a query from me: 'As far as my family are concerned they did not have a wedding reception in the sense of a gathering of loads of friends – it was simply the family who witnessed the ceremony and presumably had a meal afterwards … a few days later there would be a steady stream of visitors attending at the home and "taking tea". Equally the happy couple appear to have received invitations to dine at the houses of friends in the locality. No mention of wedding presents in any of the diaries – it doesn't mean that there weren't any.' The Jane Austen Centre webpage on weddings supports this: https://bit.ly/JACWeddingInfo.

[57] National legislation required each parish to appoint 'overseers of the poor' to be responsible for provision for poor people who lived within its bounds. The appointee held the post of overseer for one year. The poor rate was a locally administered tax, payable by landowners or their tenants, based on property value and collected twice yearly. Payments and disbursements were recorded in the Overseers' Account Book, known in St Nicholas as the Poor Book.

[58] The word 'vestry' can refer either to the room in which clergy and acolytes put on their vestments for the service, or to the group of people who run the parish, including the vicar, churchwardens and overseers.

[59] See **Appendix 2a – Shuart on a fifteenth-century map** p. 131.

[60] For a description and images of Shuart Farm, with accompanying photographs, see **Appendix 2b – Shuart Farm buildings and land** (p.133).

[61] Eliab Breton was one of a succession of that family whose surname is spelt in different ways in the parish records of St Nicholas-at-Wade. See **Appendix 2c – The owners of Shuart Farm** (p. 141).

Alighting from the carriage, Thomas and Catharine would have walked past the end wall of the adjacent Shuart Farm Cottage, with its beautiful Dutch gable, and perhaps stood for a moment outside the ancient front door of the farmhouse,[62] Fig. 11.

Fig. 11. **The entrance to Shuart Farmhouse**

The festivities over, Catharine fades into the background; her main role, besides bearing children, was running the house.

Whereas she and her sister had been the only young people in her childhood home, Thomas I was leaving what had been a much larger household. At the time of his marriage he had ten living siblings, and his rambling childhood home, Ham Manor, 6 miles from Deal, would have been full of bustle and busy-ness, so he was probably expecting to sire a similarly large family.

The Curling men generally married women from prosperous local families. Catharine would have brought a significant dowry with her, which would have helped to set her and her husband up well in their new home and have been sufficient to make an investment in stocks and shares as an insurance for the future.

Catharine went back to her childhood home in Deal to give birth to their firstborn, a son, Thomas Oakley Curling, baptized on 27 September 1781. In the era before maternity units and childbirth technology, first-time mothers often went to their

---

[62] For a detailed outline of Shuart Farm homestead, see **Appendix 2b – Shuart Farm buildings and land** (p. 133). Four buildings on the Shuart Farm homestead are 'listed buildings'. Search the Historic England website http://bit.ly/Ch3HistoricEngland, which has separate entries for Shuart Farmhouse, Shuart Farm Cottage, the granary and the barn. The cottage is in a more original state than the farmhouse, which has been much altered in the 400+ years since the beginnings of the house were first raised on the site.

parental home for the first confinement and birth. Catharine's father, Thomas Oakley II, was no doubt pleased that his latest grandson was to carry the Oakley name. Both of them might have been surprised to know that Oakley as a middle name then tumbled on down the generations, and that a descendant bearing the name Thomas Oakley Curling (1894–1947), with a third given name, Delmar, signed up for the Australian army in 1915, to participate in World War I.[63]

On 23 March 1783 the second child, Catherine, arrived, making the third generation of that given name, although her mother and grandmother had spelt theirs with a middle a instead of an e. Little Catherine's birth may have been difficult in some way; her mother bore no further children.

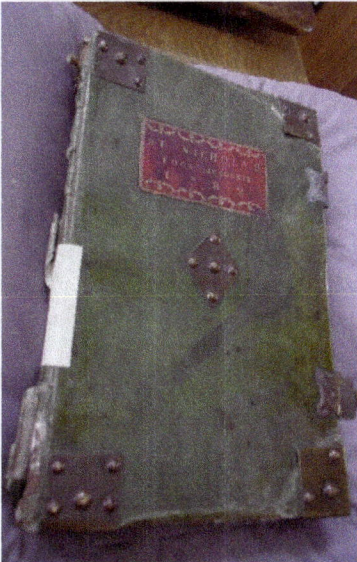

Fig. 12. **St Nicholas-at-Wade Poor Book 1782** [64]

As a major landholder, Thomas Curling I was expected to participate in the running of the parish, taking his turns amongst the vestry men as churchwarden and overseer. In September 1781 he was appointed one of the two overseers, and the following year he and his fellow overseer, John Coleman, bought a new book for the overseers' accounts, complete with tooled leather cover, reinforced at the corners with metal decoration, possibly pewter. The gilt title letters announce that it is the St Nicholas Poor Book 1782, Fig. 12.

Commencing a new poor book was a weighty matter. It had to withstand the ravages of decades, and it was an event of such note that the whole of the title page was taken to record the names of the two people who had bought it, one of whom was Thomas I, his name abbreviated to Tho, Fig. 13.

---

[63] See the enlistment record: http://bit.ly/AustEnlistTOC. (Thomas Oakley Curling II is only rarely listed in official records with his third given name.)

[64] CCA-U3-18/12/2. St Nicholas-at-Wade 'Poor Book', Front cover. Reproduced courtesy of the Chapter of Canterbury.

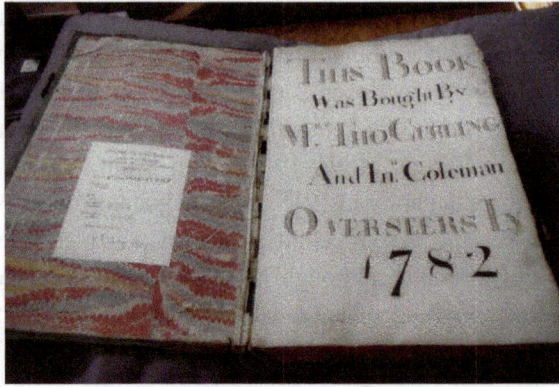

Fig. 13. **St Nicholas-at-Wade Poor Book,**[65] **flyleaf**

Celebrating the commencement of a new poor book in this somewhat flamboyant way was only following a village tradition. The previous volume had been bought almost fifty years before, in 1732, by Mr E Bridges, and he too had taken a whole page to announce his purchase.

Parish accounts include purchases of 120 dozen small sparrows (that's 1,440 sparrows!) and later, at the same price per dozen, 100 dozen large sparrows, as well as a dozen hedgehogs, a badger and a hawk. This might sound like a roaring trade in caged animals as pets, but it was in reality pest control at a time when there was no awareness of any need to conserve wildlife – and no pesticides, either.

Canterbury Cathedral Archives holds a wonderful collection of parish records for St Nicholas-at-Wade. In each parish across the land, the overseers. were responsible for collecting the poor rates. The half-yearly 'assessment' for these rates, often abbreviated in the accounts to 'Sess', listed the contributions of every parishioner of sufficient means to the running of the parish. As well as these incoming parish accounts, each expenditure was carefully recorded. They covered support for the poor of the parish, either in sickness, or in bereavement or in ways which would enable greater independence. Disbursements for the year 1781 included the following entries:

---

[65]   As above. Front flyleaf.

	£	s	d
To the widow Bradley by Order of the Meeting		3	
To clothing Eliz[th]. Kingsford fitting for Servise	1	1	
To Mr Hattoon a Quarters Rent for the Widow Knapford		1	6
To sweping the Poor Houses Chimneys		1	1
To Eliz Covell to buy Soap			1
To a coat and a pair of Stays for Eliz. Kingsford		11	3
To Goody Siblain & Eliz. Covell to buy Necessaries And staying up with Smith when Ill		4	6
To Tho[s] Young Carrying Smiths Bed & Burning it			6
To Jn[o] Willards Family by Order of M[r] Curling M[r] Gillow and M[r] Will[m] White	1	1	

Two major items of expenditure are recorded in the overseers.' accounts on Thomas I's watches as churchwarden or overseer. The first was the purchase in 1783 of a property to be converted for use as the parish workhouse.[66] The second was rebuilding the village school and constructing a new schoolhouse for the teacher and his family, Fig. 14.

Fig. 14. **School House, St Nicholas-at-Wade** [67]

---

[66] See **Appendix 2d – Vestry minute on a new workhouse** (p. 145).
[67] Photograph courtesy of Robin Webster originally posted on the Geograph website, see http://bit.ly/Ch2StNichSch1.

In the twenty-first century the old school building has become a dwelling, although the elegant stone medallion high up on the wall facing the road records its original use: Fig. 15.

Fig. 15. **School House inscription**[68]

The inscription reads:

> *THIS HOUSE*
> *belonging to the*
> *FREE SCHOOL*
> *was Rebuilt*
> *by Subscription*
> *1796.*

---

[68]   Photograph courtesy of photographer Robin Webster.

The village had made provision for educating its children since 1640, when Thomas Paramore had bequeathed to the village funds for a teacher.[69] Accommodation for the schoolmaster was inadequate, and in 1795, as the most recent incumbent of the schoolhouse had died, it was decided to rebuild it for a newly appointed schoolmaster to live in. Since Paramore's day, the school had used a variety of premises, including Frost's Farm, Mrs Foster's kitchen at Chislet and the old schoolmaster's home, and, in the church, St Thomas's Chapel, the vestry room and the South Chapel. Towards the end of the eighteenth century, members of the vestry acknowledged that a purpose-built schoolroom was required, and it was decided to build one adjoining the schoolhouse. Financial constraints on the parish purse meant that the building work was postponed, and the parish waited a further thirty years for the work to be completed. To add to the parish's burden in 1795, the vestry felt that it would be appropriate to provide a higher salary than previously for the new teacher, and it was agreed that the members of the vestry would contribute to this. The amounts committed varied according to income, and were recorded in the overseers' accounts. Their choice of teacher, a Mr Holmes, was given a year's salary in advance, so he was able to settle in and get down to work teaching the children.[70]

Thomas I's primary concern was his family and the farm. In the archive of St John's College, Cambridge, there is a remarkable large-scale map of Shuart Farm,[71] drawn in 1826 for the landowner Eliab Harvey Breton, the third generation of Breton owners. The map includes in its legend a list of all the fields, some with evocative names like Little Crow Hop and Horseshoe Marsh, and it shows that the seawall is the northern boundary.[72] The property covered about 450 acres, of which about 154 acres, or a third of the farm, was marshland.[73]

Tucked away as it is in a remote seaward part of the Isle of Thanet[74] with the nearest neighbours living 2 miles down the road in St Nicholas, it seems impossible that Shuart Farm should have been affected by the vagaries of worldly upheaval, but this is an illusion. The most telling and least controllable influence on the

---

[69] All information on the history of St Nicholas school is taken from *The Schools of St Nicholas-at-Wade, 1640–1957* by Richard Parker, privately published in 1957.

[70] Parker, pp. 28–29.

[71] St John's College, Cambridge, is the current owner of the farm. Archive reference: SJCA/MPS723: plan, with reference, of Shuart Farm, St Nicholas at Wade parish, Thanet, Kent, owned by Eliab Harvey Breton, occupied by Henry Pett, by C. A. Hally of Sandwich, Kent (1826). See **Appendix 2e – The map of Shuart Farm, 1826** (p. 147).

[72] See **Appendix 2c** as above.

[73] Calculated using Eliab Breton's map of Shuart Farm, drawn in 1826, see **Appendix 2c** as above.

[74] See map of the Isle of Thanet, by Thomas Moule, 1836, **Appendix 2f – Maps showing Shuart Farm** on the Isle of Thanet (p. 156).

prosperity of the farm was, as it still is, the weather. Records for the period show that there were very few years in which the sun co-operated to give them an optimum harvest, and in June 1795 sixty sheep belonging to Thomas Curling and his neighbour Mr Evernden died; the animals had just been shorn and the weather had turned very cold.[75]

Politics too had impacted on agriculture, both nationally and internationally. Conflict around the empire was a significant influence on the fortunes of farmers at home. The American War of Independence (1775–1783) and, closer to home, the Napoleonic Wars (1803–1815), brought significant changes to the demographic of east Kent, as local young men joined the forces and the coastal areas became holding grounds for regiments awaiting transport to the continent. It was then that the vast encampments mentioned earlier sprang up on Barham Down[76] and at Shorncliffe.[77] Significant numbers of men were also posted in readiness to defend the coast in case of invasion, east Kent being a primary target because of its proximity to Calais and the European mainland. Feeding these large numbers of men both before they sailed and as they fought for their country in other lands required constant supplies of farm produce. The price of grain increased, which was good for farmers – but there were still the usual fluctuations governed by the weather, and much continued to depend on how well the farmers managed their crops in the face of uncertain temperatures and excessive rain.

During the eighteenth century landowners began to come together, forming an independent support group called the Board of Agriculture, but it was not until the mid-nineteenth century that this became a government body. In the meantime members of the Board sought to form an overview of land management nationally, and they appointed representatives from amongst their number to write reports on each of the counties. The person who is chiefly remembered in Kent for this activity is John Boys of Betteshanger, whose book *General View of the Agriculture of Kent*, published in 1796, is available online.[78] In it he mentions Thomas Curling:

> The polled Scots cattle are frequently brought into this county for summer grazing … they are very hardy and will soon fatten on indifferent land. Mr Curling of Shuart, in the Isle of Thanet, an excellent grazier, has them generally to fatten among sheep in his salt marshes: they weigh from 12 to 25 score each.[79]

---

[75] *The Isle of Thanet Farming Community*, p. 88, RKI Quested, 2001 revision, self-published.

[76] http://bit.ly/Ch2BarhamDown.

[77] http://bit.ly/Ch2Shorncliffe.

[78] http://bit.ly/BoysKentAgric.

[79] *General View of the Agriculture of the County of Kent*, John Boys, p. 172. The updated edition, published in 1806, is available on Google Books: http://bit.ly/2BoysAgricUpdateGoogle.

John Boys' note gives us the impression that whatever the problems of running Shuart Farm it was not lack of skill, effort or knowledge on Thomas I's part.

The farm income was not huge. Correspondence with banker Francis Cobb and Co. shows only occasional large deposits; and the available bank's ledgers (not complete), now in the archives of Lloyds Bank,[80] show a similarly modest income. Thomas I certainly grew hops, offering them for sale to Francis Cobb's own brewery and, when he received no response, further afield in London. The hop pockets[81] were taken to the capital on the Margate hoy.[82]

Thomas I's father John Curling I, who had farmed the land round Ham Manor, moved in his final years to live with his eldest son John II at a small farm in Goldstone in the parish of Ash-next-Sandwich. John I died on 11 October 1797. Thomas I and his brother acted as executors for their father, administering the straightforward will. This in itself is not particularly noteworthy, but six months later Thomas I was executor for his brother John II's will; losing his brother, who was aged only forty-five, so soon after their father's death must have been a shock. When the dust had settled, Thomas I found himself with two farms to manage, Shuart and Goldstone. He continued to participate in the St Nicholas vestry, so he probably continued living at Shuart until his son Thomas Oakley Curling (Thomas II), married in 1804.

---

[80] Lloyds Banking Group Archives, LBA GB 386 A/20 Cobb & Company (Margate) Records.
[81] Pocket was, and is, the name given to the long narrow sack in which hops are stored for transport to the brewery. For the history of hop growing, see http://bit.ly/Ch4Hops.
[82] Hoys were small vessels which specialized in ferrying goods and passengers from ship to shore and from ship to ship. Larger hoys were coastal vessels, used to carry freight of all kinds between the provinces and cities.

Chapter 3 – My Beloved Friend Mrs Kelly

Elizabeth Oakley married Francis John Kelly at St Leonard's church in Deal on 21 February 1782.[83] Francis was forty-nine at the time of the marriage and Elizabeth just short of her seventeenth birthday, so he was three times her age. He was a captain in the 18th Regiment (of Foot), which at the time was posted to Barham Down,[84] and just before the wedding he was leading recruitment parties in various towns in Kent.[85,86] Unlike her sister Catharine, Elizabeth was not going to a beautifully prepared and stable home, but as an army wife would move homes frequently according to her husband's postings.

We don't have a record of where they began married life, but the baptism records of their five children show that Elizabeth gave birth to two in Deal, one at St Nicholas-at-Wade, one in Maidstone, and finally one in Hythe. The Deal births (Eliza in December 1782 and Agnes in July 1790) probably took place with the Oakley family around, to care for the mother and newborn, and Mary's baptism at St Nicholas-at-Wade in 1789 tells us that Elizabeth was staying with her sister Catharine at Shuart. Henry was baptized in October 1800 in Maidstone, his parents' names given as John and Elizabeth. Catherine, the last child, who lived for only three months, was born in 1803 in Hythe, where Francis had been appointed barrackmaster to the recently formed Royal Staff Corps (RSC), one of the earliest incarnations of the Royal Engineers.

We do not know how Francis was able to provide for his family between his retirement from active service in 1790 and 1804 when he arrived at Hythe, but he had found this comparatively comfortable post, still serving in the army. The RSC had only recently been founded by Prince Frederick, Duke of York, the Commander in Chief, who wanted to fill a gap in the army's provision for building military works. His plan was to train a group of officers in engineering, who would then feed into each regiment to oversee any necessary engineering works at home or abroad, bringing a greater degree of skill and expertise to the minimal provision

---

[83] Deal parish records, CCA U3-95-1-19 p. 113

[84] Two units of the 18th Regiment of Foot, the Royal Irish Regiment, were posted to the camp at Barham Down; see http://bit.ly/Ch3FJKellyBarhamDown.

[85] TNA WO 12/3501 and WO 12/3502 Returns of the 18th (Royal Irish) Regiment of Foot. Reference from *Protecting the Empire's Frontier*, Steven M Baule, Ohio University Press, 2014.

[86] For a biography of Francis John Kelly, see **Appendix 3a – Francis John Kelly, a brief biographical note** (p. 160).

previously available through the artificers. The nascent engineering officers were posted to Hythe for this training.[87]

Finally the Kelly family had stability, with a home which became a social hub for the young men of the new regiment, two of whom were to play major roles in the future of the Kelly family and, tangentially, that of the Curling family too.

Charles James Napier, although only twenty-four years old, was already an experienced soldier, having been taken in 1794, at the age of twelve, by his father Colonel George Napier to sign up as an ensign in the army. He joined the RSC[88] in the January of 1804, and Samuel Laing from Papdale in the Orkneys followed soon afterwards. In later life Laing wrote a brief autobiography for his children in which he described being introduced by Napier to the Kelly home: '*Their cottage was a small wooden tenement down a lane leading out of the main street of Hythe, and in this little habitation with one sittingroom there was more elegance and refinement of manners and ideas than in the more magnificent abodes of the wealthy.*'[89] Laing was prone to expressing himself with patronizing pomposity, but you should also be aware of the nuance of the word 'tenement' in this period; it had been used for centuries to mean simply a property holding (from the Latin *tenere* to hold); it did not at the time have the derogatory connotations which came to be associated with it from the mid-nineteenth century on.

Charles Napier gives us a glimpse of the fun the soldiers had on their visits to the Kelly house. Elizabeth, aged about forty, no doubt saw herself as a mother figure to the young bucks, and encouraged Napier to consider a young woman recently moved into the area as a possible fiancée. He wrote to his mother on 18 September 1807:

> *I can tell you at least Mrs Kelly says I am to fall in love at first sight with a most beautiful girl arrived at Hithe and her name is Rob of all things! Well Miss Rob is middle sized, very finely shaped has the sweetest countenance ever seen, is most perfectly easy – and withal quite unassuming, has features without a fault and an ocean of countenance in short, they can discover no fault in her person and as far as they see on a short acquaintance her mind is equally admirable they say I must fall in love with her and so with Gods help I will when I see her –*

---

[87] Information about the evolution of the Royal Engineers comes from *The First British Combat Engineers* by Major J T Hancock RE, article in *The Royal Engineers Journal*, vol. 88, no. 4, December 1974, pp. 204ff. With thanks to Gerald Napier for the signposting. See **Appendix 3b – The Royal Staff Corps** (p. 161) for extracts.

[88] See **Appendix 3b – The Royal Staff Corps** (p. 161).

[89] *The Autobiography of Samuel Laing of Papdale, 1780–1868*, edited and supplemented by R P Fereday, p. 101.

Earlier in the same letter Charles wrote

> *Mrs Kelly is fond of Partridges and she says every body has sent her game so that she won't condescend to eat brown meat and has lived on wings of Partridges ever since the 1st of Sepr this I tell her, does for a sick old lady of 41 but really if a fair damsel like her Daughter Agnes was to do such a thing there w^d be no escaping alive!*[90]

One might imagine the partridges to have been the gifts of grateful men who had shared the Kelly repasts. He ended this letter in jocular fashion:

> *17th Sepr wish you joy old Lady. Copenhagen taken, your two beasts*[91] *alive and no unnecessary apertures in their hides I am quite delighted I wish we knew the particulars – God bless you, ever yours*
>   *Boon*[92]

The RSC 'officers in training' were detailed to oversee the building of the Royal Military Canal from Hythe in Kent to Cliff End in east Sussex, part of the country's defences against French invasion during the Napoleonic Wars.[93] This gave them plenty of practical experience in the planning and execution of a major defence feature, one of the purposes of the canal being to slow down invading forces landing on the Kent coast.

The painting, Fig. 16, of Hythe by J M W Turner, executed twenty years after Napier's time in the town, shows a group of soldiers looking down from a height on the Royal Military Canal and the barracks.

Training over, the first intake of RSC officers dispersed. Napier transferred to the 50th Regiment, and Laing went briefly to 'the drawing room at the Horse Guards where I was employed for a short time drawing and copying plans' before joining 'an expedition setting out for some secret service under General Spencer'.[94]

---

[90] BodL MS Eng Lett 236/f137.
[91] 'Beast' was a term frequently used at this time in an affectionate way, to mean a child, particularly one's own offspring.
[92] BodL MS Eng Lett 236/f137. Napier's brothers William and George were involved in the second battle, or bombardment, of Copenhagen (16 August–18 September, 1807), and were, according to this account, uninjured. He signed several letters from this period 'Boon'.
[93] For a history of the Royal Military Canal see http://www.rmcp.co.uk/the-royal-military-canal/
[94] *The Autobiography of Samuel Laing of Papdale, 1780–1868*, pp. 102–103.

Fig. 16. **Hythe, Kent 1824 by J M W Turner** [95]

The Kelly family stayed in Hythe, where Francis continued to be barrackmaster. On the night of 18 March 1807 fire broke out in the stables of the RSC mess-house at Hythe. The stable building was very old and 'was soon in an awful blaze'. The town's engine arrived quickly, only to be damaged. Elizabeth and F J Kelly's son Henry, aged nine at the time, went up the hill to the barrack with an order to send down the barrack's own fire engine.

> with admirable presence of mind this very fine boy applied for a party, and with the ready assistance of the officers and men of the 43d regiment, proceeded to the engine-house, and helped to put on the chains, pipe, &c. and then joined the now numerous party under the direction of an officer of the Royal Staff Corps, to get the engine down the new military road to the scene of action. The water was readily supplied from the military canal; the engine continued to play till six this morning, to prevent any accident from sparks, and we are happy to find no material injury was done, and not a single life lost. The horses were removed at the first alarm, and providentially there was no wind until after the fire was extinguished, or the whole range of huts, as well as the mess-house, and several other old buildings, must inevitably have been destroyed.[96]

Soon afterwards, Elizabeth wrote to the Commander in Chief, His Royal Highness Prince Frederick:

---

[95] LPA 11328 © Guildhall Art Gallery, Corporation of London, UK.
[96] *Kentish Gazette*, 20 March 1807.

Hythe 21st June 1807

Sir

I have hitherto refrained from addressing your Royal Highness, to thank you for the favorable reception with which you have condescended to honor my request in behalf of my son Henry, from a fear of troubling you and from a reluctance to occupy that attention which has so many more important claims on it – but I am as uneasy under the idea of wearing the appearance of ingratitude that my unwillingness to be thought troublesome loses its weight and I again presume to intrude on your Royal Highness.

You have been graciously pleased Sir, to lay me and mine under the most serious and lasting obligation – you have confer^d on my boy the highest honor and the greatest [form] he could hope for and you have bound to you forever the attachment of a whole family by the strongest of all ties – those of a grateful ... respect – Receive then, Sir (what I am satisfied will be most acceptable to your heart) the assurance that your promise of appointing my son to a[n] ensignsy in a favorable opportunity has given joy and pride to an old and not unmeritorious officer, has made glad the heart of an anxious mother, and has helped to cherish in their son, that ardour for military fame, and that devotion to the duties of a soldier which it has been their chief pleasure to see grow with his youth –

That God may defend you from sickness and sorrow, & that honor and glory may attend the British Army under your Royal Highness's command Is the sincere prayer

Of your Royal Highness's
Grateful & most devoted servant
Eliza Kelly[97]

Elizabeth addressed this letter to:
His Royal Highness
The Commander in Chief.

And Prince Frederick had indeed been the Commander in Chief since 1795. To have written a 'petition letter' was not unusual at a time when a defined career path depended on having 'connexions' further up the social scale. What was surprising

---

[97]   BL Add MS 49112 f11.

was that Elizabeth's original petition appears to have had sufficient traction for it to be successful. This might be because someone like Napier, whose mother's family moved on the fringes of royal circles, had put in a word on Henry's behalf, or it might be that Prince Frederick had visited his new regiment in their training quarters to inspect their progress both in their studies and on the ground with the military canal, when Elizabeth might have had the opportunity to present him with her petition in person. Her reference to Francis (the 'old and not unmeritorious officer') is noteworthy. Clearly he had not abandoned his family, as Priscilla Napier wrote.[98] Although Elizabeth described her husband as 'old', aged fifty-five, he was not what we in the twenty-first century would consider old, but this illustrates well the shorter life expectancy of the period.

The battle of A Coruña

Sunday 16 January 1809 found Napier with Lieutenant General Sir John Moore's troops at A Coruña. Moore's entire army was in retreat from Napoleon's men, under Marshal Ney, in pursuit, and Napier was leading the 50th in that retreat.

The British army was pushing down the last few miles to the beach at A Coruña. British naval ships were under sail to rendezvous with the troops there and take them to safety, but the French caught up with the soldiers and battle lines were drawn. Napier had already received one wound when, leading his men through the village of Elvina, he and three others were attacked in the street. Napier was again wounded, badly, and captured. His own extended account of events, written many years after the battle but still vivid in his memory, was transcribed and included in the biography written by his brother William.[99]

As it seemed that Charles had been slain on the battlefield, his family was thrown into total disarray and grief. His mother's sister, Lady Louisa Connolly, was distraught. Napier and his siblings had spent much of their childhood playing on the Connolly estates at Castletown, County Kildare, only fifteen minutes' walk from their home in the village of Celbridge. Three Napier brothers – Charles, William and George – had fought at A Coruña in different regiments, and William was missing as well. Lady Louisa wrote a long and eulogizing letter, pouring out her grief over her nephew Charles's death to his brother George. There seems to have been a writing style particularly dedicated to such mourning letters, florid, melodramatic and extended. This is an extract from Louisa Connolly's letter:

---

[98] *Revolution and the Napier Brothers*, p. 77, Priscilla Napier, Michael Joseph 1973.
[99] *Life & Opinions*, vol. 1, pp. 94–117.

O! my Dearest Dear George –

Neither my expressions or my Pen, can give you an Idea, adequate to the feelings of my heart. I know how much like my own children I have loved you all, from your Birth, but I did not know, how much it would cost me to lose my beloved Charles! Nor did I think, that after what my heart has gone thro' of sorrow, that I could ever again feel, what I have done on this severe Blow – Your account of the fatal 16th Jan ... thrilled me with horror, to think on the effusion of Blood – think then my Dr George, what I felt for you, who saw it all; good God! What a scene it must have been! – ... The loss of that Heavenly Moore, (for such I understand, he was) I felt most deeply, until all my sorrow was absorbed in that of my dear dear Charles, whose Character, & age had not had time, & opportunity, to show himself the full deserving Companion of his General ... It is his Family & friends that must record his private Virtues, and they were so many, that one may say, he wanted none ... He never gave them a moment['s] uneasiness, but filled the measure of happiness to his Family, by an over flowing Affection, tenderness, & kindness towards them all – His elevated soul towards his God, the rectitude of his principles, his generosity unbounded (to the privation of his comforts) his charity & good nature to the lower Ranks, with an un-impeached moral conduct, are virtues that can be attested as belonging to him by all Persons that lived with him ... with what pleasure may we not look back, to the strength of his understanding, to the amiableness of all his ways, the sweetness of his temper, & the chearfulness of his spirits, which brought joy along with him, whenever he came to his Family – But we have lost him for a time, & grievous will be those days on Earth, that are passed without him – His dear Mother is certainly the foremost in suffering, but then she has not so much time to be parted from him as the rest – the Accounts of your dear sister Louisa, go to my heart, but I rejoice in your being with her, my Dearest George, because I know how very dearly she does love you – poor Caroline had so little recoverd [at] the loss of her darling Cecilia, that I am not surprised at hearing how much this second misfortune has overcome her ... I grow quite uneasy at not hearing of Dr Williams safe return, every blast frightens me, but I hope that tomorrows Post may bring us an account of him, as some Vessels at Plymouth have been heard of ...[100]

---

[100] BL Add MS 49169 f10.

Louisa wrote a second letter in the same vein on 5 February 1809, and in the meantime there was another letter-writer. Emily, the second of the eight Napier siblings, felt herself to be especially close to Charles. What follows is an extract of the letter which she wrote to George.

Castletown

Jan: 29th 1809

> *My beloved George, the only wish I have upon earth is to see you, to hear from you every heart rending particular of my adored Brother's neverfailing Glory. Yes my George I feel it as I ought, I know He is gone to reap the bright reward of all his virtues, he has fallen as the son of our father should fall, but my George He was the idol of my heart, the favourite of my childhood, the friend of my riper years. To Him since my dear Fathers death I had look'd for support, for advice, for guidance, & oh God how amply did I find all I look'd for, in his angelic character, his unbounded tenderness. – ... my poor William how I long to hear of his arrival, for alas! I cannot now feel security in any thing. – Your letter & Mr Ogilvies describing my Angels glorious conduct are never from my sight, they are only my consolation, for they only raise my thoughts to the bright rewards that awaited Him – Adieu my beloved George & May the Father of all Mercies preserve you long to our afflicted hearts! your affect^e Sister Emily Napier*

> *I must not forget in my own grief the [damaged original] of others & I beg you to inform me as soon as you can if Serjeant Fell is alive, his wretched Wife is here & I cannot relieve her anxiety.*[101]

Although Napier's brothers (their full <u>given</u> names George Thomas and William Francis Patrick) had also been on the battlefield at A Coruña, they had not been near Charles. William must have returned at some point, because we do not hear of his being missing again. George had searched the terrain thoroughly afterwards, hoping to find Charles and save him, but without success, so he joined the rest of the retreating army on board ship and sailed home. In the published gazette, Charles was listed as killed in the battle, but although as days became weeks George continued not to believe this and to make enquiries at every level, most of the family eventually accepted what seemed to be the fact, and Charles Napier's first-made will was proved.

---

[101] BL Add MS 49169 f14.

Eventually George heard from a French prisoner of war that his brother was held by Marshal Ney,[102] and petitioned for his release. To press home his plea, George was able to persuade someone in authority to commission a frigate to take him to A Coruña to speak personally with Ney on his brother's behalf. That he was able to do this speaks volumes for the standing of the Napier family in both England and France; it was without doubt principally their mother's connections.[103] On his mission of mercy, George Napier took with him, as well as a flag of truce, a letter from his elderly, blind mother, addressed to Charles:

27th March 1809

If you receive this letter my dear son you will know the bad writing of your blind & unhappy mother & will have the consolation of knowing that the health of your family, all assembled here now, & that of your dearest friends have not suffered [materially] from their severe affliction on the report that you were no more!; and since the moment in which Hope was held out to them that you were a prisoner, tho' badly wounded, we have been revived & live on anxious expectation of hearing from yourself the present state of your health & situation. – If this blessing is granted to them, they can never cease giving thanks to the all merciful God for giving you back to your affectionate mother
Sarah Napier

PS Mr Couts has written to Mr. Perigord Banker at Paris to answer your draft & to make all possible enquiry after your welfare.[104]

She supplied a French translation with an additional request in French that her son be shown the original English.

---

[102] Marshal Michel Ney was the commander in charge of French forces at A Coruña after the battle and tasked with occupying the whole area of Galicia. (Wikipedia)

[103] Lady Sarah Lennox Napier, daughter of the 2nd Duke of Richmond, had been seriously considered as a possible bride by King George III before his rise to the monarchy. Her great-grandmother, Louise de Kérouaille, had been a mistress of King Charles II, and he had settled land and several titles on their son, creating him 1st Duke of Richmond and later Duc d'Aubigny. See *Aristocrats Caroline, Emily Louisa and Sarah Lennox 1740–1832*, p. 7, Stella Tillyard, Vintage, 1995.

[104] BL Add MS 49089 f226. NB This letter is dated 27 March 1809, but it must have been written in February as Napier was released on 20 March. It may be that Sarah Napier simply made a mistake or it could be that she was dating the letter for the day she hoped it would be delivered. Sarah Napier would have had a fair knowledge of French because her grandmother was French. 'Mr Couts' was probably one of the Coutts brothers, James and Thomas Coutts, who gave their name to the eighteenth-century incarnation of the bank which is in the twenty-first century called simply Coutts.

Marshal Ney proved most magnanimous, and on hearing of the letter from Napier's mother allowed him to be released on parole not to fight again until exchanged for a French prisoner of war. Napier refused to leave unless he could take a group of other British prisoners of war with him. This was also permitted. On 20 March 1809 he set off with his brother and the other freed prisoners to be taken to the frigate, and in one week they arrived in Plymouth.

But at home, the news was slow to make its way to the family. Another Louisa – the eldest of the Napier siblings, Louisa Napier, the only offspring of their father George Napier's first marriage – wrote what was not really a reassuring letter to Lady Sarah's dearest friend, Lady Susan O'Brien, on 9 March:

> *My Dear Lady Susan, — Don't believe any reports you may hear about our dear Charles; if I can tell you he is a prisoner you will hear from me, & if you don't, conclude all is as it was; a flag of truce has been sent to Corunna. to find out the truth of many reports, & we hourly expect its return. L^y L and Emily are come. & we are all better for that meeting being over; L^y Sarah keeps wonderfully well. Adieu, my dear Madam; depend on my letting you know any good news, & excuse this hasty letter, but I have been much agitated to-day from some particular circumstances of L^y Sarah and Emily being told the reports, which we have carefully been keeping to ourselves this fortnight past 'till the return of the flag of truce. & now unluckily they know it all, & must share the anxiety of the suspense it keeps us in.*
>
> *Once more, believe me,*
>
> *Your Ladyship's sincere & obliged.*
> *L. Napier*[105]

Aware of the high likelihood of his death in battle, Charles had made a will on 12 September 1808, appointing his brother Richard executor. As George and William had reported that they had been unable to find Charles and there was no news from other quarters of his being alive, the family must have come to the conclusion that it would be best to prove the will. Richard did so on 10 February 1809.[106] The army also clearly thought the balance of evidence was against Charles being still alive as the *Kentish Gazette* of 24 January 1809, in an account headed 'Battle at Corunna', announced that 'Major Napier of the 50th and Lieut.-Col. McKenzie of the 43rd

[105] *The Life and Letters of Lady Sarah Lennox, 1745–1826*, p. 222, eds. the Countess of Ilchester and Lord Stavordale, pub. Charles Scribner's Sons, New York, and John Murray, London. See archive.org website: http://bit.ly/Ch3LNapierletter.
[106] BL Add MS 49112 f13. The will and its proof are in this one document.

were killed.' So great rejoicing broke out among the family as soon as they heard the news. Brother Richard wrote from Cadogan Place to William O'Brien:

Monday Even^g. Eleven O'Clock.

I have just time & senses, my dear Sir, to tell you that Charles is alive & well of his wounds, come from Corunna., and now at Plymouth, where his own letter is dated 28th; he says he is still weak. George, Emily, & Louisa are gone down to Exeter to meet him. You may well suppose that nobody is ill here. He finished his letter by Hudibras, you lie —

For I have been in battle slain,
and yet I live to fight again.[107,108]

In those two lines, Charles triumphantly twisted Samuel Butler's poem in which his hero Hudibras says:

For those that fly may fight again
Which he can never do that's slain.[109]

Butler's poem was hugely popular when it first appeared, Canto I being published in 1662. A new edition of the complete work was published in 1727.[110] It might have been among the poems which Napier studied at school in Celbridge in the 1790s. When he arrived in Plymouth with George, he had probably heard from Emily and Louisa that his will had been proved, effectively declaring him dead, hence Charles's Hudibras parody.

Lord Napier,[111] the Napier clan's chief and a first cousin to Charles Napier and his siblings, wrote to Richard from 27 St James's Street, London.

I enter with the utmost Sympathy into the feelings of Yourself, and all your family on the happy news you have received of your Dear Brother's safety and I fervently feel the deepest Gratitude to the Almighty, for this instance of his goodness to You all. May the same watchful Providence ever shield you all, from every possible Evil, and bestow on You every comfort. I feel, that I cannot write; but, if possible, I will endeavour to call in Cadogan Place tomorrow. You

---

[107] For the full epic poem by Samuel Butler see http://bit.ly/Ch3Hudibras.
[108] *The Life and Letters of Lady Sarah Lennox*, as above, p. 223. This letter is undated in the book text.
[109] *Hudibras* Canto III (Kindle Locations 8288-8289). Samuel Butler. Standard Ebooks. Kindle Edition. Original pub. 1680.
[110] See https://en.wikipedia.org/wiki/Hudibras.
[111] Francis Napier, 8th Lord Napier of Merchiston, was in 1807 chosen for the third time as a representative peer in the House of Lords, so was based in London.

will not find me at home, as I am forced to be at the Parliament Office from half past Ten, till two. Give my best Love & kindest congratulations to your beloved Mother, your Brother and Sisters. None can more truly participate in your happiness than, My Dear George,

Your ever affectionate
Cousin, Napier[112]

Lady Sarah wrote ecstatically to her dear friend Lady Susan O'Brien:

Cadogan Place, April 1, 1809.

My beloved Charles is alive and recovered from his wounds; a letter from himself confirms it from Plymouth. Think what joyful happiness for me; he is on his parole I believe. Louisa, Emily, and George are gone to Exeter to meet him, as he must rest there a day or two, being weak at least; he is at a person's house only 7 miles from Exeter. My joy is too great to say more, so God bless you !

Ever yours,
Sarah Napier[113]

Charles was delighted with this outcome, but he was still rather frail from the five extremely serious wounds he had received in the battle and its aftermath, so he went to stay with a family friend, Mrs Brown of Combe Satchfield, Fig. 17, not far from Plymouth. Mrs Brown was an extraordinary woman; her sister was the wife of James Coleridge, elder brother of Samuel Taylor Coleridge, and by the time Napier visited her she had been a widow for many years.

Charles had Mrs Brown's address in a tiny little notebook which he had kept with him, even during the battle and his imprisonment.[114] Who should be at Combe Satchfield but Mrs Elizabeth Kelly, and 'she poor girl, betrayed the strength of their relationship by falling in a dead faint as he arrived'.[115] She and her daughters were staying at the Kelly family home, 16 miles away, in an initial attempt to heal the rift between her husband Francis and the rest of his family. What a coincidence that they happened to be visiting Mrs Brown on the afternoon of Charles's return.

---

[112] BL Add MS 49169 f32.
[113] *The Life and Letters of Lady Sarah Lennox, 1745–1826,* p. 223, as before.
[114] The notebook is in the Napier Papers of the British Library, catalogue reference: Add MS 49141.
[115] *The Sword Dance – Lady Sarah Lennox and the Napiers,* p. 223, Priscilla Napier, pub. Michael Joseph 1971.

Fig. 17. **Combe Satchfield, the seat of Mrs Brown (Dorothy Ayre Taylor)**[116]

Samuel Laing had also returned to Plymouth after A Coruña, and had been very active in arranging a new life for himself. Having visited the Kelly family at Kelly House in Devon to propose to Agnes, the second of the three daughters of Elizabeth and Francis, he travelled to his family home in the Orkneys, left the army – because, so he said, it was no life for a wife – and returned to marry Agnes on 21 March 1809 in the church attached to her ancestral home in the village of Kelly, the nearest town being Launceston in the county of Cornwall, although Kelly itself is in Devon. Laing wrote that he and Agnes went to stay with Mrs Brown of 'Combe Sackville' as he calls it, so it is very likely that he crossed paths with Napier there.

After an interval of recuperation Napier returned to the Peninsula as a volunteer, breaching his exchange agreement. He fought at the battles of the Coa and Busaco, where on 27 September 1810 he received another serious wound. Edward Beasley tells us that Napier's cousin Charles John Napier was present at the battle, and in later years, speaking in parliament of the event, said 'At the battle of Busaco

---

[116] This sepia image of a painting of Combesatchfield, artist unknown, is taken from *The Story of a Devonshire House*, London, 1905, Lord Bernard John Seymour Coleridge KC, p. 68a. This is the story of the family of the Rev. John Coleridge, one of whose eight sons was the poet Samuel Taylor Coleridge. Digital image from the National Library of Australia, call number 920 COL.

[Charles James Napier] … was shot through the nose, and the ball fell into his jaw'. Enlarging on the event Beasley wrote 'the bullet passed diagonally through Napier's face and he began to suffocate. The bullet was extracted, but he lost part of his jaw and some of his teeth. He would feel the pain of the wound every day until his death forty-two years later.'[117] Yet again, in March 1811, he returned to the Peninsular fray, only to find that both William and George, his brothers, had been wounded, but neither of them fatally. In January 1812 Charles took up a new command with the 102nd Regiment, joining them in Guernsey. From there they were ordered to Bermuda, where they arrived in September 1812.[118]

Over many years Napier liked to keep a sketchbook with him. Two such books have survived, one in each of the Napier Papers Collections at the British and Bodleian Libraries. See Fig. 18.

Fig. 18. 'George Town Bermuda 1813 from Town Cut'[119]

In this next letter, it is not entirely a surprise to discover that Napier had Henry Kelly under his care in the regiment in Bermuda. On the other hand, it is a revelation to find that Elizabeth Kelly was in direct contact with Charles Napier's

---

[117] *The Chartist General*, Edward Beasley, 2017, quoting as sources William Napier, Alexander Craufurd and David Gates.
[118] Beasley, as above.
[119] Sketchbook of Charles James Napier, BodL MS. Eng. Misc. e. 603 41264, f26.

mother, to whom she wrote of her family's gratitude to Napier for his care and protection of Henry, who had been ill with fever but was now on the mend.

Upminster Feb^{ry} 18th 1813

I thank very sincerely dear Lady Sarah for forwarding our most ... letters from Bermuda – I do not attempt to express (what is indeed inexpressible) the grateful feelings which Col Napiers great tenderness & care of our beloved Henry give us – You dear Lady Sarah could understand our emotion & our sentiments of gratitude – if you had a son so young – so ill – so watchd & nursed – but you could not I believe express these feelings to your own satisfaction neither can I – we have another cause of gratitude to your excellent son – who fosters our Henrys best affections with the care of a true tender friend – Henry having been thought fit to have the payment of a company has received this favor – and he sends a present to his sisters (a Christmas gift he calls it) – as the first fruits of the oeconomy his Commanding officer has taught him – this present is no less than twenty pounds – & is I believe no less uncommon than it is creditable to him –

Such news and the assurance that the fever had intirely left the Island had cast a ray of comfort over our circle – which the information of my dear sister having been seriously ill has alas! in some degree obscured – She is I trust now better – but your ladyship will forgive my hurried scrawl – it was meant merely to tell you that the wine merchant at Portsmouth, Mr Sharp – has offered to forward any thing for us to Bermuda – and if you have any thing to send to Col Napier that cannot go in a letter as the Septre *is shortly to sail – we can send it to Mr Sharp – I shall write through ... [paper torn away in two places] the Admiralty desk ... by the* Septre *& if y^r ladyship will let me have y^r letter by Monday next I will enclose it*

I hope you have had good accounts of Major Napier & that he is quite well Our family are pretty well the dear children benefiting from the country air & fine weather – I gain strength I hope tho' slowly and am Ever dear Lady Sarah

Most truly

Elizabeth Kelly[120]

---

[120] BodL 237/f54–55.

This letter was addressed to 'The Rt Honble Lady Sarah Napier' at the family's city home, 13 Cadogan Place, Sloane Street, London.

Here we learn that the Kelly family had moved from Hythe. Elizabeth was writing from Upminster. Francis John Kelly had been posted as barrackmaster to Romford Barracks in 1811, Romford being less than 4 miles from Upminster.

As mentioned earlier, Priscilla Napier wrote that Elizabeth was abandoned by her husband Francis John Kelly.[121] Evidence of this has not so far surfaced, and when Francis died in 1826 he was buried in Cookham, which is where Elizabeth was living at the time.

As well as writing to Lady Sarah, Elizabeth was also communicating with two of Charles's siblings, Emily and Richard. There is this little note to Emily at a time when Elizabeth was clearly feeling so unwell that she thought she might die:

26ᵗʰ Feb 1817

There is a paper in the enclosed little packet directed for me which as it was intended for you by your beloved brother it is my particular & last wish that you should see and there is also a little miniature which only [you] can value I would rather yʳ brother did not see the little [relick] I have treasured – you will perhaps keep them
Elizabeth Kelly

On the reverse:

To Miss Emily Napier in case of Death to be sent to her immediately
26 Feb [rest obliterated by smudge][122]

The extreme formality in the next letter may have been occasioned by Elizabeth's deference to Napier's brother Richard's status as a lawyer. After a mundane opening paragraph, the rest of the letter is rather mysterious.

Upminster 6ᵗʰ August 1813

Mʳˢ Francis Kelly's compliments to Mʳ Napier –

She finds on enquiry that among the many London coaches that pass her gate every day there is one called the Upminster coach – & that it leaves the Bull Inn in Aldgate every afternoon at five o'clock Mʳˢ Kelly has received many large packages by this coach very safe and without any delay and she believes a small parcel will come equally safe.

---

[121] *Revolution and the Napier Brothers*, p. 77, Priscilla Napier, Michael Joseph 1973.
[122] BL Add MS 49109 f50.

> *Mrs Kelly is much obliged by Mr Napier's informing her of the Dukes opinion she is quite ignorant of military matters however as she understands from Mr Napier that H R H^s disapprobation is by no means strong she trusts there is no fear of its being officially announced to Col Napier and of course that he will not hear of it during the expedition at least as she is sure the very smallest disapprobation will very much annoy and distress him.*
>
> *As Col Napier has not limited the time Mrs Kelly concludes she may keep the papers (unless Mr Napier particularly wishes them returned sooner) a week or two when she will have an opportunity to send them by a person who will pass the Temple or by her own servant.*[123]

Throughout Elizabeth's life we are aware of her physical frailty; she is rarely completely healthy. There may have been a genetic factor at work, for we already know that her sister Catharine had only two children and that one of those two, Catherine, lived to only 23 years of age. Furthermore, Elizabeth's last child, another Catherine, had died in infancy.

Charles Napier's letter to his mother (no date, but possibly 1819 as it was kept with other letters of that date) gives us our next window into the lives of our characters. We have no evidence of what was happening in the life of the Kelly family during the six-year gap.

> *I stay with Mrs Kelly to the last as I shall see her so little She sends you her best love and w^d like to see you again but cannot as they do not go by London – she also sends her love to Dudeny – she is quite harrassed by worries of all sorts and has been very ill but is better and I hope the journey will do her good for, unlike Ann, She likes travelling, – I have given George a direction to get you a stuff that is very good for Rheumatism – it is called "heal all" and may be had at Hastings the Chymist in g^t Hay market – I send you a paper that I cut out of the times it will amuse you – God bless you my dearest mother do be careful of y^r Rheumatism and believe me ever y^r affectionate son*
>
> *C J Napier*[124]

---

[123] BL Add MS 49111 f57.
[124] BodL MS Eng Lett 237/f51.

And to his brother Richard:

London, 11th April 1819

*I go away with some points of great satisfaction to me ... my beloved
friend Mrs Kelly is in better health than she has had for years. these
things give me a lift.*

This letter was addressed to Richard Napier at 24 Marlborough Buildings, Bath.[125]

For a brief moment all in this little circle seemed to be well and happy, and to have
come to a point of communal rest. However, in June there was more upheaval.
Elizabeth wrote to Lady Sarah:

Albro' Hatch June 11th 1819

*I know not indeed, dear Lady Sarah, how to reply to your letter of
yesterday, which I have just received and I am sure you will before
this have recollected that whatever I have, or might have, done about
the purchase of a House or land, could only be by Col^l Napiers
express desire You wish to know the purport of my letter to Geneva,
it was not to inform him of my being in treaty for a House, but to tell
him, that insted of going to look at a House in Berkshire (as he
supposed) the day he left London, I was carried into Kent, by the
dangerous & sudden [illness] of my Sister. You wish my answer, I can
only inform you that all I have done in the enquiries I have made
about Houses etc, has been by Col Napiers particular, and written
directions, at his repeated request, and has been undertaken, very
reluctantly, by me.*

*The report your ladyship mentions must have originated in some
mistake, I have certainly not compleated, tho' I had begun, a treaty
(by Col Napiers desire) for a place in Berkshire, about which I wrote
(also by Col^l Napiers desire) to M^r. Napier [Richard Napier] – the
surveyors opinion of this place does not authorize the purchase and I
have written by this post to decline it –*

*I trust your Ladyship will pardon my not entering into more
particulars, as I am much hurried, and I hope the above will make
you perfectly satisfied with*

*Dear Lady Sarah
Your most faithful &
Most ob^{nt} ser^{nt}*

---

[125] BL Add MS 49111 f59.

46

When you favor me by writing, will you have the goodness to tell me how good Mrs Frosts health is?

Pray do not trouble yourself about Franks – it makes no difference to me as we are within the 3 penny post, & the letter man charges the same for franks as other letters –[126]

Addressed to:
The R^{t} Honble
Lady Sarah Napier
13 Cadogan Place
Sloane Street[127]

So Catharine had been seriously ill in Kent, and Elizabeth went to take care of her. The illness must have been protracted, as the next we know of the sisters is that Catharine has been staying with Elizabeth at the Kelly home, Hainault Cottage at Aldborough Hatch in Essex.

---

[126] Postage was paid by the recipient until the introduction of the Uniform Penny Post in 1840, when payment became the duty of the sender.

[127] BodL 237/f56.

Chapter 4 – A Hospitable Roof

Thomas Curling I was the second son and third child of twelve born at Ham Manor. As mentioned earlier, in 1798 his elder brother John died only a year after their father, at his farm in Goldstone, Ash-next-Sandwich, and since then Thomas I had been managing that property as well as his own at Shuart. No doubt the responsibilities of his son Thomas Oakley Curling (Thomas II) increased markedly in his late teens, as he would have been learning the details of husbandry on the Shuart property and the administration of farm accounts. As he reached adulthood, the two men would have had many discussions on the state of their fields, the crops and the livestock in their care. Together they would have visited the fields of both farms, so Thomas II would have been well known in the area round Goldstone. The old rectory there was occupied by Michael Becker II and Jane his wife, née Belsey, who had moved from Dover in 1798; the Beckers are thought to have been immigrants from Prussia.[128] On 23 November 1804, at the age of twenty-two, their daughter Jane Becker II married Thomas Oakley Curling in St Nicholas Church, Ash.

Thomas II took his bride Jane to Shuart, the family home where he had grown up. His main ambition would have been to follow in his father's footsteps, husbanding the land and attempting to ensure a prosperous home for what he hoped would be a large and healthy family, with a long-term future secured for his descendants. Making a viable living may have been an uphill struggle, possibly almost every year, for Thomas II and his wife Jane, but five days after his marriage a secure financial foundation seems to have been laid when he wrote from London to the family bankers, Cobbs of Margate:

> *Sir, I have placed eight hundred pounds in Sir James Esdale's Bank on your account and I will thank you to pay a Draft of four hundred and forty eight pounds nineteen shill[s] and sixpence which will be presented to you next Saturday by my Father –*
>
> *Tho[s]. O. Curling*
>
> *Adelphi Hotel – Strand, Nov 27 – 1804* [129]

---

[128] For details of our Becker ancestors see **Appendix 4a – The Becker-Solley family of Kent** (p. 165) Extracts from *The Wilkinson-Becker and Kelleher-Hogan Families in Australia: 1822 to 2017*. Peter Wilkinson, unpublished paper 2017.

[129] KHLC EK/U1453/83/15/482.

Addressed on the reverse to:

Francis Cobb Esq[r] Margate[130]

The letter gives us a glimpse of Thomas II administering the family's financial affairs, but this was too big a deposit to be the result of a successful sale of grain or cattle in London. £800 was a considerable sum of money in 1804, but it is difficult to discover an exact equivalent. There are several websites offering conversion of historic sums to current equivalents. The one which best illustrates the difficulty and provides figures is the Measuring Worth website.[131] Entering the data on this site gives (amongst other possibilities) the following results:[132]

In 2018, the relative price worth of £800 0s 0d from 1804 is:
   £69,100.00 using the retail price index
   £63,100.00 using the GDP deflator.
In 2018, the relative wage or income worth of £800 0s 0d from 1804 is:
   £790,000.00 using the average earnings
   £918,000.00 using the per capita GDP.
In 2018, the relative output worth of £800 0s 0d from 1804 is:
   £5,040,000.00 using the GDP.

Whatever its value, this sum was either a nest egg carefully accumulated over many years in preparation for Thomas II's marriage or, more likely, a dowry from his new wife's family. Jane's father, Michael Becker, had been a shrewd businessman and at his death had left his wife Jane, née Belsey, comfortably off.[133] Thomas's request to Francis Cobb that half of the funds should immediately be transferred to his father's account might indicate that the family had needed him to marry well in order to keep them afloat financially.

Around the time of their son's marriage, Thomas I and Catharine moved to live permanently at Goldstone, giving the young couple the space to establish themselves at Shuart.

---

[130] KHLC EK/U1453/83/15/482. The placing of the date and the sender's address varied for a considerable period, and such information was often written at the bottom of the letter, as here. Envelopes were not in general use, the letter paper being folded in such a way as to provide a central panel on the outer side of the paper for the addressee and a second panel for the sender's name and address. The edges were folded inwards and the whole was sealed with sealing wax.

[131] www.measuringworth.com

[132] The data are taken, with permission, from the Measuring Worth website, Copyright © 2019 MeasuringWorth.

[133] Jane Belsey was a direct descendant, through her father and his mother, of John and Mercy Curling of Chilton, Thanet.

The St Nicholas overseers' accounts[134] show half-yearly poor rates payments listing rental value and individual assessed payments due. These accounts record that although he was now living in Goldstone, Thomas I was from 1804 the owner, rather than the tenant, of a small plot of land in St Nicholas whose rental value was £34. Looking at these accounts we can see that the two Curling men together occupied the largest portion of land in St Nicholas parish. The next largest was Mr Gillow's.

As the kingdom continued to take the strain of the Napoleonic wars Thomas II stepped into his father's place in St Nicholas-at-Wade's vestry. In a run of poor seasons[135] he kept the farm afloat, while between 1805 and 1822 his wife bore him on average one child every two years. The firstborn, a boy, was inevitably christened Thomas Curling, the third in the line of that name. Thomas III was baptized at St Nicholas Church, Ash-next-Sandwich, on 6 October 1805,[136] his mother Jane having returned to her childhood home for her first confinement.

Here is a full list of Thomas II and Jane's children with their baptism years. All except the eldest and the youngest were born at Shuart Farm and baptized at St Nicholas-at-Wade parish church:

Thomas III	1805	Charles I	1810	Jane II	1819
Edward I	1807	Robert	1814	Catherine III	1820
Henry	1809	John III	1817	Arthur I	1822

Arthur was baptized at the church of St John-in-Thanet, Margate. The reason for this will become apparent later in the story. Our 2× great-grandfather was the second child, Edward I.

Life was generally ruled by the seasonal farming routines, but there were occasional 'alarums and excursions'. Newspaper reports of the time shine chinks of light on the lives of our family:

> In the night of Friday last a male ass, the property of Mr. Petman, butcher, of Hearn, was stolen from a field, about a mile from that village; early in the following morning, however, Jack returned home, loaded with a tarred sail-cloth nearly new, a brewing copper bent together, also nearly new, and a sack, having on it the name of Mr. Curling of St Nicholas, and doubtless greatly disappointed the thieves in the loss of their booty.[137]

---

134 CCA-U3-18/12/2 St Nicholas-at-Wade parish records, 1781–1815, no page numbers inserted in original.

135 *The Isle of Thanet Farming Community*, pp. 88–104 RKI Quested, 2001 revision, self-published.

136 Information originally supplied in a 'family reconstitution form' kindly supplied by David Cave, former parish archivist of St Nicholas parish church, Ash-next-Sandwich. Ash parish records are now held at CCA.

137 *Kentish Gazette* 25 July 1806.

This could well have been a smuggling expedition when the smugglers had acquired more contraband than they could transport and needed an extra animal in a hurry. Shuart Farm, with its track leading through the fields directly to the seawall and Minnis Bay, would have been ideally situated. Even the Curlings' banker, Francis Cobb, is known to have been on the wrong side of the law at least once:

> evidence suggests that Francis I was involved in some 'shady' enterprises: he was certainly not averse to operating outside the law, being fined £26 of 'Lawful English Money' for avoiding custom duties in 1799 and preventing an officer searching his premises. Living on a coastline renowned for smuggling, it is not unlikely that substantial capital was accrued through this activity.[138]

And further west along the coast, William Baldock, started life as a cowherd, and

> in the space of just sixty years, this allegedly dirty, uncouth cowhand on the Seasalter Marshes had amassed an estate said to be worth £1.1m and was building the largest private house in nineteenth century Kent at the time of his death. ... If William had been a cowherd on the Seasalter Marshes, this would have given him an unrivalled knowledge of the marshland topography which would have been very useful in his smuggling career.[139]

Metaphorically closer to the Curling home, Thomas I's father-in-law, Thomas Oakley, would certainly have known of and dealt with the smugglers of Deal; as a shipping agent he could not have avoided doing business with them,[140] and the track from the sea to the farmhouse at Shuart would have offered an ideal route for smugglers landing from Minnis Bay.

Thomas II was as active a participant in the administration of local community concerns as his father had been. As well as taking his turns in the parish administration, through participation as churchwarden, overseer and surveyor, he took an interest in the development of the local area. With the improvement of road-building techniques, an expanding web of turnpike roads made travel smoother and quicker, but also imposed increasing charges on road users. At the beginning of the nineteenth century the tolls at Sandwich Bridge were viewed as already excessive by local farmers bringing their produce and stock to market.

---

[138] 'The Cobbs of Margate : Evangelicalism and Anti-Slavery in the Isle of Thanet, 1787–1834'. Toby Ovenden *Archaeologia Cantiana*, vol. 133, 2013. http://bit.ly/Ch4OvendenAntiSlavery. With thanks to Kent Archaeological Society.

[139] 'William Baldock 1748/9–1812 Smuggler, Property Tycoon and Gentleman' © Peter Osborne, 2015.

[140] For information about smuggling in east Kent, with a significant section on Deal, see Richard Platt's website *Smugglers' Britain*, http://bit.ly/Ch4Smuggling.

On Tuesday 6 January 1807 Thomas II was present at a meeting in the Brick-layers' Arms, Minster, where he was chosen as a member of the committee elected to

> prepare a Petition to the Honorable House of Commons ... in opposition to the Bill now in Parliament, for the obtaining of a Turnpike Road from Sandwich to Ramsgate.[141]

The proposed road was to stretch from Margate via Ramsgate to Sandwich; a similar meeting had been held the previous day in Margate. Local opinion was less concerned about the turnpike road than about obtaining a reduction in the already exorbitant Sandwich Bridge toll. There was a unity of feeling between those attending the two meetings. They opposed the turnpike road if it meant an increase in tolls, and moreover appealed for a reduction. Their petition was successful; the Sandwich, Margate and Ramsgate turnpike road was enacted in 1807, the title of the act being 'A Bill for repairing the Road from the Town and Port of Sandwich in the County of Kent, to the Towns of Margate and Ramsgate in the Isle of Thanet in the said County; and for reducing for a limited Time the Tolls and Duties payable at Sandwich Bridge.'[142] At a later date, the tolls were reinstated. The toll-gate entrance to Sandwich, through the sixteenth-century Barbican gate (Fig. 19) still exists as part of the Barbican in Sandwich, and the last tolls levied are still displayed inside the arch, dated 1905, Fig. 20.

Fig. 19. **View to toll bridge on leaving Sandwich through the Barbican gate**

---

[141] *Kentish Gazette*, Tuesday 13 January 1807, front page, final column, via BNA.
[142] Website *Turnpikes in England and Wales* http://bit.ly/Ch4Turnpikes.

SANDWICH TOLL BRIDGE
TABLE OF TOLLS

For every Chariot, Landau, Berlin, Chaise, Chair, Calash, or other Vehicle:

	TOLLS AUTHORISED BY ACT OF PARLIAMENT		TOLLS NOW PAYABLE	
	s.	d.	s.	d.
drawn by 6 or more Horses or other beasts	2.	6.	2.	3.
drawn by 4 Horses or other beasts	2.	0.	1.	6.
drawn by 3 Horses or other beasts			1.	1½.
drawn by 2 Horses or other beasts	1.	0.		9.
drawn by 1 Horse or other beast		9.		6.

For every Waggon, Wain, Dray, Car, or other Carriage:

drawn by 4 or more Horses or Oxen	1.	6.	1.	0.
Less than 4 Horses or Oxen	1.	0.		9 for 3
				6 for 2
				4½ for 1

For every Horse or Mule laden or unladen, and not drawing	2.			1.
Ass laden or unladen and not drawing	2.			½.
Drove of Oxen, Cows, or Neat Cattle per Score	1.	8.		10.
and after that rate for any greater or less number.				
Drove of Calves, Hogs, Sheep, or lambs per Score	4.			2½.
and after that rate for any greater or less number.				

	TOLLS AUTHORISED BY ACT OF PARLIAMENT	
For every Locomotive weighing 2 Tons or under, having 4 wheels	1.	0.
having 3 wheels		9.
having 2 wheels		6.
For every Locomotive exceeding 2 Tons and not exceeding 4 Tons	1.	3.
4 Tons 6 Tons	1.	6.
6 Tons 10 Tons	2.	0.
10 Tons 14 Tons	2.	6.
For each wheel of any Waggon, Wain, Cart, Carriage, or other Vehicle, drawn or propelled by any Locomotive not exceeding 6 Tons		2
exceeding 6 Tons		3.

Guildhall
Sandwich
June 19th 1905

E.C. BYRNE,
Town Clerk.

Fig. 20. **Sandwich Toll Bridge charges 1905**

In September 1807 Thomas II is listed in the *Kentish Gazette* as having 'a licence to kill' – game.[143] Although for the elite the shooting of game had evolved into a leisure pursuit in mediaeval times, with game hunting in nineteenth-century Kent considered a sport by some, it was also a way of contributing significantly to the farm's larder.[144]

Wooden ships, relying as they did on wind and sail, were far more at the mercy of storms than the later vessels built of iron and powered by steam. In an almighty storm on 12 February 1808 many vessels in the Channel and North Sea were either badly damaged or completely wrecked:

> It is feared the crews of these vessels have all perished except the captain
> of one of them, with his wife, who committed themselves to the mercy

---

[143] *Kentish Gazette*, 22 September 1807. This indicates that the killing of game was regulated even before the Game Act of 1831.

[144] Wikipedia has a comprehensive page on hunting and shooting in the United Kingdom, which includes a section on the history of shooting, and a list of animals which are permitted targets: http://bit.ly/Ch4HuntingandShooting.

of the waves at the risque of their lives, they were both driven on shore and taken up alive, though much bruised, and conveyed to Mr. Curling's at Shuart, under whose hospitable roof they at present remain. It is mentioned as an instance of pure humanity worthy of record, that when the lady was taken up perfectly naked, a wagoner stripped himself of his cloaths in order to protect her from the inclemency of the weather.[145]

Fox-hunting was seen as essential to preserving the smaller livestock such as fowl, a food source on which families relied heavily. Thomas II was elected to be the inaugural secretary of the Isle of Thanet Hunt:

On April 2nd 1813, a meeting was held at Mount Pleasant Inn, attended by most of the principal gentlemen in the neighbourhood, to form the Isle of Thanet Hunt. Mr Thomas Oakley Curling was chosen [as secretary]; a liberal subscription entered into, and a committee appointed, to receive the names of those who might wish to become members thereof. It was also agreed that every member should wear a green coat, and buttons with T. H., so that a uniformity among the members might be observed. The huntsman to wear a scarlet coat, and black velvet cap.[146]

Fig. 21. **The Isle of Thanet Hunt, mural in Margate Caves (1)** [147]

---

[145] *Kentish Gazette*, 16 February 1808.
[146] *Mockett's Journal* p. 84, by John Mockett, pub. 1836. Search result for Thomas Oakley Curling at this URL: http://bit.ly/Ch4Mockett1. See also **Appendix 4b – History of hunting in East Kent** (p. 175), Thanet and Herne Hunt.
[147] Photographs Fig. 21 & Fig. 22 kindly supplied by Frank Leppard, Margate.

Fig. 22. **The Isle of Thanet Hunt, Margate Caves (2)**

The mural in the chalk caves at Margate, Fig. 21 and Fig. 22, provides a contemporaneous painting of the Isle of Thanet Hunt, although the artist appears to have taken licence with the hunt colours. Here is the story of the caves and their murals:

> In the latter half of the 18th century, a gentleman named Francis Forster built a large red-brick house above the caves, which at the time he did not know about ... In 1798 his gardener, whilst digging behind the building, discovered the Caves by having the ground give way beneath him. One account of the discovery stated that he died from the injuries sustained falling into the caves ... Forster started to adapt the underground space to his own use. He was known to be a rather eccentric character and engaged a local artist named Brazier to create some carvings and to paint the various figures and scenes on the chalk walls that can still be seen today.[148]

If the images in the murals are of the same 'Thanet Hunt' which was inaugurated in 1813, the murals must have been executed after that date. A century later, in Baily's Hunting Directory the name had changed to the Thanet and Herne Hunt, but the members were still wearing green, and the buttons still had the initials TH. (Fig. 23)

---

[148] R F LeGear, as above.

THANET AND HERNE.

Hunt Uniform—Green coat with black velvet collar; the Master wears a red coat.

Master — (1905) B. Prescott-Westcar, Esq., Strode Park, Herne. **Hon. Secretaries**—G. T. Adams, Esq., Alexandra Road, Margate (for Thanet); (1910) Mr. F. A. Tomkins, Rayham Lodge, near Whitstable (for Herne). **Huntsman**—The Master. **Whippers-in**—1st and K.H. (1909), T. Garratt; 2nd (1906), A. Breed. **24** couples of foxhound bitches and half Stud Book harriers. **Kennels**—Strode Park, Herne. **Telegraph Office**—Herne. **Railway Station**—Herne Bay, 1 mile. **Days of Meeting**—Tuesday and Friday; and Thursday.

This pack hunts the whole of the Isle of Thanet and district of Herne to Whitstable. The Canterbury to Sandwich road is the S. boundary. It is chiefly plough, but of recent years much land has been laid down in grass; large woodlands in the Herne district. The quantity of wire is considerable; it is well marked, and arrangements are made for its removal. No foxhounds hunt over the country N. of the River Stour. In season 1910—11, the pack hunts the WEST STREET country (q.v.) by arrangement.

A subscription pack; the Master has a guarantee. The hounds belong to the Master.

The THANET Harriers were first kennelled at Cleve Court Minster about 1762 and were maintained and hunted by Mr. J. F. Farrer. In 1775 the kennels were moved to Gore Street, Monkton, and in 1813 the ISLE OF THANET Hunt was established and carried on by a Committee till 1849, when Mr. John White took the country till 1873. (In 1895 the name was changed to THANET and HERNE.)

Masters (after Mr. White): Capt. Tomlin, 1873—75. Capt.

15

Fig. 23. **Baily's Hunting Directory 1910–11**[149]

Thomas Oakley Curling's father, Thomas I, continued to farm at Goldstone, although it looks as though he found the trade in hops to be slow in 1814. He wrote to Francis Cobb:

> *Dear Sir*
>
> *After I left my sample of Hops with you at Margate, I waited a month in expectation of hearing from you, when concluding that you were sufficiently provided and fearing the sale for Pockets would be over, I sent them on board the Hoy for London on the 28th ult – had*

[149] With thanks to Nick Onslow, the historian of the East Kent Hunt, for this clip. See also **Appendix 4b – History of hunting in East Kent** (p. 175) for further insights provided by Nick.

*this not been the case I should have been very glad to have now dealt
with you for them*

*I beg my Comp^(ts) to your Son
and remain Dr Sir
Yours truly*

Thos. Curling

Goldstone 7 Novr 1814

Hoys were local vessels providing a regular service between Margate and London, carrying goods and passengers: Fig. 24.

Fig. 24. **Margate, with the Arrival of the Hoy, 1801** [150]

The sea inevitably played a significant role in the lives of coastal farmers. A major source of fertilizer for the land was seaweed. As mentioned earlier, tracks at Shuart Farm led through its fields right to the seawall, so harvesting the marine material was relatively easy. Horse-drawn carts carried it back to the farmyard for layering with animal manure and other materials.

---

[150] Image of *Margate, with the Arrival of the Hoy* (**1801**) P J de Loutherbourgh. Pub. R Bowyer, Historic Gallery, Pall Mall, London, 1801. Sculp. J C Stadler. http://bit.ly/Ch4MargateHoyPrint. From Margate Local History website, With thanks to Anthony Lee for permission to use material from his website: www.margatelocalhistory.co.uk

In July 1815, Thomas II was one of the two churchwardens at St Nicholas-at-Wade who followed up the King's edict that provision should be made for the families whose menfolk had been killed or wounded at Waterloo. The following historic note, recorded in July 1815 after the battle, was probably matched in every parish in the country:

> *In Consequence of a letter to the Archbishop of Canterbury from the Prince Regent in the Name and on the behalf of his Majesty, authorising a subscription for the benefit of the wounded & the families of those that were killed in the ever memorable Battle of Waterloo fought on the 18th June 1815, & another letter from the Arch-bishop recommending the same to his clergy, a subscription for that benevolent purpose was* [erasure, ink stain] *entered into in this Parish & the Vill of Sarr on Monday the 31st July, when the following Sum was collected £38/15/6 was paid, as directed in the Arch-bishop's letter, into the hands of Mr. Abbot, Proctor & Deputy Registrar at Canterbury on Saturday 5th July by I. D. Vicar.*[151]

A list of contributors and their contributions follows; it includes 'Thos. O Curling Esqr. £1/1/='.[152] In the original, the February 1815 church rates follow that entry, indicating that the use of the pages of the churchwardens' account book was rather random, as the Battle of Waterloo took place in June. The account summary is presented by '*Thos. O Curling and Wl^m Champion, churchwardens*'.

The daily lives of our ancestors were remarkably like those of the inhabitants of any small twenty-first-century village. The vestry has morphed into the parish council, but its members are still volunteers. We get the impression of the nineteenth-century St Nicholas-at-Wade community being a settled one, caring for its more needy members; the lives of everyone were touched nonetheless by the tectonic shifts of power both nationally and internationally. Certainly there have been changes. In our ancestors' times tea and fabric were among the prizes to be obtained at 'tax-free' rates via a swift trip to the coast, whereas these days, more often than not, the contraband is illegal drugs. It should be noted too that as well as importing goods illegally, smugglers traded *out* items such as wool and even gold.[153] Changes came by degrees, and the next chapter lays the foundation for a major change for Thomas Oakley Curling's family. (In a class of its own is the indescribably appalling twenty-first century trade which takes advantage of desperate people's vulnerabilities, often called 'people smuggling' which we hear of on a daily basis.)

---

[151] St Nicholas-at-Wade parish records. CCA-U3-18/12/2, no page numbers inserted in original.

[152] In imperial currency, £1/1/= was known as a guinea, and prices were often expressed as multiples of one guinea.

[153] See Richard Platt's website *Smugglers' Britain*, section under Deal on this page: http://www.smuggling.co.uk/gazetteer_se_14.html.

Chapter 5 – A Letter from Shuart Farm

Despite the 1815 victory at Waterloo, things looked bleak for farmers across the country. The army had required considerable food supplies during the Napoleonic wars, and the Kent farmers had been particularly well placed to supply it. But this market had now dried up, and the surviving soldiers had returned to their homes around the country, worn out and unfit for work. The decreased demand for the Kent farmers' agricultural produce greatly reduced their incomes, which affected employment.

In 1816 the Board of Agriculture published its report *The Agricultural State of the Kingdom*.[154] The Board was not a government body but a national association of landowners and tenant farmers with large acreages, originally established 'to promote agricultural improvement'.[155] Its 1816 report was a county-by-county survey of the state of agriculture in the immediate aftermath of the Napoleonic wars. To achieve this the board had sent a questionnaire to farmers and landowners across the United Kingdom. Thomas Oakley Curling (Thomas II) was one of 326 farmers who replied.[156] His response was published in the report. What follows here is a modern rendering of the points he made.

Thomas II wrote that farmers with bigger enterprises had initially diversified their sources of income. This had enabled them to manage for longer – but for several of his friends bankruptcy was finally looming.

> [*T*]*here are many of them now in great distress, who at one time might have made from 5000l. to 10,000l, by the sale of their stock and crop; their friends obliged to call money from them by their own necessities, which the farmer finds impossible to replace in his business.*[157]

Farmers were not keeping as many animals as before, and every acre devoted to arable was '*cropped, to produce something* [however small the yield] *towards preventing total ruin*'.

The result was that the stackyards, where harvested supplies were stored, were empty. Graziers could not keep as many animals as normal on the land. Increasing

---

[154] *The Agricultural State of the Kingdom 1816*, first published Charles Clement, London; republished 1970 Augustus Kelley, New York, with an introduction by Gordon E Mingay.

[155] See Wikipedia, http://bit.ly/Ch5WikiBrdAgric.

[156] For a complete transcript of Thomas II's letter, see **Appendix 5a –Thomas II's letter to the Board of Agriculture** (p. 176).

[157] 5000l. = £5,000. According to Wikipedia the £ symbol 'derives from the upper case Latin letter L, representing *libra pondo*, the basic unit of weight in the Roman Empire, which in turn is derived from the Latin word, *libra*, meaning scales or a balance.' I have often found lower case 'l' in place of £ in the notation of monetary value in earlier centuries, and often placed after rather than before the digits.

the price of produce would not be of any help, as there was so little to sell or to use for feed. So the farmer would thresh the next crop as soon as possible, to try to make ends meet. Thomas II thought that the only hope was for the government to take 'more decided steps than any yet adopted' to relieve farmers, by keeping the price of corn high. The first Corn Laws had been introduced the previous year, but were being inadequately implemented. He warned that another year like this would bring many who might formerly have been described as 'men of property' to complete ruin.

With little work for agricultural labourers, unemployment increased. The unemployed were given support from the poor rates, similar to the present-day benefits system in the UK but administered at parish level. To receive this they had to do whatever work could be found for them by the parish overseers, such as mending the roads. Thomas II's meaning is not clear at this point in the letter. He seems to have implied that the men were not suited to this work, their labour only worthy of a payment of the number of pennies equivalent to the number of shillings they were actually given. Alternatively he might have meant that the men were only receiving as many pennies as the number of shillings that they would have earned in farm work. Either way the men were earning a pittance compared to their normal wage. Thomas II went on to say that men who would normally have been reliable workers fell in with 'the worst of labourers and broken down smugglers', who were a bad influence. They became the first to be sent from farm work to the parish to receive 'relief'. This in turn put additional financial pressure on the parish and its large farmers locally, because it was they who paid the Land Tax, administered at parish level, to fund the poor rates.

One of Thomas's observations has overtones of the attitudes to the unemployed young couples prevalent in the 1970s and 80s: 'The young are not deterred from marrying by the present want of employment ... knowing they must always receive sufficient for existence from the poor-rates.'

The old Kent ploughs required four horses, a man and a lad to work the field.[158] But in order to economize, farmers had started using two-horse ploughs which needed only the man, not the lad. Young unmarried men who cost the farmer less were employed in preference to the more experienced married labourers. So the income of whole families was jeopardized, further adding to the burden on parish funds. Thomas mentions that 'some benevolent characters' had taken on unemployed labourers, thinking that the crisis would be temporary, but Thomas thinks they were wrong, as their being unable to support these labourers long term would ultimately send them to the parish, too.

---

[158] There is a beautiful painting of a four-horse Kentish plough by John Duvall in the Ipswich Museum and Gallery collection, currently in storage. You can view it on the ArtUK website: https://bit.ly/Ch5KentPlough

His recommendations include
- – a prohibition of all corn imports for two years
- – high duty on imported materials and seeds
- – an alteration to the poor laws
- – standardization of rates, and no farmers to be exempt
- – the poor being supported by the nation rather than the parish, and factories being established in places where the poor might find work.

Thomas II's suggestions had no direct channel to decision makers. The best he could hope for was that some members of the Board – landowners with influence in government circles, many of them MPs – would press for agricultural reform.

From the landowners' standpoint, taxing imported grain was to their advantage. The first incarnation of the Corn Laws, imposing exorbitant import taxes on corn, had been introduced the previous year, 1815. During the Napoleonic wars Britain's farmers had been protected from the effects of cheap foreign grain by mutual blockades imposed by Napoleon against Britain and by the British against the import of French goods. This, along with other influences such as several poor harvests, had the effect of keeping the price of grain excessively high in Britain. Then after the war the government, made up largely of landowners who wanted to prevent these high prices from dropping, introduced the Corn Laws, which imposed restrictions and tariffs on imported grain.[159]

Thomas got his wish that the laws be enforced more rigorously. He and the many MPs who supported these laws in parliament either failed to anticipate or determinedly ignored the disastrous effect which the higher cost of grain would have on the price of bread, the staple diet of thousands of city-dwelling factory workers and rural labourers alike. A vicious circle ensued in which landowners succeeded in keeping corn prices high, bread remained expensive, workers could not afford this basic food and demanded lower prices – but high corn prices were seen as essential to the country's economy. Reformers in parliament struggled for thirty years to get the Corn Laws repealed, succeeding only in 1846.

Any joy the community might have felt over the cessation of the Napoleonic wars was dampened by the depression in agriculture which was having a serious effect on everyone – the landowners, the tenants and the agricultural labourers – and its effect was long-lasting.

Having sent off his response to the Board of Agriculture's questionnaire, Thomas II returned to the pressing local concerns. He had stepped into his father's shoes in the vestry, and the schoolmaster, Mr Holmes, was proving difficult to manage. We do not know exactly where the fault lay, but Holmes was struggling financially. Although the vestry had paid him his first year's salary in advance, when it came to subsequent payments some of the vestry members were less than

---

[159] See https://en.wikipedia.org/wiki/Corn_Laws.

punctual with their contributions to it, leaving Holmes himself in pecuniary difficulty. He was either too embarrassed or too cowed by his employers to tell them of
his problems; he got deeper and deeper into debt, and ended up in the debtors'
prison in Maidstone in April 1816, from where he wrote to Mr John Bridges at St
Nicholas Court, asking for help to pay the carpenters and bricklayers. (These days,
to expect an employee living in a tied cottage to pay for the upkeep of the fabric of
the house would be considered grossly unfair.) Having rescued Mr Holmes from
gaol, the vestry continued to employ him as the schoolmaster for the time being.[160]
Thomas II's children do not appear to have been educated at this school, as there
are no Curling names on the 1821 list of pupils.[161]

Two years after Thomas Oakley Curling wrote his letter to the Board of
Agriculture, the depression in agriculture was creeping closer to home. His father,
Thomas I, was becoming frail, and struggled to balance his books. It was unusual
for a farmer to write a will long before he died if he was in full health (although
local mariners of the period did so routinely, because their mortality rate was much
higher). Thomas I drew up his will on 21 June 1809, opening with the time-
honoured phrase 'This is the last will and testament of me Thomas Curling' and
said he was 'of Goldstone in the parish of Ash-next-Sandwich Gentleman'.[162] It
seems that following the drawing up of his will, he may well have been in failing
health for almost a decade. In 1818 he wrote the following note to his bankers,
Messrs Cobb & Co of Margate:

Delf Street Sandwich

Nov^er 7 1818

Sirs

*I was from home when yours of 3rd inst[163] was delivered here – I
removed from Goldstone last spring to this place – I have been very
sorry that it has not been convenient to me to settle the account
between us, but you may depend on my doing it immediately that it is
in my power, and I shall have great satisfaction in waiting on you for
that purpose and remain Sirs very truly Yours*

Thos. Curling[164]

---

[160] *The Schools of St Nicholas-at-Wade*, Richard Parker, pub. Mill Bank, 1957.
[161] Parker, pp. 28–29.
[162] TNA prob 11/1617.
[163] '*inst*' is an abbreviation of the Latin word '*instanta*'. This abbreviation was in regular
use until the late twentieth century, meaning in this context 'the present month'. The
previous month was indicated by a similar Latin abbreviation '*ult*' from '*ultimo*', and
the following month by '*prox*' from '*proximo*'.
[164] KHLC EK/U1453/83/15/482.

It must have been excruciatingly difficult for this diligent man of 'good family' to make such an admission to his bank manager. Less than four months later, on 4 March 1819, Thomas I died, leaving Catharine, after thirty-eight years of marriage, a widow, living alone in Delf Street, in Sandwich. He was buried in the family vault at Ham, for which he had applied to the Archbishop of Canterbury,[165] twenty years previously.

---

[165] See **Appendix 5b – The Curling family vault at St George's Church, Ham** (p. 178).

Chapter 6 – Epistolary Intercourse

Commentary on three Curling letters, Autumn 1819

We now come to another exciting family history treasure. In June 2009, I was introduced, as mentioned in the Introduction, to Carey Bayliss, a descendant of Thomas Curling III, who lives in Australia. She sent me transcripts of all three nineteenth-century letters in her possession, and digital images of one.[166] The first is from our 4× great-grandmother, Catharine Curling, writing from her sister Elizabeth Kelly's new home, near Cookham in Berkshire, to her grandson Thomas III; the second is a reply from him, written from Reverend Abbot's boarding school in Ramsgate, where he and his brother Edward were pupils; and the third is another from Catharine, written after her return home to Sandwich. What follows here is a commentary on the letters.

All three letters give us a wonderfully detailed insight into the writers' lives. Thomas III's letter names several individual family friends, relations and acquaintances, and we can begin to build a picture of life for the rural 'middling classes'[167] of 1819 in Kent. Things were not so bad that the Curling family had tightened its purse strings completely.

For all the gloom of Thomas II's 1816 letter to the Board of Agriculture, the Curling family was comfortable, even though by then there had already been financial difficulties, as Thomas II had hinted in his letter.[168] This leads to speculation that he was getting assistance for the school fees from elsewhere in the family. It is evident from Catharine's letters that a good education was of paramount importance to her, but her husband Thomas I had died in March 1819, and although she had obtained probate of the will she had not administered it. Unless she had funds of her own which had reverted to her control on her husband's death, she might not have been in a position to do much for her grandchildren financially. So the funding could well have come from the boys' maternal grandmother Jane Becker I (née Belsey), who had been a widow since 1796; Michael Becker I had

---

[166] Complete transcripts of the three letters can be found in **Appendix 6a – The letters of Catharine and Thomas Curling** (p. 180). I am immensely grateful to Carey Bayliss for sharing these with me.

[167] In earlier centuries, people in the broad middle band of society, between the rich élite and those who were either on a low and uncertain income or unemployed, were called the 'middling classes'.

[168] See Chapter 5 and its **Appendix 5a –Thomas II's letter to the Board of Agriculture** (p. 176).

left her financially secure.[169] It is more than likely that she gave her daughter Jane money to help with the elder boys' education while she was still alive, Certainly, on her death Jane Becker I bequeathed to her daughter Jane Curling the considerable sum of £1,000.

The Reverend George Abbot's boarding school in Ramsgate catered for thirty boys. Thomas III was coming up to his fourteenth birthday, and Edward was aged twelve. The school gets a brief mention on pp. 18–19 of *Hunter's Directory* of 1815 – note the opportunity for students to swim in the sea as a marketing point, Fig. 25.[170]

Mr. Abbot's seminary for a limitted number of young gentlemen, is on a liberal plan, situated at the upper part of High-Street, in an airy situation, with an excellent play ground attached:— youth are instructed in the different branches of education and the classics; and every attention is paid to render the establishment worthy the support of those families who may have occasion to place their young gentlemen at Ramsgate for the advantage of sea-bathing.—

Fig. 25. **Reverend Abbot's advertisement** [171]

The boys at Mr Abbot's school were expected to be hardier than many twenty-first-century teenagers. Thomas III wrote that they were still swimming in the sea at Ramsgate towards the end of September, and he expected to continue possibly even into October. From the late eighteenth century, sea bathing had led to the blossoming of seaside towns as destinations for restorative and invigorating holidays or even prescribed cures. 'Thalasso-therapy' had been available only to the middling and upper classes until Dr John Coakley Lettsom built the Royal Sea Bathing Hospital in Margate, 4 miles from Ramsgate. It opened in 1796, receiving

---

[169] The will of Michael Becker was transcribed by Reverend John Hovell (1937–2014), who was a 2× great-grandson of Michael Becker II. The original of the will is at Kent History and Library Centre, PRC/31/266 B/1.

[170] An online version of the original directory can be read via this link: http://bit.ly/Ch6ThanetHunter-GoogleBooks.

[171] *Hunter's Directory*, 1815, pp. 18–19.

large numbers of patients, particularly children suffering from tuberculosis and other ailments associated with poor living conditions.[172,173] Five years later, on 28 September 1801, a report in the Kentish Gazette recorded that Jesse Curling and his son, also Jesse, were among the governors of the Sea Bathing Infirmary, and contributed £25.0.0 each to the purchase of further land for the institution. Jesse senior had been born in Ramsgate, son of John and Katherine Curling.[174] By 1793 he was living in Rotherhithe and his son Jesse lived in Bermondsey, but both maintained their connection to their Kentish roots.

Reverend Abbot appears to be offering to middle-class parents the benefits of sea bathing for their sons, presumably as a preventative for childhood ailments and the opportunity to build a healthy physique. Catharine also mentions in her second letter her pleasure that the boys were playing cricket. These were healthy, active lads, with horse-riding, swimming and cricket as part of their lives.

Three more children were at home with their mother, too young yet for school; a further two grandsons, Robert, aged four, and John, two years old (neither of whom Catharine named in her letter) together with baby Jane, only five months old.

At the beginning of September 1819, Catharine was staying with her sister Mrs Elizabeth Kelly, who had recently moved to a house called Stone House in Cookham, near Great Marlow. In fact the two places are separated by the River Thames and while Cookham is in Berkshire, Great Marlow is in Buckinghamshire; see the two maps of the area, Fig. 26 and Fig. 27. I particularly like Thomas Richardson's 'close-up' of the Winter Hill area, because he labels the field where Stone House was built 'a House & Land belonging to Mary Medwin call'd Stone House'.

---

[172] See Kingston University's Historic Hospital Admissions Records Project [HHARP], which researched admissions to Victorian and Edwardian Children's hospitals and provides background historical information for the earlier period. Website http://bit.ly/Ch6RSBHMargate. Thalassotherapy or the 'sea water cure' is also mentioned in connection with the hospital in A Sakula's review of *The History of the Royal Sea Bathing Hospital 1791–1991*, Journal of the Royal Society of Medicine, vol. 84, October 1991. http://bit.ly/Ch6RSBHMarHist.

[173] A generation or two later, the list of Fellows of the Royal College of Surgeons (RCS) includes 'Henry Curling, Surgeon to the Margate Royal Sea-Bathing Infirmary and the Ramsgate Seamen's Infirmary, Ramsgate, Kent elected to the RCS in 1846.' This Henry was a direct descendant of the Curlings of Ham Manor. In the RCS listing directly below Henry was 'Thomas Blizard Curling, F.R.C.S., Surgeon to, and Lecturer on Surgery at, the London Hospital.' The latter was a distinguished member of the RCS as described in his lengthy obituary in the *British Medical Journal*, March 1888. He was a descendant of another branch of the Thanet Curlings.

[174] Baptism in the records of Ramsgate Ebenezer Chapel from FindMyPast https://www.findmypast.co.uk/.

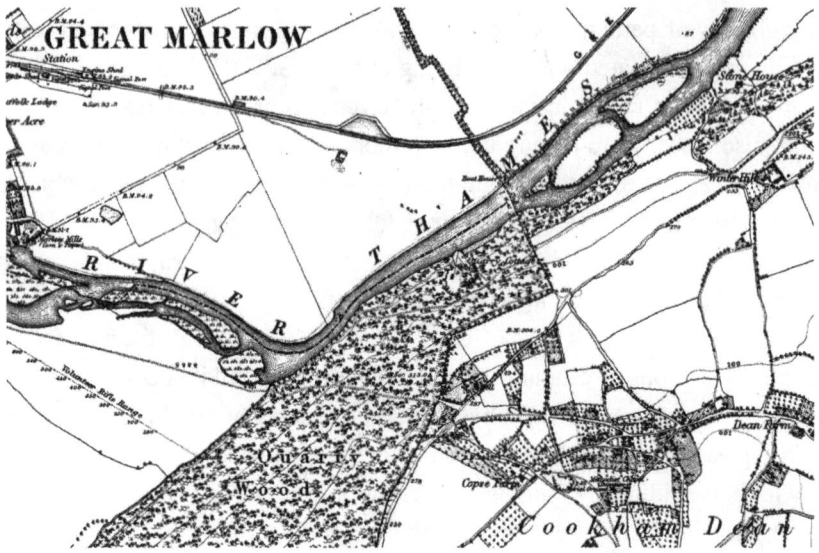

Fig. 26. **Marlow and Cookham on the Ordnance Survey, 1876–1886**

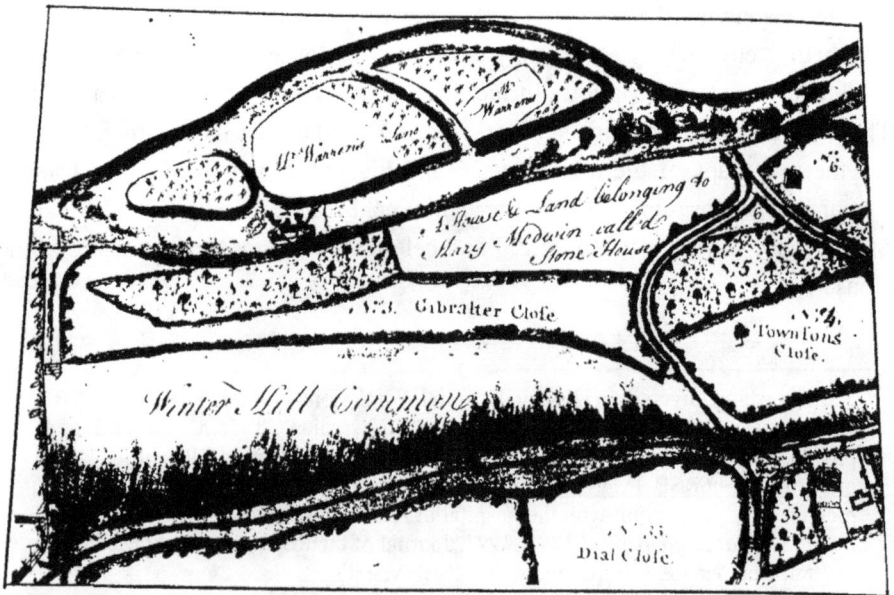

Fig. 27. **Winter Hill in 1744** [175]

[175] 'Winter Hill in 1744', cartographer Thomas Richardson. Stone House was at the bottom of a steep road down Winter Hill, Cookham Dean, in Berkshire. Thomas Richardson's map, drawn seventy-five years before the Kelly family's arrival, shows the area as it probably still was in Catharine's time. *The Royal Hundred of Cookham*, p. 84, Luke Over and Chris Tyrrell, 1994, Cliveden Press.

Prior to the move, Elizabeth had been living in Hainault Cottage in Aldborough Hatch with her son Henry. Catharine mentioned 'Mr Kelly's family', giving the impression that Elizabeth's husband was also present for the move although we have no other concrete evidence of this. According to biographies of Napier,[176] Francis John Kelly abandoned his family at some point after his time at Hythe. However, military records show that he transferred from his post at Hythe Barracks in 1811,[177] to become the barrackmaster at Romford, and that he retired on an annual army allowance in 1817.[178] Letters written by Elizabeth are headed with addresses first in Upminster in 1813 and then Hainault Cottage, Aldborough Hatch, in 1819. Both these addresses are 4 miles from Romford, an easy horseback commute for Francis, although he may have lived at the barracks, returning home only infrequently.

When he died in 1826, he was buried at Cookham. If he and Elizabeth were estranged for the nine years prior to his death, it would still have been she who arranged his final resting place, near her home, because she was still legally married to him and the responsibility would have been hers whether they were together or not.

Although the language is more formal than letters (or emails) between family members these days, there is real affection in them, and Catharine's demonstrates how attentively she has read Thomas III's previous letter. We discover that there were three steeds allocated to Thomas III and Edward; Catharine had heard from her daughter-in-law Jane, Thomas's mother, that his younger brothers were being prevented from attending school despite having recovered from an illness. Catharine was a bit tight-lipped about the schoolteacher's caution; we are introduced to the 'sagacious' Neptune, a great name for a seaside dog (dogs were often 'sagacious' in the nineteenth and early twentieth centuries[179]) and she was delighted that Thomas III had visited her friend Miss Stewart in Sandwich. We can deduce that Miss Stewart was a close friend, as she had visited the sisters at Hainault Cottage before the move to Cookham, a not inconsiderable journey for a friend to make by public transport from Sandwich even today, never mind doing it by coach and horses in 1819, requiring at least one change of transport, in London. Catharine finished her letter by encouraging the boys in their latest educational

---

[176] See: Priscilla Napier *Revolution and the Napier Brothers*, 1973, p. 77; Rosamond Lawrence *Charles Napier, Friend and Fighter*, 1951; Edward Beasley *The Chartist General*, 2017.

[177] TNA WO 54/715 f13 Appointments in the Barrack Department

[178] Ibid, f28

[179] See this online example, found on VictorianWeb.org, an illustration by Robert Seymore, from Chapter 2 of Charles Dickens's *The Pickwick Papers*, published in 1836, http://bit.ly/SagaciousDog. Googling 'sagacious dog' yields other examples.

foray, French, and in their sporting activities, namely cricket; and she finally asked for another letter from Thomas's brother Edward before she left Stone House.

All three letters give a wealth of insight into the social life of the rural middling classes of the time, and it is clear that the Curlings were a family of some standing in their community, with Thomas III and Edward's father throwing a party after the races and Catharine visiting friends and relations both near and far. Her account of the Cookham–Sandwich journey highlighted the arduous nature of travel in those days, the distance of 32 miles from Cookham to the Strand in London apparently taking much of the day on 18 September. She was met in London by her son Thomas Oakley Curling (Thomas II). The following day the journey took eleven hours from London to Sandwich (75 miles from the Strand in London to the Guildhall in Sandwich) where Thomas II, having accompanied his mother to her home, travelled on, in the Margate coach, to the village of Sarre. It would then have been a walk of less than 2 miles from Sarre to Shuart Farm. These days, the whole distance from Cookham to Sandwich is a mere 2 hours 8 minutes by car – traffic permitting.[180]

Catharine's account of the Royal Military College's move from Marlow to Sandhurst gives us an interesting glimpse of what cadet life was like at the old site and the reasons for the move.

Thomas's and Edward's schooling was obviously quite sophisticated, including, as it did, the Classics and French. Their aunt Elizabeth Kelly was proficient enough in French to write a letter to Thomas III. Catharine's letters highlighted Elizabeth Kelly's active interest in the Curling boys from their youth, a fact which became significant in Edward's life less than ten years later.

On Saturday 25 September,[181] Thomas III sat down to write his reply to his grandmother. She had asked him to tell her about the boys' trip to the races. Boarding schools these days might be reluctant to allow their pupils out midweek to attend races with their father, but at the time the Margate races were a major social event for the Isle of Thanet.

Thomas III's excitement about the outing shines through the careful writing style of his 'dutiful grandson' letter. He and Edward must have been delighted that their father 'was so kind as to send for us on Wednesday', and we learn that the boys attended races on both days of the race meeting, and went home overnight. It is more than likely that other families withdrew their sons from school for the occasion, so Mr Abbot and his wife would have had an unusually quiet midweek in school. The boys who were not so lucky were no doubt miserable that they had to carry on with their lessons.

---

[180] Calculation taken from the RAC Routeplanner.
[181] Google search result for day of the week.

The walk from Ramsgate High Street to Dandelion Field would have taken about an hour and a half[182] and such a walk was obviously unworthy of comment at the time, when country folk were accustomed to walking several miles in the course of a week. Thomas III told Catharine that Mr Friend[183] estimated that 23,000 people attended the event – an astonishingly large crowd. If Mr Friend's assessment was accurate, then the Isle of Thanet Races were perhaps Kent's answer to Ascot. The newspaper report in the *Morning Post* of Saturday 25 September 1819 certainly corroborates his estimate:

MARGATE, Sept. 23.

THE RACES

We question whether the Isle of Thanet ever saw such a concourse of people as were assembled on her Downs yesterday. The Course is a mile in circuit, and situated to the south of the far-famed Dandelion. Nearly in line with the grand stand were equipages of the gayest description, consisting of landaus and landaulets, chariots, curricles, barouches, cabriolets, tilburies, and dennets; stage coaches, caravans, donkey-carts and waggons, branched off nearly as far as the eye could reach. Perhaps twenty thousand persons were there, of whom at least five hundred were horsemen. Sir GILBERT HEATHCOTE, and many other Newmarket leaders were present. The first race commenced at half past one o'clock, for the Powell Stakes of five guineas, with thirty from the fund:

Captain COMBERATCH's	Belerophon	Lilac and white
Mr PALMER's	Lucretia	Pink and black
Mr CURLING's	Maid of Kent	Light blue
Mr PAGE's	Hap Hazard	True blue

Six to four on Lucretia at starting, and she came in in grand style.

I was lucky to find this newspaper report as Thomas III did not mention the names of the horses at all, probably thinking that his grandmother would be more interested in the people she knew in the area.

The couple whom Thomas III named, separately, as Mr John Curling and Mrs Curling, lived at Ozengell,[184] and one gets the impression that they were the senior, or at least the wealthiest, of the Curling families in Thanet: this was John, grandson of John Curling I of Ham Manor. One cannot help feeling there is the merest hint

---

[182] Google Earth calculation.

[183] 'Mr Friend' was possibly Matthew Curling Friend, a man of many talents; for a brief biography, see **Appendix 6b – Mary Ann and Matthew Curling Friend** (p. 192). A Mr Friend also occupied land adjoining Shuart Farm; see **Appendix 2e – The map of Shuart Farm, 1826** (p.147).

[184] Ozengell Grange still stands. It is a Historic England listed building, dating from 1711. Its listing can be seen here: http://bit.ly/Ch6Ozengell.

of poetic justice implied in Thomas's dead-pan anecdote with its nicely placed punchline about Mr Curling's jockey, from the Prince Regent's own stables,[185] who was 'quite ignorant of the manner of training a horse' and 'consequently lost'. Mrs Curling said she would invite Thomas and Edward to Ozengell, but she postponed the visit almost as soon as the invitation was issued. Mr Gillow, to whose house Mr Duihampton was taken after his nasty fall, owned land which shared a boundary with Shuart Farm, and Mr Gillow's house was in the village of St Nicholas-at-Wade. Thomas III and Captain Clowes [186] visited Mr Duihampton there the morning after his fall, when he seemed much better. Julia Clowes, one of Thomas III's many cousins, was staying with Mr and Mrs Curling at Ozengell for the races. Thomas III mentioned several other owners and riders: Messrs Ashenden, Palmer, Page and Pullen. The Neame brothers, from another prominent farming and ancient Thanet family, merited a special mention, as in Thomas III's opinion they ran the strongest equine contenders that day. A generation later members of the Neame family joined the Shepherds to become Shepherd Neame, which today claims to be Britain's oldest brewer,[187] and is still based in Kent.

Thomas III said that one of the two boy jockeys was 'so very small that I do not think he was higher than my brother Robert's shoulder'. This must surely have been an exaggeration as Robert was aged only four at the time, but it is quite likely that some of the jockeys were very young boys, as education was not compulsory[188] and they would have been employed as stable hands. These days jockeys have to comply with weight restrictions, and this would have been true by convention in earlier times, it being obvious that a horse carrying a heavier rider would not have been able to move as fast; so jockeys were, and still are, people of slight stature.

A twenty-first-century teenager would probably not remark on the death of a local politician in his email to grandparents, and Thomas might well have omitted this event had it not been that the death of Sir Edward Knatchbull,[189] local Conservative MP, had an impact on the school community, where two of his sons were pupils. They went home to join their mother and sixteen siblings for the funeral.

---

[185] The Prince Regent's stables were in Brighton. More information is available on the Brighton Dome website: http://bit.ly/Ch6RegentStablesBrighton.

[186] Captain Thomas Clowes was Thomas III's great uncle, married to Ann Curling of Ham Manor. Their daughter Julia is mentioned in this letter, too.

[187] Information from the Shepherd Neame company website: http://bit.ly/Ch6ShepherdNeame, see also Neame Family history page: http://bit.ly/Ch6NeameFamily.

[188] Education of children was not made compulsory until the 1870 Education Act, http://bit.ly/Ch6EducationAct1870.

[189] See Sir Edward Knatchbull's biography in the History of Parliament Online here: http://bit.ly/Ch6KnatchbullBiog. Sir Edward Knatchbull, 8th Baronet of Mersham Hatch, Kent, died on 21 September 1819, four days before Thomas III wrote his letter. Knatchbull's son, the 9th Baronet, inherited the title and the parliamentary seat.

Even by the standards of the day, a family of eighteen surviving offspring was unusually large.

In Thomas's letter we discover the name, occupation and nationality of the Ramsgate character Catharine had referred to in her first letter as 'your new acquaintance at the seaside'. Thomas reported that Mr Diggs, who we gather was the Watch Man, found the restrictions of the role too great, being obliged to stay in the Watch House permanently unless he obtained written permission from Margate, and that he left his post and went home to Ireland, being replaced by Mr Drake.

The boys were allowed to keep caged birds at school with them. One of Thomas's goldfinches managed to escape due to the carelessness of a servant and Edward's bird died, so it looks as though the school environment was not a safe one for pets. Edward was to buy another bird when at home for the 'Christmas Holydays' (surprising to see this old spelling of holiday still in use in the nineteenth century, but a nice reminder of the origin of the word). Thomas, merely disgruntled at the servant's carelessness, demonstrated that he did not consider himself responsible for the welfare of the creature.

Keeping pet finches was, apparently, common in the nineteenth century; see Fig. 28.

Fig. 28. **The Pet Goldfinch** (artist: Henriette Browne) [190]

---

[190] V&A, Museum of Childhood Collection, London, accession number 1083–1886. The work has the alternative title of 'A Girl Writing'. Henriette Browne was the pseudonym for Madame Jules de Saux, née Sophie Boutellier.

The boys were looking forward to the Christmas holidays, when they were going to have the use of their uncle Michael Becker's pony to go hunting. Thomas was particularly pleased about this as the family pony was growing too old and too small for him and Edward. They were no doubt proud of the fact that their father was the secretary for the Isle of Thanet hunt.[191] Becker attended both days of the races, staying at Margate and giving the boys a half crown (2s.6d.) to share. He was their mother Jane's brother, Michael Becker III.[192]

Thomas acknowledged the content of his grandmother Catharine's letter, saying he would like to see such a big river as the Thames, and although the original of this section of his letter contains several damaged passages we gather that he was commenting on her description of the visit to Hainault Forest, to which he responded with an anecdote of his own former nutting outings in woods at a place called Nye, which does not appear on any maps, period or current. It may have been near their home in Shuart or – as he described it as a 'half holyday' activity – some-where close to Mr Abbot's school. He wrote of it as though it was unlikely to happen again, possibly because he was in his final year at school.

The closing sentences of Thomas's letter betray his awareness of class divisions and (from a twenty-first-century perspective) an unattractive snobbery. He high-lighted the 'inferior quality' of many of the summer visitors to Ramsgate, but noted that 'Sir John Honywood's and Sir Henry Ahenden's sons are coming very soon'.

In his postscript Thomas confessed to a repetition in his letter. He knew his grandmother would be reading it with a critical eye to style and content. He must also have known that crossing out the repetition would not have been well received, either. His mention that Catharine had recently written two letters to their mother underlines her prolific letter-writing activities; Catharine, the matriarch of this branch of the Curling family, was thoroughly engaged with all the members of her family. Thomas's endearing sign-off overstepped the customary formality, asking his grandmother to write and let him know when she has safely arrived at her home in Sandwich and sending her his 'most sincere love'.

Catharine's second letter is dated 26 October 1819, written a month after Thomas wrote his. We can see that it must have been the next letter in Catharine's communications with Thomas as she thanked him for his concern about her journey home. *The Farmers' Almanac* lists Brentwood Fair as occurring on 15 and 16 October each year.[193] Catharine had arranged to meet her son Thomas Oakley Curling (Thomas II) in London and return to Kent with him after the fair. She

---

[191] See **Chapter 4 – A Hospitable Roof** (p. 54).

[192] For further details of Michael Becker III, see **Appendix 4a – The Becker-Solley family of Kent** (p. 170).

[193] http://bit.ly/Ch6BrentwoodFairRef. No online version of the almanac could be found for 1819.

apologized for the delay in replying, excusing herself with illness and near-daily visits from friends and relations.

Outlining her journey home, which had taken two days, Catharine told Thomas that she had set out from her sister's house on 18 September, meeting her son Thomas II that evening, in the Strand, London. Maybe they stayed at the Adelphi Hotel in the Strand (from where Thomas II had written to Cobbs in 1804).[194] They left the capital the following morning at eight o'clock, Thomas II accompanying Catharine as far as Canterbury, where he took the Margate coach to Sarre.[195] He would then have either walked the final stretch to Shuart Farm, or hired a horse at the Crown Inn in Sarre with the promise to return it the following day. Catharine continued her journey from Canterbury to Sandwich and 'reached Sandwich at seven in the evening'.

The pride in her grandson's letter-writing skills is evident in Catharine's sharing of the contents with Thomas's 'uncle [Francis John Kelly], aunt and cousins'.[196] She marvelled at the size of the Thanet race crowds. Her warm appreciation of Thomas's account of Sir Edward Knatchbull's death, both for her own information and as a demonstration of Thomas's interest in current affairs, must have been pleasing for him. We wonder what the boys' reaction was to the letter to them written in French by their great-aunt Elizabeth, enclosed in Catharine's, although in a later volume of the story we will see that Elizabeth had a keen awareness of the appropriateness of educational material, and no doubt chose her topics and words with care to make it easy for the boys to understand. We do not know how Elizabeth was able to acquire her knowledge of French, nor why her sister Catharine was deprived of the opportunity. Their father Thomas Oakley had clearly thought language skills important, as he had ensured that his son Thomas Oakley III had sufficient linguistic ability in Dutch to become the shipping agent for the Dutch East India Company.[197]

The conveying of letters to their recipients was still an uncertain business. Catharine mentioned that she was planning to take her Sandwich letter, together with Elizabeth's, for Thomas III and Edward when she visited the boys' mother the following day, 'as I know she will have the goodness to get them sent to Ramsgate on Saturday by some of the marketing people'. In her postscript she said that she and Miss Stewart would travel to Shuart by post-chaise.

---

[194] See Chapter 4, letter dated 27 November 1804, p. 48.

[195] The village of Sarre is less than 2 miles from St Nicholas-at-Wade. In earlier centuries the spelling was 'Sarr', as in Catharine's letter.

[196] This little phrase tells us that Captain Kelly was indeed still living with his family in Cookham.

[197] SR http://bit.ly/Ch1ThOakleyDutchLetter The catalogue detail for this letter is 'Collection City Archive Rotterdam / Coopstad & Rochussen, inv. 63 original letter from Thomas Oakley written in Dutch' (translation by Martijn Verbon, SR archivist).

Catharine's turn of phrase makes us smile sometimes. She said she was pleased to know that Thomas had paid such attention to her account of the Hainault Forest trip and of the activity on the River Thames. She was quite self-deprecating and hadn't thought it would amuse the boys at all, writing by way of excuse that she had not much 'epistolary intercourse'.

Although her careful response to the tale of the cage-birds was sympathetic and tactful, she encouraged Thomas to take care of the birds himself at least in the holidays – and she highlighted the feelings of the servant girl, too.

Finally, Catharine signed off with blessings and affection for her 'dear boys', implying that she had expected the letter would be read by Edward as well as Thomas.

latter consideration that I saw was near Chigwell Row, in Essex, but it was not freehold – the house not brick built, and was just suited to its owner, an old very respectable haberdasher – the land was luxuriantly rich close round the House, & the situation good & healthy, tho' not equal to this – Upminster is the cheapest place I have seen yet – I hope Col George Napier is pretty well and that his dear little children continue to grow and improve.

Blanco [202] *arrived here safe last Thursday he is looking in high beauty; he has just been led down to the window to see me, & had a piece of bread for his trouble. He is so full of play and spirits that the servant could scarcely hold him, I fear it will be some time before there is any grass for him, poor fellow, how ever he don't suffer for he has a good stable*

Adieu dear Lady Sarah. Pray do not forget how much pleasure it gives me to hear from you & believe me ever truly

Etc etc

Elizabeth Kelly

Addressed to:
The Rt Honble
Lady Sarah Napier
Castletown
Celbridge
Ireland [203]

Celbridge House, in the village of Celbridge, County Kildare, was the Napiers' family home. It was near Castletown, the home of Lady Sarah's sister Lady Louisa, and her husband Thomas Connolly. The Napiers had moved there from England when Charles James Napier was only four years old. 'From there he had travelled with his mother and step-sister Louisa to Southampton already gazetted an ensign in the 33rd though small for his eleven years.'[204] Fortunately, he did not have to join his regiment at such a tender age, but returned home to school in Celbridge until he was sixteen.

Elizabeth's letter to Lady Sarah holds the stark contrasts of her deep sorrow at the sudden and unexpected death of her beloved sister Catharine and the quiet

---

[202] Blanco was one of a grand succession of horses owned by Napier.
[203] BodL MS Eng Lett C237/f63.
[204] *The Sword Dance – Lady Sarah Lennox and the Napiers*, p. 109, Priscilla Napier, Michael Joseph, 1971.

pleasure of her present situation. She is dealing with the one by focusing on the other.

Catharine Curling was buried in the Curling family vault in the chancel of St George's Church, Ham, near Deal in Kent, on 9 November 1819. She must have died within a week of writing her final letter to her grandson Thomas. Along with Elizabeth, the whole Curling family would have felt the terrible wrench of losing such a devoted mother and grandmother. However, Catharine, despite enormous efforts to busy herself with family and friends, must surely have found widowhood to be a lonely and 'foreign' state after almost forty years of marriage; her husband Thomas I had died only seven months previously.

When Catharine's friend Miss Stewart died nine years later, Catharine would perhaps have been pleased to know that she had been mentioned in the will of Miss Stewart, who left 'the portrait of my late dear friend Mrs Curling' to Miss Eliza Kelly, Elizabeth's daughter.[205] Miss Stewart's further bequests included one for a godson, Robert Curling, possibly the Robert who was one of Thomas Oakley Curling's seven sons, and for three daughters of another Robert Curling, Catharine's brother-in-law, who had been a surgeon and mayor of Sandwich but who had died in 1810. These young women were the Misses Jane and Roberta Curling, and 'Mrs James Boys', Mrs James being their sister Mary. Clearly, Miss Stewart was an extremely close friend of Catharine's.

Napier in the Ionian Islands

Napier was now based in Corfu, and answerable to the lord high commissioner of the islands, the irascible Sir Thomas Maitland. The islands, having been a French possession at the end of the Napoleonic Wars, had become a British protectorate and 'in 1817 Britain had granted the islands a federal constitution with an elected assembly and senate whose role was to advise the lord high commissioner.'[206]

Napier was therefore corresponding from a considerable distance with Elizabeth, in particular about the alternative possibilities of rental or purchase for Stone House. Elizabeth loved everything about her new home. She was in much better health than for many years; the property was in a beautiful location, and the house 'is so convenient', by which she may have meant that the floor plan suited them – it certainly was not in a physically convenient location, being quite secluded and some distance from the village of Cookham, never mind the river which runs between the Stone House site and Marlow, their nearest town of any size. This was not just any river: it was the Thames. Napier had asked Elizabeth to investigate the possible purchase of this and other properties, but she had had no success – finding

---

[205] TNA PROB11/1746/'67.
[206] Walter Little, see footnote 199, p. 76.

the high asking price an obstacle which twenty-first-century purchasers would recognize – so Napier was clearly renting the property, initially at least.

One event which must have pleased Elizabeth was the arrival of Napier's stallion Blanco. Napier had a special affection for each of his steeds, but he was particularly fond of Blanco. We don't know why the horse was sent to Cookham – perhaps because, surrounded by pasture, it was a better environment for him than stabling in London, although Elizabeth said that there was no grass for him at the time, possibly because it was winter. The letter is addressed to Lady Sarah at Celbridge, fifteen minutes' walk from where her sister Lady Louisa Conolly lived. By this time Sarah was living mainly at 13 Cadogan Place, London, but occasionally she still travelled to visit friends or family, and in 1819 she had made the arduous journey to County Kildare to stay with her sister Louisa.

Elizabeth's quietly familiar tone in her correspondence with Lady Sarah is remarkable. It is apparent from this and other correspondence that she had met Charles Napier's family, mentioning, as she did here, his brother George's children, and remembering that she had already corresponded with both Charles's brother Richard and sister Emily. One cannot help but feel that a person of her social class would not at this time have mingled naturally with the families of peers. It should be noted however, that the Lennox family, their male line being the Dukes of Richmond, had received their not inconsiderable estates in both England and France in a rather unusual way.

> [T]he first Duke of Richmond [Charles Lennox], was born in 1672. He was the youngest of Charles II's many illegitimate sons. His mother (Lady Sarah)'s great-grandmother, was Louise de Kéroualle[207] who as a young woman of twenty, was sent over to England with Louis XIV's courtiers and diplomats conducting the negotiations for what became the secret and notorious Treaty of Dover. Louise ousted Charles's reigning mistress, and, over the years did the King, her country and herself stout service. The Treaty, signed in 1670,[208] bound England and France to peaceful coexistence, and held till the revolution of 1688 brought William of Orange to the English throne. Louise was created Duchess of Portsmouth by Charles II. Louis XIV, for his part, recognised her service to his country by granting her the Stuart family lands in France.[209] With the land came two chateaux, Aubigny and La Verrerie.[210] Louise eventually retired to Aubigny.[211]

---

[207] Louise de Kérouaille's name is variously spelt with or without the 'i'.
[208] This treaty, known as the Secret Treaty of Dover, was made between King Charles II and Louis XIV of France. See http://bit.ly/Ch7DoverTreaty.
[209] For detail of the Stewart lands in Aubigny, France, see this Stewart Society web page: http://bit.ly/StewartlandsAubigny.
[210] See the official website of La Verrerie: http://bit.ly/Ch7Verrerie
[211] *Aristocrats Caroline, Emily Louisa and Sarah Lennox 1740–1832*, p. 7, Stella Tillyard.

The manor house in Aubigny is known not as a chateau but as Castle Stuart. The town's website tells us that 'The beautiful Louise had arranged England's neutrality during the Franco-Flemish War':[212]

> In return for royal largesse, Louise gave Charles years of service in the bedchamber, and a son [Sarah's grandfather] named Charles Lennox. During his boyhood the child was given a plethora of titles to cover his bastardy. He was created Duke of Richmond, Baron of Settrington and Earl of Marc in the English Peerage, and Baron Methuen of Tarbolton, Earl of Darnley and Duke of Lennox in the Scottish peerage. When his mother died he added the title of Duc d'Aubigny to this list and did homage for it to the French crown. To this sonorous but worthless panoply Charles II added something more substantial: an annuity of two thousand pounds and a royalty of twelvepence per chauldron on coal dues at Newcastle.[213]

Sarah's own relationship history was colourful to say the least, starting with a royal flirtation with George III, followed by an unconsummated marriage to Sir Charles Bunbury, an affair and elopement with Lord William Gordon, which never became a marriage, an illegitimate daughter and social exclusion for eleven years in a retreat built for her by her brother, the 2nd Duke of Richmond at Goodwood – and, finally, marriage to the love of her life, Colonel George Napier, with whom she bore eight children, the eldest being 'our' Charles James Napier.

---

[212] See http://bit.ly/Ch7Aubigny.

[213] *Aristocrats Caroline, Emily Louisa and Sarah Lennox 1740–1832,* p. 7, Stella Tillyard.

Chapter 8 – Total Ruin

The saga of Mr Holmes the schoolteacher

As late as 1820, it was necessary for Thomas II to follow up the long-running saga of Mr Holmes the schoolmaster. He wrote a letter to the vestry's bankers, Cobbs of Margate.

> *Sir*
>
> *I am in correspondence with Messrs Benbow & Alban relative to Mr Holmes, and I think it will much assist me, in getting him his deserts, and prevent him troubling you again on a similar occasion; if you would do the favor to furnish me with a copy of the account he charged you with – the bearer can call on you in an hour, if convenient to you to have it written at once; or it may come by the coach at night to the cottages at St Nicholas*
>
> *Yours obediently*
>
> Tho. O. Curling
>
> Shuart, April 6th 1820[214]

Holmes appears to have approached the bank directly for money, possibly due to him from the vestry, for his teaching services, but having successfully acquired funds he seems to have absconded. The conclusion of the story is unknown – was Mr Holmes apprehended? Was he justified in his actions? Did the vestry get its money back? The way in which Holmes had been treated in the early days of his tenure seems unreasonable, but perhaps there was more to the story than the vestry records reveal. Either Holmes managed his personal finances badly or the administrators of the parish made unreasonable demands on him. Possibly both sides were at fault and poor communication was the problem.

The post-Napoleonic War agricultural depression

With Catharine's death, the Shuart Curlings should have been better rather than worse off, as there should have been an inheritance to distribute. Unfortunately, however, Catharine had not administered her husband Thomas I's will. She was the sole nominated executrix and she herself died intestate. On 14 July 1822, their son, Thomas Oakley Curling, Thomas II, was sworn to administer his father's will. From this point the task should have been straightforward, but Thomas II had life-

---

[214] KHLC EK/U1453/83/15/482.

changing plans in train which were already far advanced and were taking up his every waking moment.

Since 1816, when he had written his letter to the Board of Agriculture, the agricultural depression had continued to worsen. The Saracen's Head Inn, Ashford, was the venue for a meeting of the Ashford Association for the Relief and Protection of Agriculture, held on Tuesday 5 December 1820. Members of the association expressed their deep concern at the alarming depreciation of farm produce, which would, if allowed to continue, lead to the total ruin of everyone in the agricultural community. They blamed the inefficiency of the administration of the current Corn Laws, which had recently allowed the ports to be opened for the duty-free import of oats. This meant that the home market was inundated with foreign produce from places where it was much cheaper to produce the grain. It had happened at a time when a bumper crop had given British farmers and landowners hope that they would have had a fair income from their capital outlay and labour – but they now had to sell their crops at enormous loss. The Ashford Association, aware of the urgency of obtaining relief and protection in law, appealed to neighbouring farmers to unite with them to petition the House of Commons for an investigation of their claims, and they asked the government to grant farmers relief and protection. In the meantime they would continue to co-operate with the national association based in Westminster. A petition was to be ready for signatures by Tuesday 19 December at the Saracen's Head, the Royal Oak, and the George in Ashford. The committee would reconvene at twelve o'clock on that date, and in the meantime the resolutions of this meeting were to be published in three local newspapers and the *Farmer's Journal*.[215]

The names of those attending are listed, and include Thomas Curling. This newspaper article illustrates dramatically the further serious deterioration in the agricultural economy since 1816. The stricter application of the import duties on corn which Thomas II had wished for had not brought the benefits he had expected. These laws may have been advantageous to the middle and upper classes in the short term, but in the long run their effect was to keep the price of bread – the staple food of the working classes – so high that after paying their rent many of the poor had barely enough to pay for their food. Many died of starvation, and those who survived had no money to buy anything else. This meant that fewer manufactured goods were sold, and the overall effect on the economy was a downward spiral.

Thomas II and Jane concluded that as they could no longer make ends meet at Shuart Farm they should emigrate to Australia and set up as farmers on virgin

---

[215] Resumé of an article in the *Kentish Weekly Post* 12 December 1820, page 4, column 1, article title 'Ashford Association'. Transcription taken from the newspaper image available on the British Newspaper Archive website.

territory there. It took them two years of considerable persistence to jump through all the administrative hoops and arrive at the point of departure.

Providing for seven sons

A novel of the period gives us real – and, as will be fully understood later in the story – particularly special insights into the extraordinary effort and commitment involved by early settlers as they prepared for their odyssey. In his introduction to *Tales of the Colonies*,[216] the author Charles Rowcroft, a settler who had arrived in Van Diemen's Land (VDL), (now Tasmania) in 1821 gave an overview of the reasons for emigration from England at this time:

> It seems, indeed, that there must be some strange neglect or ignorance on the part of the government or legislature of a state when a large portion of an active, industrious, and intelligent population, willing to work, and capable of producing more than sufficient for their own subsistence, and of adding immeasurably to the national wealth, cannot make the wealth-producing power of their labour available. It is painfully vexatious to behold in one part of the national dominions an excess of population wanting land to work on, and in continual apprehension for the next day's food, and in another part an excess of land wanting a population to work it.[217]

Although it is a work of fiction, Rowcroft's book supplies much of the detail for many aspects of the settlers' all-consuming life changes: the emotional tensions between family members, what it was like to make the preparations for the journey to a new colony, and the many obstacles and dangers which settlers endured once they arrived. Rowcroft had arrived in Hobart with his brother Horatio only one year before the Curlings. Charles was aged twenty-four on arrival, and Horatio seventeen. They had taken up a land grant of 2,000 acres, so they must have brought substantial assets to the territory. Rowcroft's account of the settlers' experience is therefore particularly relevant to our story.

Life at Shuart Farm must have become precarious to the point of desperation for Thomas II to have uprooted his family and taken them halfway round the globe. With Rowcroft's help we can almost eavesdrop on the discussions he and Jane had

---

[216] *Tales of the Colonies or the Adventures of an Emigrant*, Charles Rowcroft 1843, Saunders and Otley, London. The complete fourth edition of the work, published in 1845, is available free on Google Books here: http://bit.ly/Ch8TalesoftheColonies. The original 1843 edition in two volumes is available on http://bit.ly/ArchivesIndexTales. In April 2007, before either of these online copies were available, staff at the University of Sidney Library kindly made a digitized pdf of the book available to me, for which I was enormously grateful.

[217] *Tales of the Colonies*, p. vii.

between them as their financial resources dwindled. In the opening chapter of *Tales of the Colonies* William Thornley, the protagonist, has been married eleven years and has five children. Written in the first person, Rowcroft's book presents William laying out the general feeling of malaise in his neighbourhood and speaking of a letter received by one of his neighbours, which tells of the wonders of life in Australia's Botany Bay, in a manner no doubt similar to the characters in Webster's painting 'A Letter from the Colonies', Fig. 29.

Fig. 29. **A Letter from the Colonies, Thomas Webster, 1852** [218]

This letter has dwelt on William's mind, and set him to making further enquiries. His business is 'not going as usual'. Rowcroft's story unfolds:

> So one evening, after a hard day's work, and no profit but all loss, I made up my mind to put an end to it. My wife was sitting alone in the parlour, and I said to her, 'Mary,' said I, 'things are going on very badly.'
>
> 'They'll get better by-and-by,' said she.
>
> 'They've been getting worse the last six months,' said I. 'I don't like the look of it at all.'
>
> 'We must work the harder,' said my wife.

---

[218] Tate. Photo © Tate.

Said I, 'I tell you what it is, Mary. I work as hard as any man can, and we both of us spend as little as we can, but we are eating up our capital; and work as I may, and pinch ourselves as we may, we can't go on at this rate. You know how many have broke, and there's no chance of our money from them; in three years we shall have nothing left, and maybe we should break down before then, for things are getting worse and worse, and the trade is like playing at hazard.'

'Why, William,' said Mary, 'what would you have us do? Shall we try a farm?'

'Not in this country,' said I. 'What with rent, and rates, and taxes, and tithes, with corn falling, and all things unsettled, I'm thinking farming never will be the business it used to be. No, Mary,' said I, speaking to her with much earnestness, 'farming won't answer here; and with our five children depending on us for bread, and for their future provision in life, I should not like to risk the little that we have left in working at a farm in this country. We must make up our minds to a great effort, and since there are too many struggling with one another in England, we must go where the people are few and the land is plenty. We must emigrate.'

'Emigrate!' said Mary, 'where to?'

'Why,' I replied, 'perhaps I have not made up my mind which would be the best place to go to, nor indeed could I make up my mind that we should emigrate at all until I had consulted with you, and you had agreed to it. But I have thought of the matter a good deal, and the more I think of it, the more convinced I am that it would be better for us to take care of what we have left, and turn it to account in a new country. If there was only you and me, we could make a shift, perhaps, to rub on; but when I consider our children who are growing up, and how to provide for them comfortably I … do feel that to be sure of house and home, and bread to eat, and clothes to wear, would be better for them than to be exposed to all the chances of uncertain trading or farming in this country.'

Well, I saw that the tears had come in Mary's eyes at this talk, and her heart was quite full; for the thought of her mother, now advanced in years, and of her relatives and acquaintances about, of the scenes of her early childhood and the companions of her youth, all to be quitted perhaps for ever, was too much for her; and all the circumstances of our own losses and difficulties crowding in upon her thoughts, her emotion got the better of her, and she burst into tears and sobbed for some time.[219]

William manages to persuade Mary that their children will have a better future if they do emigrate, although she is still upset at the thought of leaving everything and everyone she has known. Rowcroft continues in Thornley's voice:

---

[219] *Tales of the Colonies*, pp. 5–6.

I have been more particular in narrating this conversation, because it made, as may easily be supposed, a great impression on me as it related to one of the most important acts of my life; and from the circumstance also, that from that hour my dear wife never made a single complaint, nor uttered a murmur at all the inconveniences and occasional hardships which she was put to, as well during the voyage as during the first years of our settling in the colony. This deserves the more worthily to be noted, as I have been a witness, in Van Diemen's Land, of the evil effects of a contrary course of conduct on the part of the wives of emigrants. To my knowledge, more than one failure has happened from the fancies, and fine-lady affectations, and frettings, and sulkiness of settlers' help-mates; forgetting how much of a man's comfort and happiness, and, in a colony, of his success, depends on the cheerful humour, the kindly good temper, and the hearty co-operation of his wife.[220]

Jumping administrative hurdles, organizing the journey

Thomas Oakley Curling's ancestors had lived on the Isle of Thanet since at least 1463.[221] His wife Jane, née Becker's, paternal family is said to have arrived in Dover from Prussia sometime in the eighteenth century, and Jane, born in Dover,[222] had lived at Guilton Rectory, Overland in Goldstone, in the parish of Ash-next-Sandwich, since the age of eleven.[223] There was nothing like the comparatively instant worldwide communication systems that we have in the twenty-first century. So leaving the area where they had been born and bred, the close-knit community of extended family and friends, the annual seasonal events, and everything familiar, must have seemed impossibly daunting, particularly for the women whose lives were generally more sheltered than those of men at the time, and who then, much more so than now, carried the larger burden of the family's routine domestic organization and well-being. Families in those days were generally much larger; there were no electric appliances to help with routine tasks, and the management of a large household would probably have amounted to 14 hours a day, 7 days a week – far more than a 'full-time' job of the twenty-first century. Author Charles Rowcroft's acknowledgement of the importance of the wife's contribution in the venture is noteworthy at a time when women were generally invisible in domestic

---

[220] *Tales of the Colonies*, p. 7.

[221] www.curlingofthanet.wordpress.com A website exploring the Curling ancestors of Lucy Ann Curling and Clive Boyce from their joint 6× great-grandparents John Curling and his wife Mary Kirby back to Richard Curlynge of Chilton who died in 1463, in the parish of St Laurence, Isle of Thanet.

[222] Jane was born on 27 October and baptized at St Mary the Virgin, Dover, on 7 November 1783: from parish records available on https://www.findmypast.co.uk/

[223] 'The Becker-Solley Family of Kent: in England, Australia, New Zealand and North America, 1734–1913', an unpublished paper by Peter Wilkinson of Melbourne, Australia, see **Appendix 4a – The Becker-Solley family of Kent**. (p. 165).

history. The culture of the times was much more weighted towards the man being the principal member of any couple, with the perception of women as only ever playing a supporting role. The concept that a woman might have a major part, or even in some cases be the overt lead, in the success of a family would have been anathema to most, although it turned out that there were several instances of families, amongst settlers and convicts alike, where the stronger character was the woman. Even though it would have been hotly denied by the majority of both men and women in the society of the time, women's strength of spirit was often what kept families together, although they nearly always cloaked it in deferential communication and action.

Reaching the point of decision no doubt took much heart-searching, anxious conversations and sleepless nights, but that would have been as nothing for Thomas II compared to the protracted stresses of successfully negotiating a passage for his family to their 'new world'.

He had been led to believe that there was a financial incentive available to encourage farmers to migrate as free settlers (rather than deported convicts) to the southern hemisphere. A sequence of letters written between Thomas II and various government officials outlines the saga. Looking at these letters in chronological order, the first seems to indicate that Thomas II fell at the first hurdle because of his own inefficiency. An official, Thomas Hobb Scott, writing from Downing Street, at first dismissive then frustrated, finally declined to help Thomas II further. Thomas II had, Scott said, sent his enquiry to Scott in error, had not enclosed supporting documents and had misquoted Scott in a letter to Lord Bathurst. Scott washed his hands of the affair and refused to help further:

Downing St., 25 Sepr.

Sir

> *The letter you wrote me on the 24 & its enclosure I have received, the letter I return you to be conveyed in the usual way with your other documents to the proper office – I must decline all interferance on this subject first as you did not supply me with any of the letters you assured me you could procure & 2^{ndly} on account of expressions as to my line of duty you have incorrectly attributed to me in a letter written by you & transmitted to Lord Bathurst & I beg also to decline any further correspondence on this subject – I am Sir*

> *y^r ob Ser^t.*

> *T. H. Scott*[224]

---

[224] TNA C201/114 f547. For further information see **Appendix 8a – T H Scott** (p.194).

Addressed on the verso to:

> *Mr. T. O. Curling Shuart Isle of Thanet*

That must have been a dispiriting letter to receive, and Thomas II was no doubt very angry with himself, but it seems he felt he had no alternative but to persist, because fares to the antipodes at the time were

> exorbitantly high. Terms demanded for a voyage to New South Wales or Van Diemen's Land (Tasmania) on the *Skelton* … were 70 guineas for a cabin and 40 guineas for a steerage passage.[225]

In a manuscript document held at the National Archives, Kew, dated September 1821, we find that he had assembled many east Kent signatures on a testimonial of his upright conduct. From it we learn that Thomas II was 'under the necessity … of leaving his native country'.[226]

The following month Thomas II sold, by tender, the 'tenant's interest' in Shuart Farm. See Fig. 30.

TO BE DISPOSED OF BY TENDER, THE TENANT'S INTEREST in SHUART FARM. The tenders to be sent to Mr. WOOD's, at Chislet Court, on TUESDAY NEXT, the 16th instant, by 10 o'clock in the forenoon.

For particulars apply to Mr. Collard, of Broomfield; Mr. Champion, Sarr; Mr. Neame, Chislett; and at Shuart Farm.

N. B. No Tender will be received after 10 o'clock.

Fig. 30. **Kentish Weekly Post** or **Canterbury Chronicle, 12 October 1821**

From this point on Thomas II, his wife and their seven children still at home were reliant on family to house them while they pursued their efforts to emigrate. The final travelling member of the family, Arthur, was still *in utero* and although some might think that he was thus blissfully protected from the family's stressful situation at the time, there is in the present time evidence that foetuses are adversely affected by their mother's distress.[227]

---

[225] *Life and Death in the Age of Sail*, p. 81, Robin Haines, pub. National Maritime Museum, 2003.

[226] For a full transcript see **Appendix 8b – A testimonial** (p.195).

[227] 'There is considerable evidence that babies *in utero* are affected by the level of the mother's stress chemicals and that this in turn affects their behaviour after birth.' C. Petherick 2019. See this BBC News web page among many others reporting research on foetal stress: https://www.bbc.co.uk/news/health-14187905.

In February 1822, Thomas II wrote to the Prime Minister Robert Jenkinson, using his hereditary title as the second Earl of Liverpool from Margate, under a heading which indicates that he and the family had had to move out of Shuart Farm:

The Right Honourable the Earl of Liverpool,
first Lord of the Treasury &c &c &c

> *The Humble Memorial of Thomas Oakley Curling late of Shuart*
> *Farm in the Isle of Thanet, in the County of Kent*

With great regret your Memorialist feels himself called on, by the Duty he owes to a Family of a Wife and eight Children, earnestly to solicit your Lordship's attention to the failure of the hopes he was led to entertain, that, through the representation of Mr. Thomas Hobb Scott, to the Right Honourable The Earl Bathurst of his opinion on the beneficial effects, to be expected from the presence of Practical Farmers, your Memorialist and Family might have been favoured with a free Passage to New South Wales, as Emigrants wishing to settle in that Colony; – to forward which, your Lordship, through the recommendation of Sir Thomas Mantell, most kindly sent your favourable testimony to the Right Honourable The Earl Bathurst, as to the respectability of your Memorialist, about the sixteenth of September last, – a few days after which, the enclosure No. 1, was forwarded to Mr. Scott, and No. 2 was received in answer, – leaving your Memorialist, deeply to lament having inadvertently given offence to, and having lost the voluntarily offered assistance of Mr. Scott, partly by Letters favoured by your Lordship to Earl Bathurst, and partly from substituting, for Letters from the Reverend Henry Kett and the Reverend Cleaver Banks which were the only Letters expected by Mr. Scott, the Statement No. 3: which was done directly by the advice of The Reverend Henry Kett.

Under these circumstances, joined to his exceeding great difficulties, your Memorialist humbly entreats your Lordship's assistance, so, that himself and family may be permitted a free passage, as soon after April next, as may be convenient.

And your Memorialist will ever pray.[228]

Thos. O. Curling

Margate 8th. Feby. 1822

---

[228] TNA C201/114 f549.

On 12 February 1822 there is this letter, incomplete in its original form:

Lathom House. Ormskirk.

Feb 12. 1822

My dear Lord

I inclose a Petition from Mr Thos O Curling late farmer in the Isle of Thanet on a subject on which I believe you have been before applied to. He has for some time been desirous of emigrating to Van Diemens Land & made Preparations for it, under the Expectation which appears to have been held out to him of having a free Passage to that Country, & he wishes to be allowed to go free from the Expence of his Passage.

A Memorial in his Favor from the Gentlemen ...[229]

Next we find this brief letter:

Mr. Willimott presents his Compliments to Mr. Wilmot, & is desired by Lord Liverpool to send him a letter & its Inclosures, which his Lordship has received from Mr. Wilbraham, the Member for Dover –

Lord Liverpool will be obliged to Mr. Wilmot to let him know whether, consistently with the Regulations, the Prayer of the Petitioner can be complied with –

Fife House

Feby 15th: 1822

In bottom left corner of the otherwise blank verso:

M^r. Barnard to write to M^r. Willimott in my name to explain why M^r. O. Curlings application cannot be complied with – Immediate

19 Feb^y. – [initials?] [230]

Undeterred, Thomas pressed on.[231] The opportunity to set up a farm on virgin territory must have been exceptionally tempting, particularly as it had become impossible for him to make a living as a farmer in England. On 21 February 1822,

---

[229] TNA C201/114 f545. Incomplete original.

[230] TNA C201/114 f543.

[231] Thomas II was not entirely naïve in believing that it was possible to obtain a free passage to Australia. From about 1831 there were 'assisted passage' schemes to encourage free settlers to make a new life in the antipodes. See the Tasmania Maritime Museum webpage: http://bit.ly/Ch8TasmaniaEmigration and *Life and Death in the Age of Sail*, Robin Haines, pub. National Maritime Museum, 2003.

Edward Bootle-Wilbraham, 1st Baron Skelmersdale and MP for Dover, wrote to Mr Wilmot on Thomas II's behalf:

Dear Wilmot

I have forwarded a Petition to Lord Liverpool on the Part of a Person of the name of Tho[s] O Curling who having for many years farmed five hundred Acres in the Isle of Thanet, was induced to go out as a settler in Van Diemens Land where respectable men and good Farmers are wanted, on an Understanding that he was to have a free Passage there. He made his Preparations, & having done so was informed that he could not have his Passage free.

He has addressed his Petition to Lord Liverpool to whom as Lord Warden of the Cinque Ports everything in that Jurisdiction applies when anything is wanted, but as the Subject is in the Department of Lord Bathurst,[232] I write a Line to bespeak your good Word if it is a Matter which can be done, & to assure you that Mr Curling is extremely respectable, & has the highest Testimonials in his Favor & that it will be doing a Service to the Colony to get him to establish himself there...

E Bootle Wilbraham[233]

In June 1822 Thomas obtained a letter confirming his finances were sufficient to purchase a grant of land.

Canterbury June 23rd 1822

We certify that M[r] Thomas Oakley Curling upon his arrival with his family in Van Dieman's Land or New South Wales will be entitled to receive the sum of five Hundred Pounds and that the further sum of Three Hundred Pounds is appropriated to his Use as an Outfit[234]

With c/[o] our Hands

Tho[s]. Storr
Michael Becker[235]

To whom it may concern –

---

[232] Lord Bathurst was Secretary of State for War and the Colonies between 1812 and 1827.

[233] Original letter in the Derbyshire Record Office archive D3155/C6027.

[234] It is not clear what the final phrase in this line means. It may indicate that Thomas II would have available the sum of £300.0.0 to equip his new property, or that it could be added to the previously mentioned £500.0.0 to go towards the property itself.

[235] TNA C201/112 f216.

Michael Becker was, of course, Thomas II's brother-in-law. It is more than likely that the homeless Curling family, the two parents and eight children, were sheltering in his mother's capacious house, Guilton Rectory in Goldstone, in the parish of Ash-next-Sandwich; so he would have had a vested interest in helping Thomas II to obtain the passage money for their journey. It would appear that Michael was even providing some of the money which Thomas II would need once he arrived in Van Diemen's Land.

And a week later, a further letter of support:

Shuart 2ⁿᵈ July 1822

We estimate the property of Mʳ. T. O. Curling to Amount to Four Hundred Pounds independent of the document signed by Messrs Storr and Becker which he informs us he intends to apply to the purposes of Agriculture in New South Wales[236]

Thomas Neame
Thoˢ A Champion

Progress made, as we see in this next missive:

To Robert Willimott Esq
Under Secretary of State &c &c

Sir

Having engaged a passage in the Regalia which will sail on the 15ᵗʰ insᵗ, I have left the enclosed, which I hope will be deemed sufficient to procure me a Grant of Land, either in New South Wales or Van Diemans Land as I may conceive most conducive to the wellfare of my family –

As I have had the honor of a favorable mention to the Colonial Department, through the Earl of Liverpool and E. Bootle Wilbraham Esq, I have been informed, it is now only necessary for me to prove the amount of property, which I shall apply to agriculture in one of the Colonies –

I have taken the liberty to enclose two notes which you had the trouble to write in answer to some former applications in my favour and which may probably recall to your recollection the names of some friends who then kindly interested themselves for me –

---

[236] TNA C201/112 f218.

I have the honor to remain
with great respect
Your obedient humble Servt

Tho. O. Curling

July 6th 1822
Jacks Coffee House
Mark Lane
London

Finally, ten days later, Thomas must have been extremely relieved to be able to write

To
R. Willimot Esq.
Under Secretary of State &c &c

Sir

 I have the honor gratefully to acknowledge and to return you my thanks, for your kind attention in so quickly forwarding the order for the Grant of Land in New South Wales[237] – As the time for the sailing of the Regalia has been repeatedly delayed, I was absent from this place and in the country, when the favour of your enclosure arrived, otherwise the receipt of it should have met my earlier acknowledgment –

 I have the honor to remain

 Your most obliged, respectfull Ser^t

Tho. O. Curling

July 17
Jacks Coffee House
Mark Lane

Addressed on the verso:
To R. Willimot Esq
Under Secretary of State &c &c
Colonial Office
Downing Street

---

[237] Note that this order was not the grant itself, and Thomas had to take his paperwork to the governor when he arrived in order to set in motion the process for allocation of land.

Meanwhile Jane, with the eight children who were to travel, waited anxiously at the Rectory in Guilton to receive the confirmation that the journey was going ahead. She must have had great fortitude. The family had already been homeless for at least five months, having sold everything when they had left Shuart, and the thought of making such a mammoth journey with no previous experience of long-distance travel at all – not even in England – must have been daunting. The children must have been by turns excited and afraid. The three eldest who were travelling, Edward, Charles and Henry, could reasonably have been expected to help with the little ones, but what was surely most worrying of all for Jane was that her youngest child, Arthur, was barely four months old.

The single one of their offspring to be left behind in England was Thomas III. Born in Ash-next-Sandwich, 6 October 1805,[238] he was about seventeen when the idea of emigration was under discussion at home. He was an apprentice apothecary.[239] His indenture, recording the commencement of his apprenticeship, was dated 20 May 1820, and names his employers as Daniel Jarvis and John Waddington of Margate. This was an impressively substantial medical practice. Jarvis, an 'apothecary and surgeon' of considerable standing in the town, had his surgery in prestigious Cecil Square. John Waddington was his nephew.[240] Legal constraints meant Thomas III could not leave the country until he had completed at least the seven years of his training, and he may have had commitments to his employers after that too. The system was that 'indentures were drawn up, binding servant to master and vice versa, in which the master personally taught the apprentice, took responsibility for the latter's moral welfare, and provided board and lodging'.[241] For this provision of tuition and living, Thomas III's parents would have paid a substantial sum.

In Mr Jarvis's apothecary's shop in Margate, Thomas III's mind was probably in turmoil. He alone of all the family had a secure job, a substantial roof over his head and guaranteed meals every day, but being a bound apprentice meant he was unable to travel with his family, and he may well have felt abandoned in England. Judging from his brother Edward's correspondence with Napier at a much later date, it seems likely that Thomas disapproved of the radical solution which his father had

[238] Ash-next-Sandwich parish registers, FindMyPast Kent, Canterbury Archdeaconry Parish Registers Browse, 1538-1913 CCA ASH-REG-7-BAPTISMS-1800-12.

[239] Original documents at the Worshipful Society of Apothecaries in Blackfriars Lane, London, on Thomas's attendance for his final examinations to become a qualified apothecary.

[240] *A Branch of the Jarvis Family*, online paper by Janet Robinson on the HistoryofMargate website, see http://bit.ly/Ch8DanielJarvis

[241] *Skills and the English Working Class*, Charles More, Croom Helm, 1980, p. 41, quoted on the House of Commons Library website: http://bit.ly/Ch8Apprenticeship

planned for the family's long-term security. Thomas III was losing his whole family to a perilous journey and a dubious enterprise, full of risk.

From his father's standpoint, however, that was one son well set up – but Thomas II had six more sons to help into adulthood and some kind of independent living. The thought of providing them with a private education, followed by financial assistance to study for and earn a living away from the failed milieu of English agriculture, must have given him and Jane food for many anxious late-night discussions. He had managed – probably with help from either his own mother Catharine Curling, or his mother-in-law Jane Becker I, or both – to pay for Thomas III's apprenticeship, but there could have been no chance of him expending a similar sum on each of the other six boys. In fact, it may well have been that the death of Catharine intestate had created financial difficulties with respect to payment of the apprenticeship fees for Thomas III and the school fees for Edward. If that were the case it was undoubtedly a major contributory factor in planning the expedition to the antipodes and their departure from Shuart.

Thomas II had been so taken up with the process of organizing his family's departure that he had had no time to administer his father's will before he left, despite having obtained administration of the will three weeks before their departure. Why did he not appoint someone to take his place as executor? Maybe that would have been a further protracted process and a drain on his carefully hoarded funds allocated for the enterprise.

Chapter 9 – To Begin the World Anew

Fig. 31. **The Last of England, Ford Madox Brown** [242]

At the beginning of August 1822, the Curling family left the shelter of the Becker family home in Goldstone, where they had been living with Jane's brother for most of the time since the sale of the tenancy of Shuart Farm. However, baby Arthur had been baptized at St John the Baptist church, Margate, on 1 April 1822. This implies that his mother had been staying in Margate prior to the birth. The only possibility that presents itself is that Jane may have been staying with her eldest son Thomas

---

[242] © BMAG catalogue reference: 1891P24 ID10.

III and his employers, apothecaries Daniel Jarvis and John Waddington. This may seem like an imposition on the kindness of Dr Jarvis, but there was a family connection because Daniel Jarvis's mother was Ann née Oakley, a half-sister of Thomas Oakley Curling's mother Catharine.[243] Another apposite reason for Jane having her confinement in the household of Daniel Jarvis was that he was self-proclaimed 'Apothecary, Practitioner in Midwifery, and Member of the Corporation of Surgeons in London'.[244]

In preparation for the journey the Curling family probably travelled not to Gravesend, the *Regalia*'s first call after its departure from London, but to Deal, where they would have been rowed out to the ship when it anchored in the Downs.[245]

Although it was not executed until 1854–5, Ford Madox Brown's atmospheric painting (Fig. 31) *The Last of England* captures this daunting initial leg of the journey, much as it would have been for Thomas II, Jane and their children. The woman holds a baby beneath her shawl, 'whose tiny hand is just visible grasping its mother's hand',[246] as might have baby Arthur's, and there is at least one other small child, and the hand of a third holding a rope, visible behind the couple. In the foreground, upended heads of brassicas and strings of purple bean pods are stashed in a net. No matter how hard they tried to hide it from their children, Jane and Thomas II would have held apprehension in their faces exactly as this couple do as they sail past the white cliffs of south-eastern England.

Even when it looked as though Thomas and his family had jumped all their hurdles and the ship had left the London dock, its departure had been delayed at Gravesend because Customs officers had found a total of 6 lbs 4 oz of worsted in the baggage belonging to eleven passengers who had boarded in London, seven of whom were adults. According to an obscure law from the reign of Edward III, when the woollen trade had needed protection, worsted was contraband. In waiting for the inspection of these goods and for a decision, the *Regalia* was delayed five

---

[243] Margate Local History website, http://bit.ly/Ch9DnlJarvismar Janet Robinson.

[244] *Kentish Gazette* of 1 January 1788, quoted by Janet Robinson in her pages on 'A Branch of the Jarvis Family', http://bit.ly/Ch9DnlJarvisSurgeon on the blog, *Margate Local History*, Anthony Lee.

[245] I am informed by maritime historian Ian Williams of the East Kent Local History Society that it is more than likely that the Curlings and their livestock would have been rowed out to their ship, *Regalia*, from Deal rather than travelling to London or Gravesend.

[246] There are at least five versions of this painting, all executed by Ford Madox Brown; three of the earliest, done between 1852 and 1855, are in the Birmingham Museums Trust collection; one, executed in 1860, is in the Fitzwilliam Museum; and a water-colour replica is in the Tate Britain, from the online description for which this phrase is taken, see http://bit.ly/Ch9FMBrown.

days.[247] Finally, Lloyd's List tells us, the *Regalia* arrived at Deal from the Thames, and sailed for Van Diemen's Land on 7 August 1822.[248]

We have seen the administrative hoops through which Thomas II had to jump, not least of which was knowing whom his enquiries should be addressed to, and the services he should have been asking for. He wrote to the Secretary of State for the Colonies requesting an authority to obtain a grant of land, but from Rowcroft's book we learn that, in a somewhat contrary political twist, his letter should in fact have gone to the Secretary of State for the Home Department. A sealed letter, addressed to the lieutenant governor of Van Diemen's Land, was then sent to the emigrant, who was told that it contained the necessary authority to allocate a grant of land according to the applicant's means. This letter was the most important single item which the emigrants carried on their journey, and it was to be presented, still sealed, to the governor on their arrival.

In *Tales of the Colonies*, Charles Rowcroft's main character, William Thornley, says

> I found, after scraping together all I could get, that I could just manage to muster up £1,150; little enough to begin the world anew with, … Besides this £1,150 in money, we had our beds and bedding, and blankets and linen, and such household articles, in plenty; and a variety of things which lie about a house, and seem of no value, we took out with us and found them valuable, for use or sale, in the new country. As to the bulk of our furniture, we sold it all, as I was told that it would be several years before we could have a suitable place to put it in, and that I should find the money more useful; that I must rough it for some time, and think of nothing but STOCK: that is, of sheep and cattle. This advice was very good, as I afterwards found, and I was as happy, for many months, sitting on the stump of a tree, with my wife opposite me on another, as if we had reclined on the softest sofas in London … I took care to carry with us all the usual tools imperatively wanted on first settling, such as saws, axes, chisels, augurs &c. I had the good fortune to listen to the advice of the captain of a ship, and took out all the furnishing of a blacksmith's forge which I found of the greatest use to me … I was wrong in the sort of nails that I took out; they were good enough for the soft deals and other woods usual in England, but too weak for the hard woods of New South Wales. I took two pair of cart-wheels, with their boxes and axles complete. These were very

---

[247] *Public Ledger & Daily Advertiser London*, 7 September 1822 and *Bristol Mercury*, 16 September 1822. British Newspaper Archive.

[248] Hathi Trust digitized copy of Lloyds List for 1822, p. 87, republished in 1969 by Gregg International Publishers, Farnborough. http://bit.ly/Ch9LloydsList1822.

useful, but they make them in the colony now as good, and nearly as cheap as they can be imported; and the colonial wood, when well seasoned, stands the summer heat better. (Tales of the Colonies, 1843, pp. 8–9)

For real-life accounts of the rigours of the voyage for free settlers – those adventurers who had made the choice freely to submit themselves to this perilous journey, rather than convicts (transported separately in designated convict vessels) for whom the passage to Australia would have been part of the punishment for their crimes – Robin Haines's book *Life and Death in the Age of Sail: the passage to Australia*, is excellent, using many primary source letters and journals, although most of the material begins a decade or two later than the Curlings' voyage. Nonetheless, much about the voyage he described would have been identical to that of the *Regalia*. Haines has vivid pages on the advice in emigrants' manuals about the necessity of hoarding cotton fabric in advance of the voyage, to be made into disposable single-use babies' nappies (thrown overboard when removed), the horrendous smells of malfunctioning water closets, serious sea-sickness at the beginning of the voyage and on entry into the Southern Ocean after the calm of the tropics:

> Permeating the fetid air produced by numerous adults and children living in close proximity were the daily fumigants smoking away in charcoal and tar-burning swinging stoves. Other malodorous disinfectants, sprinkled liberally on the decks and bottom boards of the berths, including chloride of lime or zinc mixed with vinegar or other solutions, would be familiar to anyone who has ever smelled chreosote.[249]

… as would the restrictions on lovemaking imposed by communal living and three-foot-wide bunks.

Haines's research clearly shows that although mortality on early emigrant voyages was high, particularly in children, the British government was anxious to make the most of its investment in the Colonies by 'colonizing' wisely, ensuring that as many healthy individuals as possible survived the journey. Detailed regulations were introduced to keep conditions as hygienic as possible and to ensure adequate provision of food and water. But all this was still to come when the Curlings sailed, so the conditions may well have been worse for them. Not only that, but the *Regalia* had at the beginning of the year 1822 been used to transport goods which would have imparted a concoction of rank smells to the whole vessel:

---

[249] *Life and Death in the Age of Sail, the passage to Australia*, p. 77. Robin Haines, National Maritime Museum, Greenwich, London, 2006.

> The *Regalia,* Dixon, is arrived in the Downs from Port Jackson, with a cargo,
> the produce of the colony and adjacent islands: viz. – elephant oils,
> whalebone, seal-skins, wool, and wood.[250]

Although no doubt the whole ship had been thoroughly swabbed down between its delivery of these goods to London and its departure on the next voyage, it would have been extremely difficult to eradicate odours which had had five months to seep into every crevice of the vessel.

There are many nineteenth-century images of emigrant ships to be found on the internet, but again starting two decades later than the Curlings' journey. The main source is the *Illustrated London News* (see Fig. 32), which began publication in 1842, twenty years after the Curlings' journey, by which time the system of assisted passage was well established, with a surgeon assigned to each ship, rigorous hygiene routines and adequate food allocations.

Fig. 32. **Emigrants at Dinner** [251]

The accompanying text for this image in the Illustrated London News magazine said:

> 165 men, women and children emigrants embarked at Deptford on board the
> *St Vincent*, 628 tons, bound for Plymouth, Cork and Sydney Australia. The
> weekly allowance given in proportion daily to each adult during the voyage

---

[250] *Evening Mail*, 16 January 1822. (Dixon was the *Regalia*'s captain.)
[251] The *Illustrated London News* image, week ending 13 April 1844, pp. 229–230.
Courtesy of John Weedy, who owns a collection of 7,000 editions of the magazine: see
https://www.iln.org.uk/.

is 4 ½ lb of Bread, 1 lb of beef, 1 lb of pork, 1 lb of preserved meat, 1¼ lb flour, ½ lb raisins, 6 oz suet, 1 pint peas, ½ lb rice, ½ lb preserved potatoes, 1 oz tea, 1½ oz roast coffee, ¼ lb sugar, 6 oz butter, 5 gallons and 1 quart water, 1 gill pickled cabbage, ½ gill vinegar and 2 oz salt.

According to Lloyd's Register of Shipping for 1821–2, the *Regalia* had been built in Sunderland only four years earlier. She was an A1 ship,[252] but she had already needed some repairs, although this was not surprising for an ocean-going vessel. She was 'sheathed with copper over boards' (an expensive, but effective, form of deterrent to shipworm), had a 'single deck with beams'; weighed 370 tons unladen with 16 feet of draught when laden, and had been most recently surveyed in the port of London. The captain's name was Dixon and the owner abbreviation was Welbnk & LNSW.[253]

As well as Charles Rowcroft's fictional account of settler life, another author of the period had a unique knowledge of the travails of the Curling family as they arrived and followed the process of becoming settlers in Van Diemen's Land. Schoolteacher James Ross was a fellow passenger on the *Regalia*'s 1822 voyage, so he would have known the Curlings, and he probably improvised a teaching corner on deck and taught the school-age members of the onboard community. He later became editor of the *Hobart Town Almanac* in which he serialized his recollections of his first years in the colony.[254] Ross's writing includes an account of a visit to author Charles Rowcroft's house, and their combined work gives a vivid impression of our family's struggles. This chapter continues with extended extracts from both authors.

---

[252] The classification A1 originated with Lloyds Register. A vessel in class A was First Class or, as we might say, top of the range. The materials of which the vessel were made were separately classed by number, with 1 also top of the range; see introductory pages of Lloyd's Register of Shipping 1822, online here: http://bit.ly/Ch9Lloyds1822 under the heading 'Key to the Register Book for 1822'.

[253] Royal Museums of Greenwich Research Guide H5, available online: http://bit.ly/Ch9RMGRsrchGdH5.

[254] *The Settler in Van Diemen's Land*, a collection of Ross's writings published by Marsh Walsh, 1975; my thanks to Captain Troy of Hobart, Tasmania, for introducing me to this invaluable work.

Fig. 33. **Distant View of Hobart Town from Blufhead, 1825 – detail** [255]

With the help of James Ross we can witness the arrival of the *Regalia*'s passengers in Hobart, Fig. 33. He began with a vivid account of their disembarkation at Sullivan's Cove, which today is still part of the dock area of Hobart town:

"Now, gentlemen," said the Captain, "the boat is all ready for you." We had come to anchor that morning in Sullivan's Cove, and for the last hour or two had been doing our best, after a long voyage, to make ourselves look decent in order to pay our respects to the Governor. Every seat in the boat was already occupied when in my last new London-made black dress coat, bearing in spite of me, the folds and creases it had acquired by lying for five long months in the bottom of my clothes box, I was obliged to seat myself at the very bow, which I hastily did rather than miss my opportunity of going with the van of our passengers into His Honor's[256] presence. The boat was just shoving off when we were desired to stop (in a stentorian voice, which none of us dared to disobey) in order to take on board an emigrant whom we had all forgotten, and who we wished had also forgotten us, but who now appeared descending the steps. I do not to this hour know how he managed to get down, for both arms were loaded with articles of the heaviest kind. One embraced a steel mill, on the excellent machinery of which he had enlarged almost every day since he had purchased it in Oxford street – the other held, linked together in a bullock chain, a huge iron maul, a broad axe, and another very long felling, or rather falling one, as it is colonially called,

---

[255] Joseph Lycett c.1775–1828. Digitized item from Allport Library & Museum of Fine Arts, Tasmanian Archives & Heritage Office. SD_ILS:165548 SLIDES 85S; CD IMAGES23.

[256] 'His Honor' was Colonel William Sorrell, lieutenant governor of the island at the time.

and which it unfortunately for me, in this instance, too truly proved to be. For in spite of all our cries – "no room, no room" – "keep back," "wait till next time," &c., in an instant he had his foot impressed, with all the superincumbent weight of himself and his iron ware, on the gunnel of the boat, which he at once brought down to the edge of the water, and with the help of the passenger who sat beside me, and by the sweep of his arm, trying to preserve his equilibrium, depriving me of mine, I was as suddenly precipitated about ten or a dozen feet below the water. Thanks to the aquatic acquirements of my early days, however, I was soon again at the surface, where I swam until I caught the end of a rope, by which I returned on board, with the mortification of having my fine levee coat steeped in salt water, and seeing the rest of the passengers paddling smoothly on shore to get the first blush of the Governor's patronage. The only consolation I had under my catastrophe, was the finding that the whole of the heavy articles which had contributed to it, were now lying snug four fathoms under water at the bottom of the Derwent.

This accident was in so far, however, compensated to me as it gave me the advantage next day of a long and private interview with the Governor, to whom I delivered my various letters of introduction, and whose attention was the more forcibly drawn to me by the apology which my fellow passengers had made for my non-appearance the day before. He read my letters with attention, appeared pleased with my arrival, and especially with my determination to settle in Van Diemen's Land in preference to going on to Sydney. He assured me the colony wanted settlers like myself, and said I might rely on every assistance that the government could afford. He referred me to Captain Robinson of the 48th regiment, his Secretary, who would officially report to him the schedule of property I had brought with me, and he appointed next day to meet him with Mr. Evans the Surveyor General, in order to point out to me on the map the most eligible spot for my farm, and to afford me every other proper assistance.[257]

Visiting the governor was the most important task to be undertaken immediately on landing. William Thornley, Rowcroft's protagonist in *Tales of the Colonies*, did so too, presenting letters of credential and authority to be granted land. What followed amounted to an interview in which the applicant had to make a case for a grant of land.

The governor, whom I saw himself, and who was very kind in his information and advice, made a note of my circumstances, of the amount of my property, of the number of my children and family, of my views

---

[257] *The Settler in Van Diemen's Land,* pp. 1–2, James Ross, Hobart, 1836, originally published as a collection of his articles written for his annual publication, *The Hobart Town Almanac,* and republished in the twentieth century; no details of the editor or publisher are provided in the book.

in coming to the colony and he dwelt much on the bona fide nature of my intentions to go on the land and work it. I told him that I had come with the intention of settling as a farmer, and of residing on my land, and cultivating it myself. At this time, in the year 1817, this class of settlers was always specially favoured by the colonial government, as indeed it was right and politic to do, for it was precisely the class that was wanted in the colony to form its inhabitants of the interior, to raise food for the colony, and to create establishments for relieving the government of the expense of maintaining the convicts. It aided the plan, also of reforming the convicts, by removing them from the temptations of the town, and of habituating them to healthy work in new positions, where they would be removed from old habits and associations. Being one of this desirable class, I was told by the governor that he considered me entitled to as large a grant of land as was consistent with his general instructions; and that he should allot me twelve hundred acres.[258]

Did Thomas II manage to be among the first to present his paperwork to the governor? Possibly not, as ensuring the safe disembarkation of his family would have been his first concern.

Once the Curlings had found temporary accommodation in Hobart, Thomas probably set out alone to find suitable land on which to set up a home for his family as well as the beginnings of a farm. There were comparatively few residents outside the towns at this time. In a meeting with the British government's official surveyor he would have been told in what area he could choose land and would have been allowed to 'locate' or settle on it with his family until the official grant was made.[259] New settlers were instructed to plan their land running down to a river because access to water was vital and because it made the transport of goods easier.

Rowcroft's account is a particularly seductive source, given that he was in the country between 1821 and 1825, as the period ties in so well with the Curlings' arrival on the penultimate day of 1822. This is undoubtedly a true-to-life account of how it would have been for the Curlings as well.

In Rowcroft's story William Thornley has taken up with Samuel Crab, a bushranger,[260] in hopes of finding land, and the two of them hitch a lift:

> a settlers bullock cart fortunately was proceeding to Norfolk Plains, on the northern side of the island. We availed ourselves of its convenience; and partly riding and partly walking, we arrived at the large tract of level land

---

[258] *Tales of the Colonies*, p. 9.
[259] 'Land Grants in Early Colonial Van Diemen's Land', Imogen Wegman, https://bit.ly/LandGrantsVDLWegman.
[260] Bushrangers were escaped convicts; see *Bushrangers in the Australian Dictionary of Biography*, an essay by Jane Wilson, available online: http://adb.anu.edu.au/essay/12.

known by that name. From thence we proceeded to Launceston, and returning by the high road, we arrived at a place called "Green Ponds", in the district of Murray. Here at a little public house, I heard of a tract of country lying westward, on the banks of the Clyde, particularly suitable for cattle and sheep feeding, which was the line I had a mind to follow. I crossed over, with the persevering Crab, and lighted on a spot, which pleased me at once, from the back run for sheep and cattle which it afforded.

Having fixed on my land, I hastened back to Hobart Town, that I might be the first to apply for it. I had been away seventeen days, and it was with not a little delight that I saw my wife and children again, for I seemed to have been absent a much longer time. The very next day I got an order from the governor to take possession; and I was informed the land would be regularly surveyed and marked out for me by the government surveyor, as soon as his engagements would permit, and that in the meantime I might take possession and erect my buildings. My next care was to provide myself with two bullock-carts, and two teams of four bullocks each, to carry up such utensils and things as were absolutely necessary.

On consulting with my wife, I found that she preferred going on the land with me at once, with the children, to staying in the town until I had got some accommodation for her. Fortunately we had brought out with us two good tents, one a pretty large one; these served us in good stead. We were in a pretty bustle, it may be supposed, packing up and getting ready for our journey. It was about fifty miles from the town to the spot I had chosen. All our goods and traps being ready – and having had assigned to me two government men,[261] a bullock-driver and a farming-man – my wife, her children, and her mother, occupying one cart, with the woman servant, and all sorts of articles for bedding and use; and the other cart being filled with utensils and tools, and provisions, we commenced our journey on 26th February 1817, with anxious thoughts, but full of spirits and of hope, for the river Clyde.

It is more than twenty-one years since I set out on this memorable journey,[262] but the whole scene is present to me as if it was an affair of yesterday; and I remember well my sensations at the sight of my wife perched on the top of a feather bed in a bullock-cart, with her old mother sitting beside her, and the children higgledy piggledy about her, enjoying the novelty and the fun of being dragged by bullocks in a cart. There was something so droll

---

[261] Rowcroft makes it clear earlier in the book that it was considered tactless to refer to the deported convicts as such. The accepted term was 'government men'. The Curlings, too, had government men working with them.

[262] *Tales of the Colonies* was first published in 1843. Rowcroft's writing of the twenty-year gap since the events portrayed in his fictional account ties in precisely with the period when Rowcroft and the Curlings were in Van Diemen's Land – but Rowcroft was unmarried at the time of his arrival, his only dependant being his younger brother Horatio, so the novel is not autobiographical.

in the set-out, and at the same time the occasion was so serious, that my poor wife did not know whether to laugh or to cry; but the tumblings that the roughness of the road gave the children soon made them merry enough, and their joyous mirth set the rest of the party a-laughing, so that the journey was a merry one in the beginning at least. The old lady sat very quietly in her place, a little frightened, but resigned to her fate. She owned, afterwards, that she never expected to get to the end of the journey alive by such an outlandish sort of conveyance, and she was like to be right in her forebodings at one time.[263]

The family, of which bush-ranger Crab quickly became a part, broke their journey at a little wayside inn on the first night, and the second they spent in the open air.

At the first sign of light we were stirring. We had to pursue the same process to get up our provision-cart, when we made a hearty breakfast and not the less so from having gone without our supper. Our way was now all downhill by a gentle inclination; and sometimes following the faint track, and sometimes guided by the notched trees, and making our way over the dead timber and through the bushes as well as we could, we arrived in about a couple of hours at the site of my future farm.

It was now noon. The sun was intensely hot, and we very tired, bullocks and all; but we had arrived safe, and we felt in spirits. And here we were, our little party, alone in the wilderness. To the west there was no human habitation between us and the sea; and the nearest settler's residence was not less than eighteen miles. There was pasturage for sheep and cattle for scores and scores of miles, and no one to interfere with them. But I had not yet a single sheep, nor a single head of cattle, except my eight working bullocks. We turned them out to graze on the plain before us, through which ran the Clyde, then better known by the name of the Fat Doe River; we had no fear of their straying, for they were tired enough with their journey. The two men then set up the tents, without bidding.

I remember I sat on a fallen tree, with my wife and children and her mother stretched on the ground in the shade, for some time absorbed in thoughts of mingled pain and pleasure. Crab had strolled into the bush. It was a brilliant day. There was a solemn stillness around that was imposing; the sun shining gloriously in the heavens, and the prospect around most calm and beautiful. I felt melancholy. Thoughts crowded thick upon me. I had undertaken a vast task, to establish a home in the wilderness. The first stage of my enterprise I had accomplished through toil, and labour, and difficulty, and danger; but I had accomplished it. The first object was gained. I had reached the land of promise. I had taken possession of my land, and a noble domain it was. But what were the risks and difficulties that remained? I felt fearful at the work before me. No help near in case of danger; no medical assistance; no

---

[263] *Tales of the Colonies*, pp. 91–92.

neighbour. I looked at my wife and children lying listlessly on the dry and parched grass; I looked around me, and tried to penetrate into the obscurity of the future, and guess the end. Worn out with thought, and weary with travel, I insensibly gave way to the feeling of lassitude which possessed us all, and fell asleep on the grass. My wife would not have me wakened, but taking on herself, without hesitation and without delay, the duties of a settler's wife, she silently gave directions for unloading the carts, and preparing our canvass house. The smaller tent she made the temporary storehouse for our multifarious goods; the larger one was converted into a general bedchamber for herself, her mother, and the children. The store tent was destined for me to sleep in. Two boxes formed a table on the outside, and fitting logs of wood formed appropriate seats. A fire was kindled near the spot, and dinner got ready. It was quite an early settler's meal; boiled salt pork and damper[264] with tea and brown sugar, and rice for the children. All this was prepared while I slept. I was awakened by Crab, who had been absent about a couple of hours on his exploring expedition.

"Holloa!" said he; "here's a pretty settler, to go to sleep while his wife works for him. Look here, I've got something for you."

I awoke at this, and felt quite refreshed and ready for action. Crab displayed a brace of wild ducks, which produced a general curiosity among the party. Without stopping to ask questions, Crab prepared them for the spit after his way. But spit we had none, so we contented ourselves with throwing them on the hot embers, native fashion, and hooking them out with the ramrod of one of our muskets. We distributed them among young and old in equitable proportions. I had brought up with me a five-gallon cask of rum, rather in compliance with the customs of the colony than with my own inclination; but on this occasion, and to do honour to the splendour of our repast of game, I served out a moderate ration of it, much to the satisfaction of the two men, who were well pleased at the unexpected libation. We soon got very merry, and at last felt so reconciled to our new position, that I caught myself proposing three-times-three to the success of the FIRST FARM on the Fat Doe River.[265]

This is undoubtedly an almost true-to-life account of how the initial trek upcountry was for the Curlings. There is a particular reason for this assertion, which will become apparent later in the story. An important point which Rowcroft made is that settlers were allowed to begin work on their land even before it had been surveyed or a formal grant issued.

---

[264] 'Damper is one of Australia's most iconic symbols of bush life.It was made famous by drovers, who baked this bush bread in the coals of their camp fire, and has been recognised as a staple of bush life for decades.' The History of Australian Damper, Loreena Walsh, from https://www.littleaussietravellers.com.au/history-australian-damper/

[265] *Tales of the Colonies*, pp. 104–108.

Matthew Curling Friend and his wife Mary Ann were a young couple who arrived eight years later, landing first in Victoria but moving on soon afterwards to Van Diemen's Land. Mary Ann kept a journal and made sketches of their life.[266]

We can imagine that Thomas Oakley Curling and Jane would have had an encampment similar to the one Mary Ann recorded in her sketch (Fig. 34). Matthew, who had had an illustrious career, both in the navy and as a scientist, was a second cousin of Thomas Oakley Curling.

Fig. 34. **View at Swan River** [267]

The ties between settlers often began to form on the passage to the colony. The voyage was long and the passengers had time to build friendships which, since they often knew nobody in the colony, became significant in the choice of a location for their land grants. Fellow passengers chose adjacent grants so as to be

---

[266] For brief biographical notes on Mary Ann Friend and Matthew Curling Friend, see **Appendix 6b – Mary Ann and Matthew Curling Friend** (p. 192).

[267] SLNSW, Call Number Sv5B/Swan R/4, Reference code 82603. The full catalogued title is 'View at Swan River. Sketch of the encampment of Matthew Curling Friend Esq., R.N. [coloured lithograph] Taken on the Spot & Drawn on Stone by Mrs. M.C.F., March 1830', Mary Ann Friend, Dixson Library, State Library of New South Wales.

able to offer and receive assistance from well-disposed neighbours. Sometimes the idea of friendship overrode common sense in the choice of a location. Thomas Oakley Curling and Thomas Fletcher, who both arrived on the *Regalia* in December 1822, chose grants on opposite sides of the Lake River, Curling having prevailed upon Fletcher to do so, in order to have a near neighbour. The land commissioners noted that Fletcher 'was no farmer', and had lost 'both his time and Money', and been forced to quit the land, although not before he had been granted an additional 560 acres.[268]

The two sketches of the Lake River, Fig. 35 and Fig. 36, by Emily Stuart Bowring[269] show what a magnificent site Thomas II chose.

Fig. 35. **Ben Lomond & Lake River from Richmond Hill** [270]

[268] *Land Settlement in Early Tasmania: creating an antipodean England.* Sharon Morgan, Selwyn College, Cambridge, CUP, 1992.

[269] *Sketches in Early Tasmania and Victoria* by Emily Stuart Bowring, ed. K R Von Stieglitz, OBE, pub. Hobart: Fullers Bookshop, c1965. Both sketches are unsigned and undated, but the Tasmanian Archives online information gives the date as 1856.

[270] From the original sketchbook of Emily Stuart Bowring, 1856. Digitized item from Allport Library and Museum of Fine Arts, Tasmanian Archive and Heritage Office. Record ID: SD_ILS:73837.

Fig. 36. **Lake River & Western Tier from Richmond Hill** [271]

It may not have been in this pristine condition when Thomas II first found it, but no doubt as 'a farmer of many years' experience' on the Isle of Thanet, he could see its potential. One can see the resemblance which Thomas II notes in the letter he later wrote to a friend in England,[272] to 'the waves of the Sea, not the short waves near the shore but the long swells of the great Ocean which are 200 yards and more apart'. He must have hurried back to Hobart to tell Jane and the children the good news. He would then have been busy making arrangements to take his family, as well as his livestock and the goods and chattels he had brought from England, upcountry to their new home. The only inkling we can have of just how arduous these tasks were is Charles Rowcroft's account in *Tales of the Colonies*. His William Thornley sets out to find his land in the New Norfolk area not far from Hobart, but Thomas II went considerably further north for his land, to an area on the Lake River.

---

[271] Emily Stuart Bowring, as above. Record ID: SD_ILS:73838.
[272] See Chapter 10.

Chapter 10 – Land of Speculation and Hope

Creating a permanent shelter for his family as soon as possible was Thomas II's priority, but he had other things on his mind too, such as marking the boundaries of his territory and making it secure against bushrangers[273] and First Nations[274] people.

> The Aborigines seem to have been prepared in the first years of European settlement to share their land with the newcomers, but the British were determined at all costs to have the land for their own exclusive use. As settlement spread and the indigenous peoples were pushed further and further from their traditional hunting grounds, conflict soared.[275]

In November 1823, almost a year after their arrival, Thomas II wrote a letter to Sir Thomas Mantell in England.[276] The original of this letter has not so far come to light, but there is a contemporaneous copy in the Liverpool Papers held at the British Library.[277] Thomas II described how fortunate they were in the mild winter and pleasant spring weather, and outlined how he had quickly planned out the early use of his land. His letter indicates that even at the end of his first year he had had no official confirmation of the extent of his land. His anxiety on behalf of his sons concerning any bequest he would be able to lay down for them is evident, as he sent letters to several influential people asking for assistance in achieving his goal of a formal grant of land which would include allowances for the two older sons, who he doesn't name, but who were Edward and Charles, and possibly later for the four younger ones. It is clear both from Thomas II's letter and from Rowcroft's novel that the principle by which the amounts of land were granted was directly related to the existing wealth of the settler on arrival, even though they were not purchasing the land; it was, rather, an indication that they had the resources to husband it properly.

Thomas's letter portrays the family's experience to date in as positive a light as possible. It is a lengthy and detailed epistle, and only towards the end did he indicate the real reason for his writing: he needed help to get action on his grant of land. It is easy to see why: others who had arrived after him had had their grants

---

[273] For a history of bushrangers see https://en.wikipedia.org/wiki/Bushranger.

[274] Other than in quotations, I will use 'First Nations' to refer to all Aboriginal and Torres Strait Islander people, and 'indigenous' for more general references.

[275] *Land Settlement in Early Tasmania, Creating an Antipodean England*, p. 3, Sharon Morgan, Cambridge University Press, 1992. The injustice of taking land from indigenous inhabitants in the process of building empires is a topic which is the subject of many scholarly works. A useful web page on terminologies is provided here: https://bit.ly/Ch10terminology

[276] A complete transcript of Thomas II's letter can be found in **Appendix 10a – Letter from Van Diemen's Land** (p. 196), with an analysis of the letter's contents in **Appendix 10b – Commentary on the letter from Van Diemen's Land** (p. 202).

[277] BL Add MS 38299 f67.

formalized, but he had not. He also indicated that he was still short of funds, although this difficulty was universal in the colony.

It might be said that Thomas II's description of the family's new situation was skewed to give an optimistic impression to his reader. Sir Thomas Mantell was a relative by marriage, who had been a signatory to Thomas's appeal for assisted passage to Van Diemen's Land, so there would have been a pressure, conscious or unconscious, to impress this benefactor. A newspaper article from the *Courier & Evening Gazette*, dated 5 November 1824, might be considered a more objective view of the colony.[278] Reassuringly, it corroborates Thomas's assessment of the island and it highlights one of the ways in which news from the colonies was disseminated: via the coffee houses in London.

The government surveyor was a pivotal character in the life of the settler community. It was he who made the recommendations regarding grants of land, and he spent most of his time travelling the country surveying land for those grant allocations. He forwarded his recommendations to the governor, and decisions were made on his opinions as to allocation of land to settlers. The surveyor at the time of Thomas II's application was John Helder Wedge, who kept a diary of his perambulations, and wrote of his visit to the Curling homestead:

January 1825

Sat 19 – Went from Formosa to M[r] Curlings, with whom I dined – You here witness the comforts of an emigrant after a two years residence in the Colony – M[r]. & M[rs]. C. and eight children in a Hut divided into one room, which serves for parlor, kitchen, & dormitory – two years and such is the state of things in doors – nor can I perceive a greater forwardness in the business of the farm – a crop of corn entirely spoilt by cattle from the want of a fence – [279]

'A Hut divided into one room' would hardly have been a division. It is difficult to know what Wedge meant. A month later, he wrote

Feb. 19 – Thomas Oakley Curling was granted Rockthorpe at Cressy.

Finally! Thomas had official recognition of his right to the land, although we do not know exactly how much land he was granted. He, Jane and their children could pause for a celebration. Somewhere in the administrative process the name of the property had changed from their original choice of 'Guilton on the Lake River' to Rockthorpe. This latter name was for a time recorded as Pockthorpe, but, later still, records online note the sale of animals from the 'Rockthorpe estate, Cressy'.

---

[278] See **Appendix 10c – A newspaper review** (p. 208) for the full article.
[279] *The Diaries of John Helder Wedge 1824–1835*, eds Crawford, Ellis & Stancombe, Royal Society 1962.

Chapter 11 – Universally Respected by All

On 8 April 1825 this announcement (Fig. 37) appeared in the *Hobart Town Gazette*:

> **On Sunday the 27th ult., T. O. CURLING, Esq. at his farm on the Lake River, leaving a disconsolate widow and nine children to deplore his loss.—This Gentleman arrived in the Colony only about two years since, and was uniformly respected by all who knew him.**

Fig. 37. *Hobart Town Gazette & Van Diemen's Land Advertiser* 8 April 1825 [280]

Thomas Oakley Curling died on 27 March 1825 at the age of forty-three,[281] only six weeks after receiving his formal land grant. There is no information about how or why he died at this comparatively young age. Several murders were thought to have been committed in the area at the time, by the Sydney First Nations man known as Musquito.[282] However, Musquito was executed in February 1825, and although it is possible that a group of local First Nations people took revenge by murdering a British farmer, it would have been reported in the local press. Another possible theory is that Thomas might have been murdered by bushrangers. Again, there would undoubtedly have been newspaper reports. In *Tales of the Colonies* Charles Rowcroft wrote dramatic episodes where his protagonist's or his neighbour's houses and land were attacked.

There are other more or less dramatic theories for Thomas's early demise so soon after he had settled, and the truth is unlikely ever to be uncovered. He could simply have succumbed to severe infection or met with an accident while working on his land. Jane must have written to her eldest son Thomas to tell him of his father's death and she may well have written to other family members. The following death notice appeared in the newspaper *The British Press* in November 1825, indicating the length of time her letters took to reach them:

> On Sunday, the 27th of March 1825, at Gilton Farm, Van Diemen's Land, Mr. Thomas Oakley Curling, in the 43rd year of his age, leaving a disconsolate widow and nine children to lament their irreparable loss. Mr. Curling was born at Shuart, near St. Nicholas, and began his career under the most fortunate circumstances; but the great difficulties under which the

---

[280] TAHO, *Hobart Town Gazette and Van Diemen's Land Advertiser* (Tas: 1821–1825), Apr. 8, 1825, p. 3, col. 2.

[281] Tasmanian Pioneers Index: Births, Deaths, Marriages 1803–1899.

[282] See **Appendix 11 – Did First Nations people use guerrilla tactics?** (p. 211).

agricultural interest here suffered were more than commonly felt by him, and induced him, in the summer of 1822, to embark with his wife and (excepting his eldest son) children for Australasia. His exertions there were unceasing, and his arrangements calculated to have insured success; but the Almighty, in his infinite wisdom, having removed him from this transitory world, it is hoped the protecting hand of Government will exert its kind influence in behalf of the surviving sufferers.[283]

Jane Curling was now a widow with eight children in her care ranging in age from the infant Arthur who was not quite three years old, to Edward who was nineteen. She had to consider her options. The *Hobart Town Gazette* of 15 April 1825 has a public notification that she took out Letters of Administration on the estate of her late husband, incorrectly named 'John' Curling, settler, Lake River. Initially, at least, it looks as though she thought that they would be able to continue to develop the farm; Edward and Charles, the two eldest children with Jane, must have absorbed considerable knowledge of farming from their father, and no doubt, together with their four younger brothers, would have been more than willing to work hard towards securing their inheritance. Jane hired another 'government man', presumably to make up the manpower for the farm. The new man employed by the family was Thomas Richardson, ploughman.[284] However, the family's optimism did not last. The journal of the nineteenth-century Australian historian Henry Widowson tells us:

> Passing the house and farm of Mr Brumby, a very old settler, you cross a tributary stream of the Lake River known as Brumby's Creek. Crossing a plain of pretty good land with lagoons here and there, you arrive at the grant of Mr. Lawrence where a large paddock, which has been cleared and grubbed at considerable expense is now under cultivation. The improvement exhibited here is much beyond the generality of settlers. The fencing is extensive and good and I hope Mr. Lawrence will be amply repaid for his large outlay of capital. Mr Lawrence resides in Launceston. A plain road leads through the estate to a good gravely ford over the Lake River where there are several neat farms. To the right before crossing the river, is the farm of the late Mr. Curling, purchased from the widow of that gentleman by Captain Carns, commander and owner of the ship 'Cumberland'.[285]

---

[283] *The British Press*, Saturday 19 November 1825. Transcribed from the article available on the British Newspaper Archives website.

[284] Kiama Family History Centre, Kiama, New South Wales. Microfiche references CY1273 P2, frames 78, 79 and 86.

[285] Widowson is quoted extensively in *A Short History of Cressy and Bishopsbourne with some notes on the Lake River Pioneers* by K R von Stieglitz, Hobart DBM, 1976.

So Jane had sold up, and the next record we come across is the embarkation list for the *Cumberland* on a voyage to England. The original lists them thus:

Mr Robert Carns	*Passenger from Hobart Town*
Mrs Jane Curling	*do[286]*
Edward Curling	*do*
Henry Curling	*do*
Charles Curling	*do*
Robert Curling	*do*
John Curling	*do*
Jane Curling	*do*
Catherine Curling	*do*
Arthur Curling	*do[287]*

The full list begins with the commander Mr Charles Palin and crew. The first passenger on the list is Mr Carns, the *Cumberland*'s owner travelling as a passenger, he who had purchased Rockthorpe from Jane. His name is followed by the whole Curling family, listed individually in chronological order. There were eleven other passengers, including a family with two children (not named individually) and three freed convicts, their liberation details listed. Finally, in a hastily scrawled addition right at the end of the list on the reverse of the folio:

Charles Rowcroft Esq	*do*
Mr Robert Gregory	*do*
Full 40 Persons	*Sailed 17th September 1825*

Artist Emily Stuart Bowring provides a postscript to the Curlings' time in Van Diemen's Land. Her finest contribution to the Curling family history is undoubtedly the picture in Fig. 38. She shows us the Rockthorpe (Pockthorpe) property as it was thirty years after their departure, the site of the house on a little rise by the river. K R von Stieglitz had included the image in *Sketches in Early Tasmania and Victoria*, his collection of Bowring's work. Two more sketches, Fig. 35 and Fig. 36 (pp. 110, 111), also by Bowring, are from an album now held by the Tasmania Archives and Heritage service in Hobart, and were easily found on their online catalogue. Tracking down the original of the Pockthorpe sketch took some years, but I was wonderfully fortunate in coming across Michael von Stieglitz, grandson of K R von Stieglitz. In February 2021 Michael, after considerable

---

[286] 'do' here is an abbreviation for 'ditto'.

[287] Information from original *Cumberland* record held by Tasmania State Library and Archive Service, archival reference: CSO63/1/1: Copies of Clearances Issued to Ships Leaving Hobart, p. 157.

sleuthing, located the sketch in the Victoria Museum and Gallery in Launceston, Tasmania. With Michael's assistance and that of museum staff, I was finally in possession of a high resolution digital image of Bowring's sketch of the site which Thomas Oakley Curling and Jane had named 'Guilton on the Lake River'. I suspect that only another family historian can truly appreciate the level of excitement I felt on receiving it, and the gratitude I feel to everyone involved.

Fig. 38. Pockthorpe and the Western Tier, Emily Stuart Bowring, 1855 [288]

In editing his publication of Emily Stuart Bowring's sketch, K R von Stieglitz wrote:

> Pockthorpe, or Rockthorpe as it is now called, was originally granted to that "practical Kentish farmer", Thomas Oakley Curling, who arrived 30th Dec., 1822. He named the property Guilton.[289]

---

[288] Emily Stuart Bowring's sketch of Pockthorpe, the original of which Michael von Stieglitz helped me to locate. Collection of the Queen Victoria Museum and Art Gallery, Launceston, Tasmania.

[289] *Sketches in Early Tasmania and Victoria,* Bowring, as before.

Thomas II had chosen the site of his farm well. In the following years sheep farming prospered at Rockthorpe. In 1936 when the property was sold 'under instructions from Mr J J Gatenby', 3,300 sheep came under the hammer at the clearing sale,[290] and in 1977

> [e]ight Polwarth stud rams from five Australian studs have been sold to Uruguay for $17,250.
>
> Lep Air Services Pty Ltd transported the rams, including an $8,000 ram from Mr R. E. Lawrence's 'Rockthorpe' stud, Cressy, Tasmania, in two shipments from Tullamarine.[291]

What a tragedy it was that Thomas Oakley Curling had died prematurely, and only just after making it all the way to, and clearing, the final hurdle in setting up his farm.

---

[290] *The Examiner* newspaper, Launceston, Tasmania, 5 March 1936, TROVE database.
[291] *Trade News*, 9 December 1977, p. 725. TROVE database.

Chapter 12 – Criminal Conversation with a Woman

Charles Rowcroft and Robert Gregory were last-minute additions to the *Cumberland*'s passenger list. Rowcroft was yet to write his *Tales of the Colonies*, but soon after his arrival in Van Diemen's Land he had attracted attention as a well-educated young man worthy of public office. That positive attention, however, turned later to notoriety. His entry in the *Australian Dictionary of National Biography* begins:

Fig. 39. **Charles Rowcroft, 1798–1856, artist unknown** [292]

---

[292] From a glass plate negative of the original painting, held by NSW State Archives: NRS-4481-3-[7/16034]-St16967. The location of the original painting is unknown.

ROWCROFT, CHARLES (1798–1856), novelist, was born on 12 July 1798 ..., the eldest son of Thomas Rowcroft, an East India merchant and London alderman ...` [Charles's father] became British consul-general in Lima, Peru, and in December 1824 was mistaken for one of Bolívar's revolutionary supporters and shot.[293]

Charles was educated at Eton in 1809–11. In August 1821 he arrived at Hobart Town ... with his brother Horace, and took up a grant of 2000 acres at Norwood, five miles north of the present town of Bothwell ... In 1822 he was made a justice of the peace. He was a member of the committee of the Agricultural Society of Van Diemen's Land and an original shareholder of the Van Diemen's Land Bank. In 1823 he unsuccessfully sought the position of colonial secretary. In December 1824 he was the unsuccessful defendant in a case in which E. Lord sued him for a criminal conversation.[294]

'Criminal conversation' was a legalistic euphemism for the seduction of someone else's wife.[295] Maria Lord, née Risley, had arrived in Van Diemen's Land as a convict. She already had a daughter when wool merchant Edward Lord married her, and with him she had five more children. Trading in goods between Van Diemen's Land and England, Lord was often absent from home for extended periods, sometimes taking one or more of his children with him. In October 1824, Lord, brought the law suit

seeking 1000 pounds in damages. A fortnight after winning his case, but having received only 100 pounds in damages, Lord again left for England taking with him five year old Emma.[296]

Rowcroft was unable to pay the full fine which he had incurred. He stayed on in Hobart for a year, but 'by this time he was almost a pauper'.[297] It may have been his fall from social grace which led him to decide to leave Van Diemen's Land, or he might well have thought the simplest way to deal with an unpayable debt was to leave the country; but his father Thomas Rowcroft, who was consul-general in Peru, had died in December 1824, which would have been an equally pressing reason for Charles to return to England, not least to claim his share of the inheritance which came to him and his five siblings.[298]

---

[293] Simón Bolívar led the peoples of South America in widespread and successful campaigns for independence from the Spanish Empire, resulting in the formation of the independent nations of Venezuela, Bolivia, Colombia, Ecuador, Peru and Panama. The success of his campaigns relied in part on Spain's being preoccupied with Napoleon's advances in the Peninsular War. Wikipedia page on Simón Bolívar, http://bit.ly/Ch12Bolivar.

[294] Cecil Hadgraft and J C Horner, 'Rowcroft, Charles (1798–1855)', *Australian Dictionary of Biography*, National Centre of Biography, Australian National University, pub. first in hardcopy 1967. http://bit.ly/Ch12RowcroftbiogADB.

[295] Thelaw.com dictionary: http://bit.ly/Ch12CrimConvDefinition.

[296] ADB biography of Maria Lord: https://bit.ly/39fwCTN.

[297] ADB biography of Charles Rowcroft, as above.

[298] Will of Thomas Rowcroft, proved 1826, TNA PROB11/1711/475.

Rowcroft had brought substantial liquid finance to the colony, as indicated by his land grant of 2,000 acres. He had arrived with his younger brother, but no wife or children. Lloyd Robson wrote 'Charles and Horatio Rowcroft had considerable capital and were recommended by their father, Thomas Rowcroft'.[299]

With the knowledge of Rowcroft's less than responsible behaviour in accruing debts which he could not honour, and first seducing and then abandoning Maria Lord, the reader may question whether his judgment as magistrate in the case, amongst others, of Musquito was likely to have been fully informed, impartial and well thought out.[300]

These days Bothwell is one and a half hours' drive from what was the Curling property, Rockthorpe. It is possible that Charles Rowcroft had not met either Mr or Mrs Curling prior to his embarkation on the *Cumberland*; but on the other hand, as he was a prominent member of the farming community and a magistrate in Bothwell, it seems unlikely that Jane Curling would not have known of him.

Having won the case against Rowcroft, Lord took his children to England, leaving Maria to fend for herself – which she did very capably, opening a shop which became 'the best in Hobart'.[301]

The other late passenger, Robert Gregory, is said to have been a convict, but the record of his marriage to Jane Millar in 1822 states that both he and she were 'free'. He might have been re-arrested and incarcerated again, or there might have been two men with the name Robert Gregory, one free and one a convict. The convict had arrived in Van Diemen's Land aboard the *Malabar* in 1822, convicted of 'Uttering Forged Bank Notes'.[302] Further information about him can be found in **Appendix 12 – Robert Gregory** (p. 217). If there was a second Robert Gregory, there is no further information available.

The *Australian Dictionary of Biography* entry for Rowcroft continues from the first extract above:

> His land was poor so, after hearing of his father's death, he left Van Diemen's Land in the Cumberland in September 1825, and sailed by way of Sydney to Brazil. The eight children and Jane, the widow of Thomas Oakley Curling, who had died in Hobart in March, sailed on the same ship; on 16 December Rowcroft married Mrs Curling at San Sebastian on the Rio de Janeiro.

---

[299] *A History of Tasmania*, vol. 1, p. 109, Lloyd Robson, pub. 1983.
[300] See **Chapter 11 – Universally Respected by All** and **Appendix 11 – Did First Nations people use guerrilla tactics?**
[301] http://bit.ly/Ch12MariaLordshop.
[302] Tasmanian State Archives, Alphabetical record book of convicts arriving in Van Diemen's Land, 'G': 1815–1830, Accession Number 2/144, Classification: File 2(h), p. 83.

Rowcroft did indeed marry Jane Curling, in the Anglican church 'in the city of San Sebastian, Rio de Janeiro'.[303] She had been widowed only nine months previously, and had passed her forty-fifth birthday on board ship. Mr Rowcroft, aged twenty-seven, may have had winning ways with middle-aged women: Jane may have carried her years (and her eight accompanying children) superbly and charmed Rowcroft. What were the real reasons for the marriage?

We know that Rowcroft was effectively destitute when he boarded the ship, but he had started his career in Van Diemen's Land with every advantage: good birth; what most people of the time would have considered the best education; and family money as security for a substantial grant of land. He had positions of authority giving him status in the community. He appears to have squandered it all. And then, just as he was being overtaken by his follies, he met Jane, a widow with £2,000 from the sale of her husband's property. We know that the outward fares for passage from England to Australia at the time were about £70 per person.[304] Even assuming that Jane had had to pay the full fare for all eight children and herself, her expenditure would only have been £630, so she would still have had substantial cash in hand.

Jane had needed to find not only a way of providing for her children in the long term but also someone to shelter and protect her. This young gentleman of good breeding must have seemed like a gift to a destitute woman – provided she had not heard of Rowcroft's extended dalliance with Maria Lord, nor of his financial situation. By the time of his departure, Rowcroft's standing in the Bothwell community and indeed throughout Tasmania, was low, but the Curling property was isolated and it is possible that Jane would not have heard gossip from Bothwell. She married the man who would later turn her story and his into the first novel about life in the antipodes, *Tales of the Colonies or the Adventures of an Emigrant*, the work which has been frequently quoted in telling the Curlings' story.

The family arrived back in England about five months after departure from Hobart, in approximately mid-February 1826. What happened when the ship reached London? It is likely that they went to Guilton Rectory, Goldstone, to visit Jane's brother Michael, his partner Hannah Solley and their own eight children (a

---

[303] This is verified in a present-day copy of the original marriage record in the parish register now held at Christ Church Anglican Church in Rio de Janeiro, kindly supplied by the Reverend David Weller. The record reads 'Charles Rowcroft Bachelor of the City of London and Jane Curling Widow of the parish of Ashe in the County of Kent were married in this Chapel … this sixteenth Day of December in the Year One thousand eight hundred and Twenty-Five, By me Robt. P: Crane. A:M Rector & Chaplain.' Both Charles Rowcroft and Jane Curling signed the marriage record, witnessed by Thos. Carruthers and John Ross.

[304] *Life and Death in the Age of Sail*, Robin Haines, pub. the National Maritime Museum, 2003.

further four Becker children were born in later years). Rowcroft too may have had relatives in England. As well as a sister he had three more brothers, besides Horatio, who had gone with him to Van Diemen's Land and had remained there.

Jane and Charles were anxious to ensure that the marriage in Rio de Janeiro was regarded as legitimate by the Anglican church in England and the local society which they had joined. They applied to the Archbishop of Canterbury for permission to repeat the ceremony[305] and did so on 24 June 1826 at St Mark's, Kennington; Fig. 40. Unusually, the parish record gives Jane's surname as Rowcroft, indicating that she and the vicar were agreed that she was already married to Charles. It is generally the bride's former name which is recorded, so that if the Rio de Janeiro marriage had not been seen as legitimate, then as a widow Jane would have been Jane Curling in the marriage register.

Jane and Charles Rowcroft disappear from the historian's radar for a year or so at this point. The reader might think that the foregoing adventure to Van Diemen's Land should have been enough for one struggling family, but the saga is only just taking off.

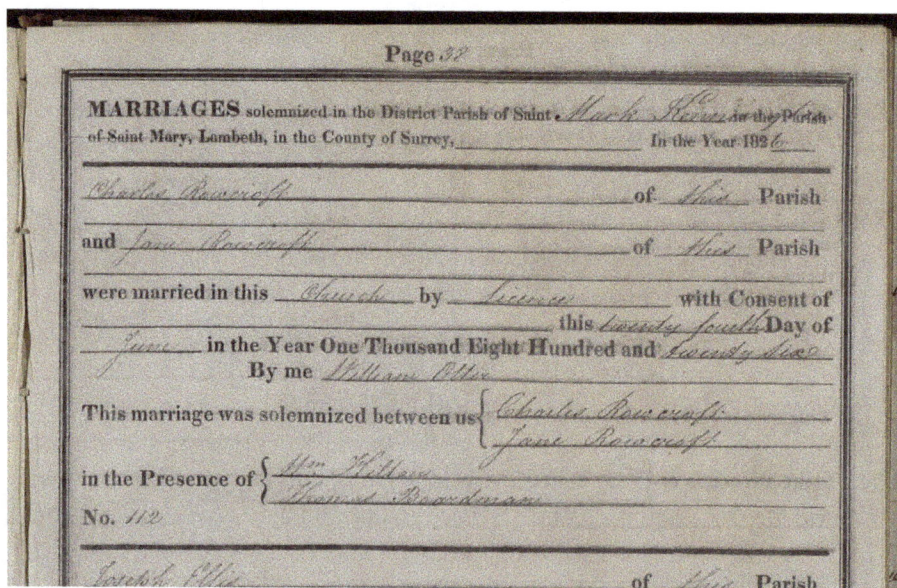

Fig. 40. **Record of the repeat marriage of Charles and Jane Rowcroft** [306]

---

[305] CCA-DbCb-PRC/18/53/129 'Draft letter stating that Charles and Jane Rowcroft (formerly Jane Curling, widow) having previously been married in St. Sebastian, Rio de Janeiro, Brazil, now wish to confirm their marriage with a Church of England ceremony and Charles Rowcroft is applying for a licence in order to do so'.

[306] Reproduced by kind permission of the Bishop of Winchester.

Appendix 1 – The Oakley family, Mayors of Deal, Kent

The Oakley family were active participants in the administration of Deal throughout the eighteenth century. Surviving records for Deal Assemblies, precursors of town council meetings, begin in 1710.[307] From the first Assembly John and Thomas Oakley are listed as attenders.

Four members of the Oakley family were mayors of Deal, and between them covered ten years in the post:

Name	Years Served as Mayor			Generation	Notes
Thomas Okely	1730			I	died in Office
Thomas Oakley	1746	1766	1769	II	
Thomas Oakley, junr.	1765	1783	1792	III	
William Oakley	1770	1771	1775	III	

In many years of the eighteenth century two or three Oakleys attended the Assemblies as common councilmen or jurats, and as the table above shows in ten of those years there was an Oakley mayor.

When two Thomas Oakleys were present, the younger acquired the tag 'junr' or 'the younger' in the records. Many documents are signed Thomas Oakley junr, but many more documents are signed just Thomas Oakley. The only occasions when 'senr' is used are when other people are writing about the elder man, for example in the parish records of his burial (see below). He apparently did not see the need to use it himself. In referring to material here recorded, all documents signed only Thomas Oakley have been ascribed to Thomas II, the context in each case strongly indicating that this is accurate.

The Thomases in generations II and III took turns as mayor, with the other in most cases being present as a jurat.

The participants at Assemblies had to hold one of these offices: mayor, jurat or common councilman. Only freemen of the town could be appointed to these roles. Both men and women could be freemen, and even infants could be nominated to receive the Freedom of the Town, although the definition of an infant at the time seems to have been anyone under the age of twenty-one. In a court case brought by the crew of the *Culloden*, a privateer part-owned by Thomas Oakley II, the list of crew includes three young men described as 'an Infant under the age of twenty one years that is to say of the age of Nineteen years or thereabouts by [father's name] of Deal aforesaid his father and next friend'.[308] 'Next friend' is a legal term, now

---

[307] KHLC De/AC1, Deal Assembly Minutes.
[308] TNA C 11/1635/31 Hartley v Fuller, Bill and Answer.

replaced with 'Litigation friend', and indicates 'a person who can fairly and competently conduct proceedings on behalf of a child or a protected party'.[309]

Freemen could be chosen by the Assembly (the precursor of the Town Council) to become common councilmen, jurats were selected from existing common councilmen, and the mayor was always chosen from among the jurats, so it was a self-regulating hierarchy.

Kent History and Library Centre holds archives for Deal Town Council. The first minutes still available are dated 21 July 1710. They are signed by all present, and the list includes John and Thomas Okely (the Oakley surname spelling often varied until about the middle of the eighteenth century).

Freemen of Deal

On rare occasions Freedom was granted as a gift in recognition of services to the community, but mostly there were charges.

It is noticeable that on at least two separate occasions children were made freemen when their fathers held the post of mayor. Here are two consecutive minutes from an Assembly held in 1767 when Thomas Oakley II was mayor. In the first not only his brother John Oakley but John's 'infant' daughter Mary are given their freedoms, and in the second, his other brother William Oakley is given his:

> It is ordered That John Oakley of Deal aforesaid, Gentleman, Son of
> Mr. Thomas Oakley who was a Freeman before his [John's] birth, be
> admitted a freeman of this Corporation in consideration of his having
> paid to Mr. Sole a Treasurer the Sum of Six shillings and Eight
> pence ... And It is further ordered that in consideration of his ...
> having several times applied for his ... freedom before his Daughter
> Mary Oakley an Infant was born, ... He be deemed free from the
> twenty sixth day of October last and his said Daughter Mary be
> intitled to her freedom ... in the same manner ...

> It is ordered that William Oakley of Deal aforesaid gentleman son
> of the said Mr. Thomas Oakley[310] ... be admitted a freeman of this
> Corporation in consideration of his having paid to Mr. Long a
> Treasurer the Sum of Six shillings and Eight pence And He was at
> this Assembly accordingly sworn a Freeman thereof.[311]

---

[309] See *Thomas Reuters, Practical Law* at: https://tmsnrt.rs/3za9NcR

[310] An instance of the spelling of a name changing. This Thomas 'Oakley' was the first generation of Deal Oakleys, whose name had been earlier spelt, in the Assembly minutes, 'Okely'.

[311] KHLC De/AC2 Deal Assembly Minutes.

The Oakley dynasty in Deal was composed of men of substance: brewers, bankers, shipping agents and merchants.

Two of the Oakleys were stalwarts of the freemasons' Royal Navy Lodge at Deal. In 1770 John Oakley submitted a list of its members to the Grand Lodge in London. He lists himself as WPM (Worshipful Past Master[312]) and brother Thomas Oakley as WT (Worshipful Treasurer). Elsewhere in the list they are 'Thos. Oakley Brewer' and 'Naval Lieutenant John Oakley'.

Thomas Okely I was one of our 6× great-grandfathers. The Assembly minutes are the first record of any kind that he lived in Deal. He was probably the Thomas Okely who married Anne Holland in Dover on 4 February 1694.[313]

Thomas Oakley II (1704–1783), baptized 3 September 1704, was the son of Thomas I and his wife Ann.

Thomas Oakley II married three times:

1 Mary Kite, 1 January 1729 at St Augustine's Church, Northbourne
2 Mary Schunzar (widow), 27 November 1749 at St Mary's Church Dover
3 Catharine Smith, 5 July 1760 at St Nicholas' Church, Deptford

Thomas Oakley II was buried on 2 September 1783 in the graveyard of St George's parish church in Deal. In the parish records, under the page headed 'Burials 1783', is the entry for his burial:

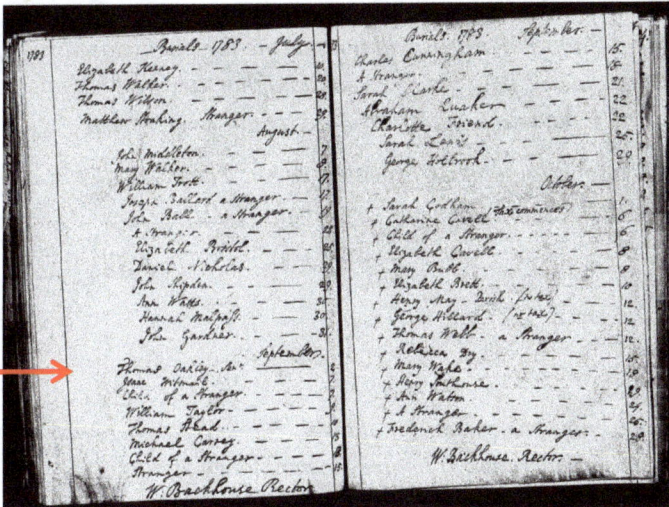

Fig. 41. **Thomas Oakley II – burial record** [314]

---

[312] LMF HC 3-E-1.
[313] FamilySearch result.
[314] Fig. 41 is reproduced by kind permission of the Chapter of Canterbury, from the Deal St Leonard parish registers, CCA catalogue reference U3/95.

Unusually, a second record, in a different volume[315] which appears to be devoted to the location of each grave, puzzlingly reads 'Thos. Oakley Sen[r] … a Grave Stone Marvel feet of His Father'. I surmise that the grave stone was marble and this record indicates that Thomas Oakley II was buried at the feet of his father.

Thomas II has proved extremely elusive to trace, and the impression is that he was a private man. The most reliably informative source for Thomas II is his will, but even that is enigmatic. It is puzzling that Thomas II does not leave any bequests for his son, nor indeed for any other children from his two earlier marriages who might still have been alive. One theory might be that Thomas II, having set his son Thomas III up in business during his earlier life, had no further arrangements to make for him. However, Thomas III is not made an executor of the will; his step-mother Catharine was the sole executrix, and she and her two daughters were the only beneficiaries.

In later life Thomas II might be imagined as an intellectual, introverted man, perhaps made so by the sadness of his previous two wives dying. It is surely Thomas II who is the 'Mr. Oakley of Deal Kent' listed as a subscriber to Deal blue-stocking Elizabeth Carter's *Translation of All the Works of Epictetus Now Extant*[316] published in 1753, although his son Thomas III would have been aged 21 that year and so could in theory have been the subscriber.

In 1755 Thomas II complained that the Deal chapel wardens had refused to pay him, but he does not say what the expected payment was for:

> *Sir*
>
> *The Deal Chapel Wardens will not pay me for the Inclosed receipts, saying they never paid but 8[d] a year, and that they owe but one Year, therefore be pleased to return me the 3[s] I paid you for them.* _____
>
> *M[r]. Joseph Iggulden, Carpenter, & Mr. Thos: Middleton, Baker, are our P[sent] Chapel-Wardens. ___ I am*
>
> *Sir*
>
> *Your very h[ble] Ser[t]:*
>
> > *Tho[s]. Oakley*
>
> *P.S: You may remember I paid you for several Persons, & you promised (if any refused) to give me my Money again._____*
>
> *To M[r]: Wellard.*

Addressed on the reverse as follows:

> *M[r]: Alex[r]: Wellard, Town-Clerk at Dover*

---

[315] CCA U3/67.Deal, St George, composite register.
[316] See online copy of Elizabeth Carter's book: http://bit.ly/App1Epictetus

The case of Thomas Oakley against the Ship *Nostra Seigniora Maij des Homems ei St: Antonio* (1760–1762)

In 1760 Thomas Oakley II, shipping agent, brought a case before the Court of Admiralty. The ship was an independent merchant vessel (not part of either the Dutch or British East India companies' fleets, nor a naval vessel). Her name may sound rather florid, but she was owned by Joze Gomes da Silva Merchant at Lisbon. On her voyage from Saint Valéry in France to Newcastle the captain was a very British-sounding Thomas Reynolds, when

> by the Violence of the Wind and Sea off Cromer [she did] lose her Cat
> Head and her small Bower Anchor and received so much Damage
> that She became very leaky insomuch that it was necessary for the
> preservation of the Lives of the said Thomas Reynolds and the Ships
> Crew and also of the Ship with the Advice of the Pilot on board to put
> back to the Downs where She arrived on the Twenty fourth Day of the
> said Month of November [1760].[317]

Captain Reynolds approached Thomas Oakley II to act as his agent to handle all aspects necessary to make the vessel seaworthy. The final account of disbursements shows the tremendous diversity of services required, from arranging 'a room for the ship's crew' with Thomas Planter, and separate lodgings for the captain with Jacob Friend, to food and beer for them from a range of suppliers, as well as all the necessary work with Deal tradesmen like John Kite, shipwright & carpenter; Henry Temple, smith; Thomas Castle, ropemaker; and Sarah Nairne for canvas, to name but a few.

A contract or 'instrument' was drawn up, signed by Captain Reynolds on 24 November 1760, witnessed by Henry Dilnot and John Cavel, appointing Thomas Oakley II as his 'lawful Attorney and Agent' and 'on his Behalf to employ a Pilot to conduct his said Ship to Sandwich Haven'.

Thomas II made all the necessary payments to ensure that the many repairs and replacements took place. He also made two payments of cash to the captain for his personal use and a further one for victualling the ship, all payments carefully noted in the account. The total of the bill presented to Capt. Reynolds was £240/5/-. Capt. Reynolds gave Thomas II a promissory note or Bill of Exchange signed and dated 2/5/1761, but *'which Bill of Exchange was protested and Returned ... for want of Payment and ... the said Thomas Reynolds ever since the Month of July last [1761] hath absconded and left the said Ship in Sandwich Haven'.*

---

[317] KHLC document reference 5CPW/AP1762/1 Case against Na. Sna. Maij de Homems – Affidavit. The KHLC reference is for a bundle of documents. I have given each document a number, and this one is document 12 of 13.

Thomas Oakley II goes to court

Having tried in vain to contact Captain Reynolds, Thomas II took the matter to the Court of Admiralty via the Lord Warden's office. 'The most noble Lionel, Duke of Dorset[318] &c, Constable of Dover Castle, Lord Warden Chancellor & Admiral of the Cinque Ports' on 17/2/1762 issued a warrant for the 'arrest' or impounding of the vessel.[319] A notice was also published requiring anyone with *'any Right Title or Interest'* in the vessel to *'appear before the judges of the Court of Admt[y] ... at the Church of S[t] James the Apostle ... Dover ... there to be holden ... on 25th day of February inst[t] at Eleven of the Clock in the Forenoon to answer to Thomas Oakley in a certain Cause civil and maritime'*.[320]

On 18 March 1762 the Lord Warden ordered a valuation of the vessel and its contents, and on 25 March a further authority was issued for their sale.

An affidavit dated 7 June 1762,[321] giving a full account of the case and declaring that the sum owed to Thomas II was £240/11/3, was signed by Thomas Oakley, Jos. Stewart, Henry Dilnot and John Cavel *'before John Iggulden Mayor of Deal in the presence of Jn[o]: Middleton Notary Publick Deal'*.

The final document in the folder is a draft summary by Thomas II's advocate for presentation to the court. History does not relate whether Thomas finally received his dues, but the court documents, especially the warrants for valuation and sale, indicate that he probably did.

The equivalent sum in 2019 as calculated on the Bank of England's inflation calculator web page was £49,714.91.[322]

---

[318] Lionel Cranfield Sackville, 1st Duke of Dorset (1688–1765).
[319] KHLC reference CPW/AP1762/1 LAC Document 3 of 13.
[320] KHLC reference CPW/AP1762/1 LAC Document 4 of 13.
[321] KHLC reference CPW/AP1762/1 LAC, Document 12 of 13.
[322] See http://bit.ly/App1BoEInflCalc

Appendix 2a – Shuart on a fifteenth-century map

Sometime between the years 679 and 1000 a chapel of ease was built at Shuart, dedicated to All Saints. A fifteenth-century map by Thomas Elmham (Fig. 42). which includes stylized images of eleven Thanet churches, has the Shuart one named, in a Latin abbreviation, as *Omū Scōrum*, for *Omnium Sanctorum*. This church was demolished in the fifteenth century, so Elmham's map would have been the last opportunity to record its existence. These days the casual visitor to the site would have no awareness of there ever having been a church there, part of a Shuart Farm field near the seawall of the north Kent coast.[323]

Elmham oriented his map with east at the top of the page, labelled in Latin, *Oriens*. At the bottom of the page, *Occidens* labels the western edge, which is bounded by the Wantsum Channel. An appealing link between the village of Eastry, where I presently live, and the Isle of Thanet as shown in Elmham's map is an old legend telling how King Eckbert of Kent authorized the murder, by his advisor Thunor, of two young cousins under his care, at his court in Eastry.[324] Requesting absolution he confessed to the boys' aunt Domne Eafe, the founder of Minster Abbey. She agreed to accept as blood money some land to establish the abbey on the Isle of Thanet. She asked for as much land as her pet deer could run round in a day. If you look carefully at the middle of the northern coast (the left edge) of the island in Elmham's map, you will see the deer delicately outlined in black, and its course is given as a green line, showing clearly the boundary of Eafe's lands.

On the Western stretch of the Wantsum Channel, the bottom edge of the map, is a wonderful scene in which a Templar knight is wading across the channel with a monk on his back, watched from a rowing boat by two other monks. St Nicholas-at-Wade village must have been the wading place in a time before Elmham's map, which would have made the island a little smaller in that area. By Elmham's time, Sarre, with its church of St Giles (destroyed in Elizabethan times) was the wade. It is just above the boat on the map. Slightly north-east is St Nicholas Church, with All Saints church at Shuart a little further north-east again.

The earliest known Curling family document is the will, dated 26 July 1463, of Richard Curlyng of 'Chylton' (Chilton) in the parish of St Laurence-in-Thanet, a will written slightly later in the same century as Elmham drew his map. The distance from Chilton Farmhouse to Shuart Farmhouse is 7.7 miles by car.

---

[323] With thanks to Bernard Clayson for showing me the site of All Saints, Shuart.

[324] Several websites recount this ancient story, referring to documentation in *The Kentish Royal Legend*, 'a diverse group of Medieval texts which describe a wide circle of members of the royal family of Kent from the 7th to 8th centuries AD.' https://en.wikipedia.org/wiki/Kentish_Royal_Legend. Eleanor Parker in her excellent blog 'A Clerk of Oxford', devotes a page to the legend, telling the story and analysing modern perceptions of it: https://bit.ly/2RxIlnM.

Fig. 42. **Fifteenth-century map of Thanet, Thomas Elmham** [325]

---

[325] UC THA MS 1, fol. 42v from *History of St Augustine's Abbey of Canterbury* by Thomas Elmham. By permission of the Master and Fellows of Trinity Hall, Cambridge. Viewable online at https://cudl.lib.cam.ac.uk/view/MS-TRINITYHALL-00001/90. See also the Wikipedia page for All Saints' Church, Shuart http://bit.ly/Ch2ShuartAllSaints.

Appendix 2b – Shuart Farm buildings and land

Today, the busy dual carriageway of the A299, the Thanet Way, branches off the M2 artery, taking traffic between the heart of London, the Isle of Thanet and the dock and freight terminus at Ramsgate harbour. Gliding along it in the luxury of our twenty-first-century, super-swift motorized carriages it is difficult to imagine the interminable time a similar journey would have taken in earlier centuries when roads were rougher, often mired, and the suspension of horse-drawn carriages infinitely less cushioned. But although it is not far away from the 'speed ribbon', the solitary remoteness of Shuart Farm heightens our powers of imagination and brings to mind the weary farmer making his way homeward on the last leg of his journey on foot or horse, after a visit to Margate, Ramsgate, Canterbury or even London – all journeys made by Curlings of past centuries.

Shuart lies north of the Thanet Way; much of the farmland in this area was marshland in the Curling family's day, but land which had been cultivated or farmed in one way or another for centuries before them. In 1800, Edward Hasted's description of the parish as a whole, including the estate of 'Shoart', summarizes the geographical location:

ST. NICHOLAS

The parish of St. Nicholas, formerly called St. Nicholas at Wade, from its situation *ad vadum*, that is, near the wading place, or ford, across the water called the Wantsume, at, or at least near where the bridge at Sarre now is, lies at the north west corner of this island.

This parish is most part of it situated upon high ground, excepting towards the west, where it consists of a level of marsh land, bounded by the water called the Nethergong. The sea bounds it northward. The church and village stand on an hill, nearly in the centre of the parish … About a mile northward from the church, near Shoart, is the borough of All Saints, in which there was once a church or chapel, long since ruinated, the parish of which is now united to this of St. Nicholas.[326]

Of Shuart or Shoart, Hasted wrote that it 'is an estate about a mile north-east from the church, in the road leading to the sea'. He listed all the owners from the time of Henry VIII to his own time, finishing by saying 'it was sold within memory to Eliab Breton, whose two sons, William and Eliab Breton, esqrs. are at this time possessed of it'.[327] This tells us that Hasted must have visited Shuart after 1785, because when Thomas Curling I took on the farm in 1780 the owner was still Eliab Breton I, who

---

[326] *The History and Topographical Survey of the County of Kent*, vol. 10, p. 238, Edward Hasted, 1800, available online: http://bit.ly/App2aStNaW

[327] *The History and Topographical Survey of the County of Kent*, vol. 10, p. 239, as above.

died in 1785. The Breton family continued to be the Curling family's landlords throughout their tenure, see **Appendix 2c – The owners of Shuart Farm** (p. 141). Below are some photographs of the exterior of the farmhouse:

Fig. 43. **The front elevation of Shuart Farmhouse**[328]

Fig. 44. **Shuart Farmhouse rear gable end with outhouses to left**

---

[328] All photographs in this appendix are by LAC or Ben Jones at Ozaru Books.

Fig. 45. **The rebuilt Dutch gable of Shuart Farmhouse**

Fig. 46. **The rear elevation of Shuart Farmhouse**

The layout of the farmstead is still much as it was in Thomas and Catharine Curling's day. What seems unusual is that there is not just one farmhouse; there are two substantial premises, built within about twenty paces of each other and both built with the elaborate Dutch/Flemish gables characteristic of a small but significant number of the historic domestic buildings in east Kent.[329] Much of the exterior of Shuart Farmhouse, the larger of the two, has been altered since the sixteenth century, as can be seen in Fig. 43, photographed from the yard, where virtually none of the original frontage is apparent, and also in Fig. 44 where, although the east-facing gable and elevation are comparatively unaltered, the end wall of the 1960s extension is visible. Dutch gable houses often have only one ornamented gable, the other being left unadorned. The Dutch gable on Shuart Farmhouse was rebuilt by the present occupiers, who found it in considerable dis-repair when they first took on the tenancy, Fig. 45. In Fig. 46, we can see that the characterful rear elevation of the farmhouse, whilst structurally comparatively unaltered, has changes in the brickwork which show where extensions may have been put up and taken down, and a metal tie marks a weakness. The endearing triangular dormer window is twentieth-century; the three large first-floor windows are possibly original.

Although the farmhouse is inevitably much altered, there are two original features of particular interest, the first being the front door, Fig. 47. The entrance is original to the earliest building and is therefore sixteenth-century. Protected by a modern porch, it is not immediately apparent that this entrance threshold is exactly the one which Thomas Curling I and Catharine would have stepped over together for the first time following their marriage in September 1780. The exterior of the door is much worn but carries a welcoming air, and the modern porch protects it. The original door has a little ledge above it which must have offered less than adequate shelter from rain for waiting callers. Inside, the door has been reinforced at some distant point in the past.

The other original feature is even more remarkable, being a repeated mural pattern, painted directly onto the plaster, Fig. 48, and, unusually, some of the timber frame, Fig. 49, in one room in the house. The sample on the plasterwork still retains some original colour. The pattern is the same on both plasterwork and wood, and it looks like a rather elaborate crest or shield.

---

[329] See http://iotas.org.uk/?page_id=151 for Isle of Thanet Archaeological Society article *The Dutch and Flemish Gabled Houses of East Kent*, Gordon Taylor.

Fig. 47. **Exterior and interior of front door of Shuart Farmhouse**

Fig. 48. **Mural paintwork on plaster**

Fig. 49. **Mural outline on interior timber frame**

Fig. 50. **Shuart Farm Cottage – Dutch gable**

The Dutch gable end of the second house, Shuart Farm Cottage, is comparatively unscathed apart from the addition at some early point of a 'carriage house'. Only two of the rafters of this lean-to are tied to the main cottage, giving it an L-shaped appearance, the rest being free-standing with the entrance forward of the cottage's front door (Fig. 50 and Fig. 51). Both houses comfortably wear the evidence of 300–400 years of daily use.

The Historic England listing[330] dates the original main farmhouse to the mid-sixteenth century, and the cottage to the mid-seventeenth. Because of the remoteness of the farm, at some point a family of occupants may have decided that rather than the younger generation moving off the home farm to set up on their own, it was better to build a second house, keeping the family together. The original gable end of Shuart Farm Cottage (Fig. 50) is still intact, as is the rear wall, with only a few small windows, perhaps for privacy but more likely because from 1696

---

[330] See http://bit.ly/Ap2bShuartLstedBldgs for separate links to pages about Shuart Farmhouse, Shuart Farm Cottage, Shuart Granary and Shuart Barn.

138

windows, being taxable, were expensive. All of the windows in the cottage have been replaced in the twentieth century. The former carriage house, seen in Fig. 51, is currently used as a garage. (It is not a big step from 'carriage' to 'garage', although the etymology of each word is different.)

Fig. 51. **Shuart Farm Cottage, front elevation**

Other farm buildings on the property listed by Historic England include an enormous sixteenth-century barn, Fig. 52. On the day I first visited, the resident barn owl flew the full length of the barn through the rafters as I stood in the entrance. A large eighteenth-century granary is also still there, mounted on eight staddle stones (which were originally intended to keep the rats out of the grain).

Fig. 52. **Shuart Farm barn and granary group**

139

A small tumble-down outhouse close to the farmhouse is thought to have been a dovecote. In front of it, one of the slabs in the path which runs round the house covers what would have been the Curling family's source of fresh water, the well. A source of fresh water near the house was essential.

The Shuart houses are full of character and are a most endearing presence, hidden as they are from the rest of the world. The interiors are as interesting as the exteriors, but out of respect for the present occupants' privacy there are no photographs of the rooms. In the farmhouse the original panelling is still in place in some of them.

The Overseers' Accounts (Poor Book) for St Nicholas-at-Wade, held at Canterbury Cathedral Archives, show Thomas Curling renting from May 1780, having taken over from a Mr Pamflett. The property was still being rented by a Mr Thomas Curling in 1805, when his first grandchild, Thomas III, was born. By that time Thomas Curling I was paying £149 rent for the property owned by Mr Breton, and the rental value of land which he owned himself was £34. When Eliab Breton I died, in 1784–5, the Curlings continued to rent from his widow and, on her death, from her heirs, Eliab Breton II and his brother William.[331] In 1871, fifty years after the Curling family had left Shuart, the property was sold to St John's College, Cambridge, which still has ownership.

---

[331] All information on rent from St Nicholas-at-Wade 'Poor Book', CCA-U3-18/12/1 1732–1781, and CCA-U3-18/12/2 1781–1815.

Appendix 2c – The owners of Shuart Farm

During the whole period of the Curlings' tenancy (1780–1822) the owners of Shuart Farm were members of the Breton family, absentee landlords whose principal domicile was Norton Hall in Northamptonshire although they also owned a substantial house near London, Forty Hall. Besides their two homes they owned other property in Middlesex as well as in Essex, Hertfordshire and Kent.

We know about the Curlings' landlords from the St Nicholas-at-Wade overseers' Poor Book records held at Canterbury Cathedral. Before 1948, when the welfare system was introduced nationally, the responsibility for caring for individuals and families who had fallen on hard times was held by each parish. The system for raising funds to assist the poor of the parish was to levy a tax on landowners or their tenants; the tax was payable by the tenant when the acreage occupied by them was significant. The names of landowners were recorded alongside the occupiers in the parish's Poor Book records, and the spelling of the Breton surname provides a classic example of the variations which were common in past centuries. In the parish records of St Nicholas-at-Wade, they appear as Briton and Britton as well as Breton. The spellings were, presumably, the parish clerk's interpretation of what he heard tenants say as he was jotting down information at tax collecting sessions. The family themselves used Breton, as, for example, on various memorials in All Saints church at Norton.[332]

When Thomas Curling I took over the tenancy of Shuart Farm in 1780 the owner was given as 'Eliab Britton'. In these same records, three years later, Eliab's surname lost a t, becoming Briton.

Who were these absentee landlords and what was their life like?

> A letter written by Eliab [Breton] in June 1770, describes an agreeable life spent fox hunting at his Northamptonshire Estate and sea bathing at the fashionable new seaside resort of Bright Helmston, (Brighton). It was the Breton family who created the lawn, shrubberies, ponds and walks that define Forty Hall today and were responsible for creating the Ferme Ornée. This was a raised pathway leading around the Estate, which allowed Ladies and Gentlemen to appreciate the grounds without muddying their fashionable gowns.[333]

---

[332] Thanks to Angela Malin of Northamptonshire Family History Society for transcripts of memorials in the church.

[333] Forty Hall is open to the public, under the aegis of the Municipal Borough of Enfield. The official Forty Hall Estate website is excellent, and this quotation is taken from their page on the Breton family. https://www.fortyhallestate.co.uk/page/the-breton-family/

Eliab was appointed one of the three sheriffs of Northamptonshire for the year 1766.[334]

When he was writing his eleven-page will, although he mentioned two farming estates, one at Hern Hill[335] and the other at Sea Salter, he did not once mention Shuart or the other two contiguous farms he owned in the parish of St Nicholas-at-Wade. Either the farm came under the two other named estates or for some reason it was not in his gift. Eliab had married Elizabeth Wolstenholme at St Anne's Soho, Westminster, in 1739.[336] They had three sons, the first of whom, Michael Harvey Breton, was born in July 1743. Eliab, their second son, was born in 1745 and their third, William, in 1749.

In 1786 the recorded landowner of Shuart Farm changed to 'the heirs of Eliab Briton'.[337] Eliab had died in December 1785. For the next four years, 1787–1790, his widow, Mrs Briton or Breton, is the listed owner until her death in 1790. Her heirs, so named, followed on from 1791 to 1798, the surname spelling still not fixed, then between 1799 and 1802 the owner is 'Mr E Briton Esq.'; the second Eliab Breton (1755–1819), son of the first. In 1803 Eliab II appears to be sharing ownership with his younger brother William, as the St Nicholas poor rates listing is 'Wlm and Eliab Breton Esq.'s In 1804 it reverts to Eliab alone, which might seem curious until we know that disaster struck William's family in that year: His daughter Lavinia with her husband Colonel George Yates and their four children 'were unfortunately drowned on board the *Prince of Wales* East-Indiaman, Capt. Price, in 1804, on their passage from Bombay to England'.[338] William's name turns up once more with his brother Eliab in the 1805 poor rates assessment records. Thomas Oakley Curling had married Jane Becker in 1804 and taken over the management of Shuart from his father.

Eliab Breton II died on 23 January 1819. At the time he was living in Phillimore Place, Kensington, London. In an unusual but not unique move, his brother William changed his surname the following year:

> Whitehall, April 26, 1806. The King has been pleased to grant unto William Breton, of Holly Hill, in the Parish of Hartfield, in the County of Sussex, Esquire, Second Son of Eliab Breton, late of Norton, in the County of Northampton, Esquire, deceased by Elizabeth his Wife, eldest Daughter, and at length sole Heir, of Sir William Wolstenholme, late of Forty Hall, in the Parish of Enfield, in the County of Middlesex, Baronet, also deceased, His

---

[334] *Oxford Journal* – Saturday 16 November 1765.
[335] Breton says specifically that his two estates of Hern Hill and Sea Salter are both in Kent. These days the name of the village of Hernhill in Kent has come to be one word, as has Seasalter. (There is also a place in south London called Herne Hill.)
[336] England Marriages 1539–1973.
[337] St Nicholas-at-Wade Overseers' Accounts (Poor Book), as before.
[338] Kearsley's Peerage, 1809, pp. 269–270.

Royal Licence and Authority that he and his Issue may take and use the Surname of Wolstenholme only, and also bear the Arms of Wolstenholme, from affectionate Respect to the Family of his said late Mother; such Arms being first duly exemplified according to the Laws of Arms, and recorded in the Heralds' Office: And also to order, that this His Majesty's Concession, and Declaration be registered in His College of Arms.[339]

Michael Harvey Breton, had been named after his grandmother Mary's brother Michael Harvey who in 1738 was 'of Clifton, Dorset'.[340] But,

Unfortunately, the Breton's eldest son Michael appears to have enjoyed a somewhat profligate lifestyle and shortly after Eliab's death, Elizabeth was forced to sell the entire estate at auction, 'due to the misconduct of her offspring'. It is not clear precisely what her children did to make Eliza Breton sell Forty Hall, but the Auctioneers, describe the house as being a *Spacious Mansion with extensive offices, an elegant greenhouse and a park of 400 acres.*[341]

However, a flier for the auction found online states that the property was close on 1,500 acres. The family even sold their main dwelling, Norton Hall. Searching for the size of that estate online, we find that Eliab Breton

was Lord of the Manor in 1755 when the last 1072 acres of the parish were finally enclosed by Act of Parliament. Breton was allotted 582 acres of the total. The church was allotted 47 acres … The Town charity was also allotted 13 acres.

Eliab's son Michael Harvey ran up debts of £22,000[342] and was forced to put the manor up for sale in 1794 by his creditors. The manor was finally sold in 1800.[343]

Michael's name commemorates his grandmother's brother Michael Harvey. The name Harvey passed down several following generations. Eliab II and his wife

---

[339] The quotation is taken from this web page: http://bit.ly/WBreton2Wolstenholme. I have verified the quotation with the College of Arms. Their reference is 'College of Arms – I37/209'.

[340] LMA ACC/1057/046 record description: 'Attested copy of lease and release made 9 March 1738 Michael Harvey of Clifton, Dorset, esq., and Benjamin Cooke of St. Christopher, London, gent., in trust for Katherine Wolstenholme, spinster, sister of Sir Nicholas Wolstenholme, according to the provisions of Sir Nicholas's will … All the manors, lands, tenements, hereditaments and premises at , Middx., and Waltham Holy Cross, Essex, late the Estate of Sir Nicholas Wolstenholme.'

[341] Forty Hall Estate website, as before.

[342] Equivalent in 2019 to £2,948,776.47, Bank of England Inflation Calculator http://bit.ly/App1BoEIC.

[343] *Norton Village Design Statement*, May 2008, p. 11, adopted by Daventry District Council.

Elizabeth, née Bullock, had a son Eliab Harvey Breton, baptized 24 April 1807 at St Dunstan-in-the-East, London. The fine large-scale map of Shuart Farm by surveyor Hailly of Sandwich, Fig. 54 on page 147, bears his name: 'Plan of Shuart Farm in the parish of St Nicholas, Isle of Thanet, County of Kent, Property of Eliab Harvey Breton Esq. and in the occupation of Mr Henry Pett. A.D. 1826.' In that year Eliab Harvey Breton would have been nineteen years old.

Appendix 2d – Vestry minute on a new workhouse

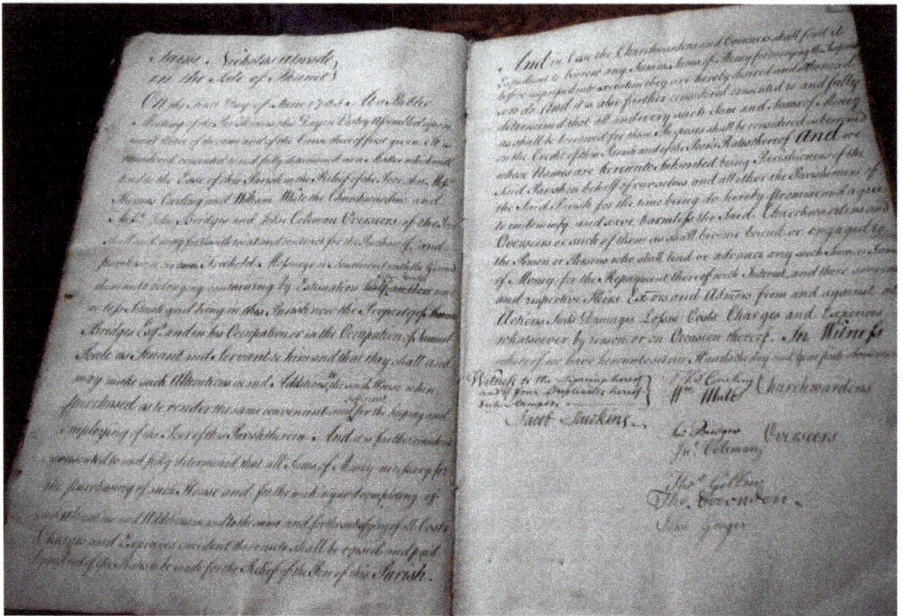

Fig. 53. **Workhouse minute in vestry Poor Book** [344]

St Nicholas atwade in the Isle of Thanet

On the First Day of June 1783 At a Public Meeting of the Parishioners this Day in vestry Assembled upon usual notice of the same and of the Cause thereof first given It is considered consented to and fully determined as a Matter which will tend to the Ease of this Parish in the Relief of the Poor that Messrs Thomas Curling and William White the churchwardens and Messrs John Bridges and John Coleman overseers of the Poor shall and may forthwith treat and contract for the Purchase of, and purchase a certain Freehold Messuage or Tenement with the Ground thereunto belonging containing by Estimation fifteen Perches more or less Situate and being in the Parish now the Property of Thomas Bridges Esqr. And in his Occupation or in the Occupation of Samuel Peale as Tenant and Servant to him and that they shall and may make such Alterations in and Additions to the said House when purchased as to render the same convenient and Sufficient for the keeping and employing of the Poor of this Parish therein And it is farther considered consented to

---

[344] Taken from the St Nicholas-at-Wade parish records 1781–1815. Reproduced courtesy of the Chapter of Canterbury. CCA-U3-18/12/2, no page numbers inserted in original.

and fully determined that all Sums of Money necessary for the purchasing of such House and for the making and completing of such alterations and Additions and to the same and for the satisfying of all Costs Charges and Expences incident thereunto shall be raised and paid by and out of the Rates to be made for the Relief of the Poor of this Parish.

And in Case the churchwardens and overseers. shall find it Expedient to borrow any Sum or Sums of Money for carrying the Purposes before expressed into execution they are hereby desired and authorized so to do And it is also farther considered consented to and fully determined that all and every such Sum and Sums of Money as shall be borrowed for these Purposes shall be considered as borrowed on the Credit of this Parish and of the Poor's Rates thereof And we whose Names are hereunto Subscribed being Parishioners of the Said Parish on behalf of ourselves and all other the Parishioners of the Said Parish for the time being do hereby promise and agree to indemnify and save harmless the Said churchwardens and overseers or such of them as shall become bound or engaged to the Person or Persons who shall lend or advance any such Sum or Sums of Money, for the Repayment thereof with Interest, and their several and respective Heirs Ex~ors and Adm~ors from and against all Actions Suits Damages Losses Costs Charges and Expences whatsoever by reason or on Occasion thereof. In Witness whereof we have hereunto set our Hands the day and Year first above written

Witness to the Signing hereof and of four Duplicates hereof duly stamped	}	*Jacob Sawkins*
Thos Curling *Wm White*	}	*churchwardens*
J^{no} Bridges *J^{no} Coleman*	}	*overseers*
Thos Gillow *Tho. Evernden* *John Gouger*		

Appendix 2e – The map of Shuart Farm, 1826

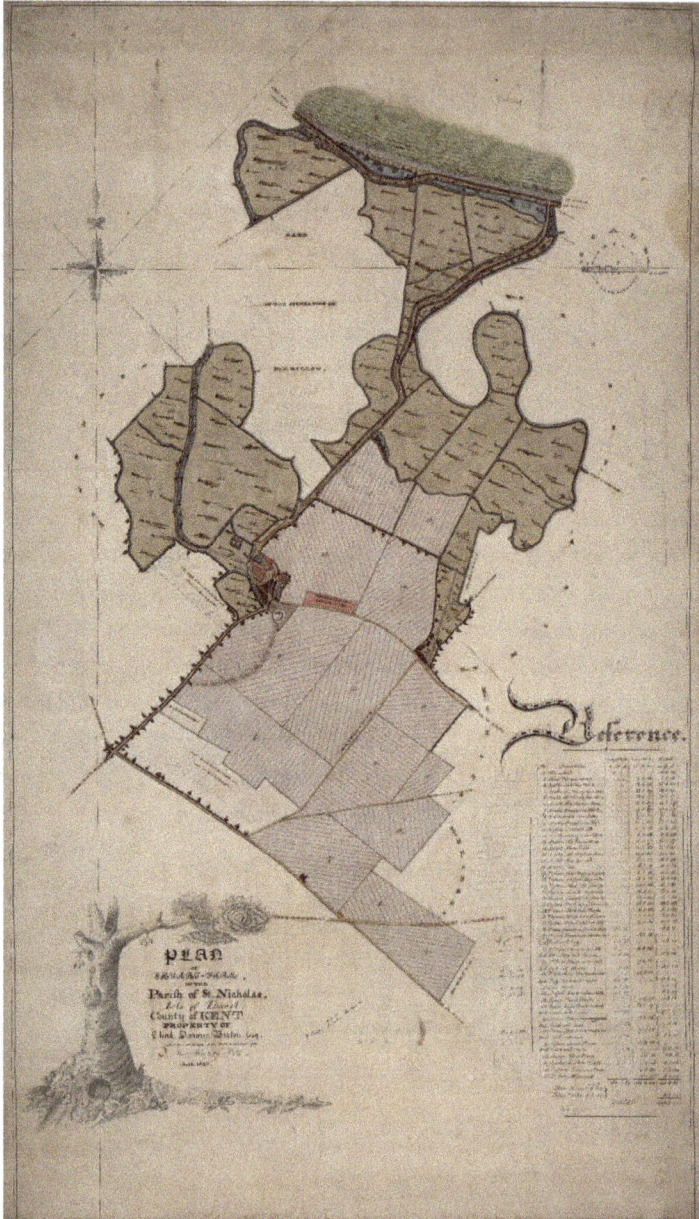

Fig. 54. **Map of Shuart Farm** [345]

---

[345] MPS 723: Plan, with reference, of Shuart farm, St Nicholas at Wade parish, Thanet, Kent, owned by Eliab Harvey Breton, occupied by Henry Pett, by C.A. Hailly of Sandwich, 123 x 73 cms (48 x 29 ins) scale 3 chs to 1 in, by permission of the Master and Fellows of St John's College, Cambridge. Photo: Maciej Pawlikowski.

This is a large-scale map of Shuart Farm showing the red buildings of the home-stead centred on the length of the map and towards the west of the property. No colour key is given, but fields are either hatched, which I interpret as cultivated arable land, or washed brown with darker rough strokes, for rough grass or reeds, indicating marshy land, as confirmed by field names in the reference list in the bottom right corner of the sheet. Fields and other features are numbered both on the map and in the reference.

Neighbouring land is 'under the occupation of' Mr Gillow, Mr White, Mr Bridale and Mr Evenden. Although one or more of them may have been owner-occupiers, much of the land in England at the time was owned by absentee landlords. Land was let to tenant farmers, and those who rented large tracts of land often described themselves (notably in their wills) as 'yeomen' or 'gentlemen'[346] who. although comfortably off. were not substantial landowners.

The seawall can be seen at the top of the map.

The map was drawn by surveyor C A Hailly of Sandwich, as he indicated within the scale legend: Fig. 55.

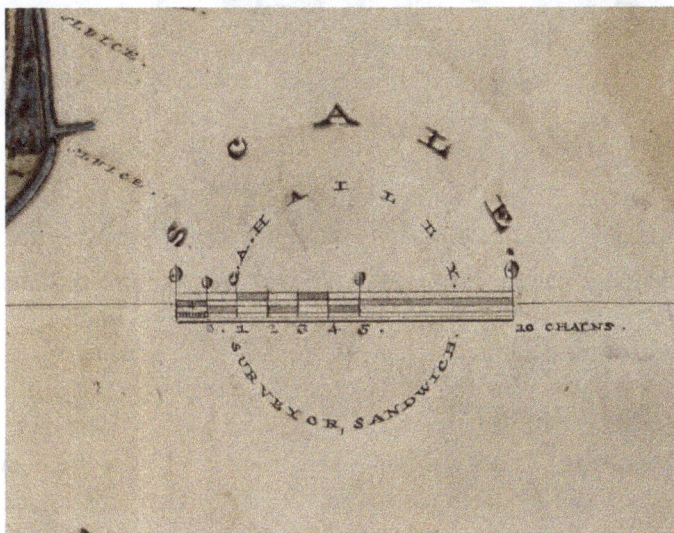

Fig. 55. **Enlarged detail of scale legend from the 1826 map of Shuart Farm**

For a close-up of the farmstead, see Fig. 56:

---

[346] In past centuries the middle classes were referred to as 'people of the middling sort'. It could be argued that it has always been the 'middling sort' who have led domestic change, improvement and even style. The Geffrye Museum in London is a 'museum of the home' dedicated to presenting how interiors have changed since the seventeenth century. See this page of its website as an introduction https://www.museumofthehome.org.uk/explore/.

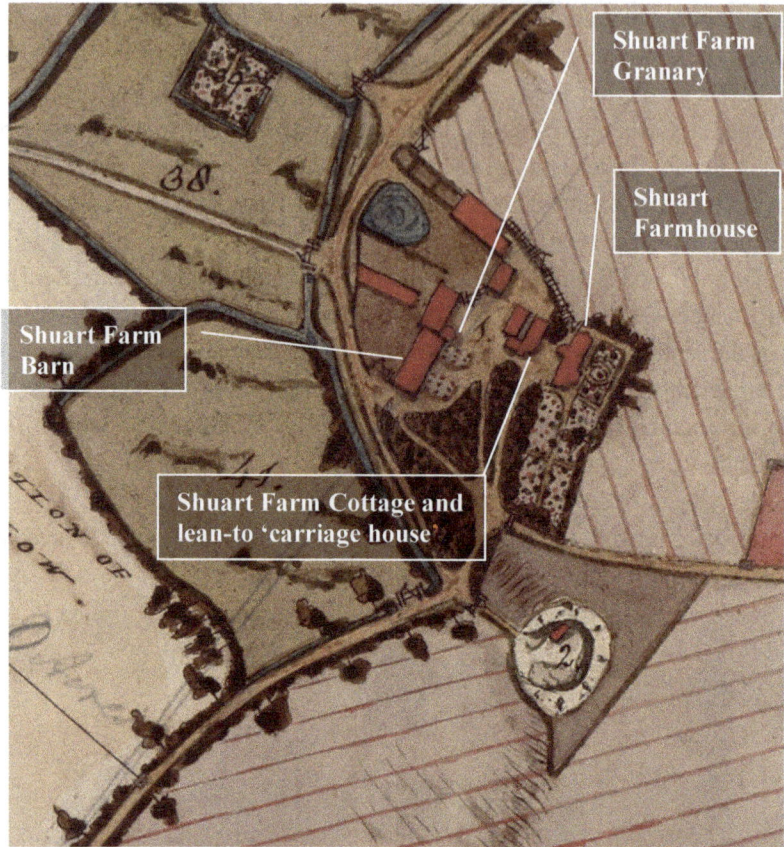

Fig. 56. **Enlargement of 1826 map of Shuart Farm, showing the homestead**

In this section of the map there are nine buildings, some of which no longer exist. On the western side of the farmhouse is its 'outcrop': an octagonal room. The ground floor of this extension is now a dining room, and it is quite possible that it was intended as such when it was built, there being at least ten family members to accommodate around the table when Thomas Oakley Curling presided. Whether this was part of the original building is unknown. The upper floor of this extension is twentieth-century. The blue disc on the northern edge of the homestead is probably a pond, not listed in the references. The reference numbers are clearly visible. The number 1, in the middle of the yard between the two houses and referring to the homestead, has a slight curve which can mislead the reader. The field marked 38 is 'Pasture Home Marsh' in the reference list, and the number 41, the marshy field adjoining 38, refers to 'Pasture Hammels'. The number 2 indicates the Chalk Pit.

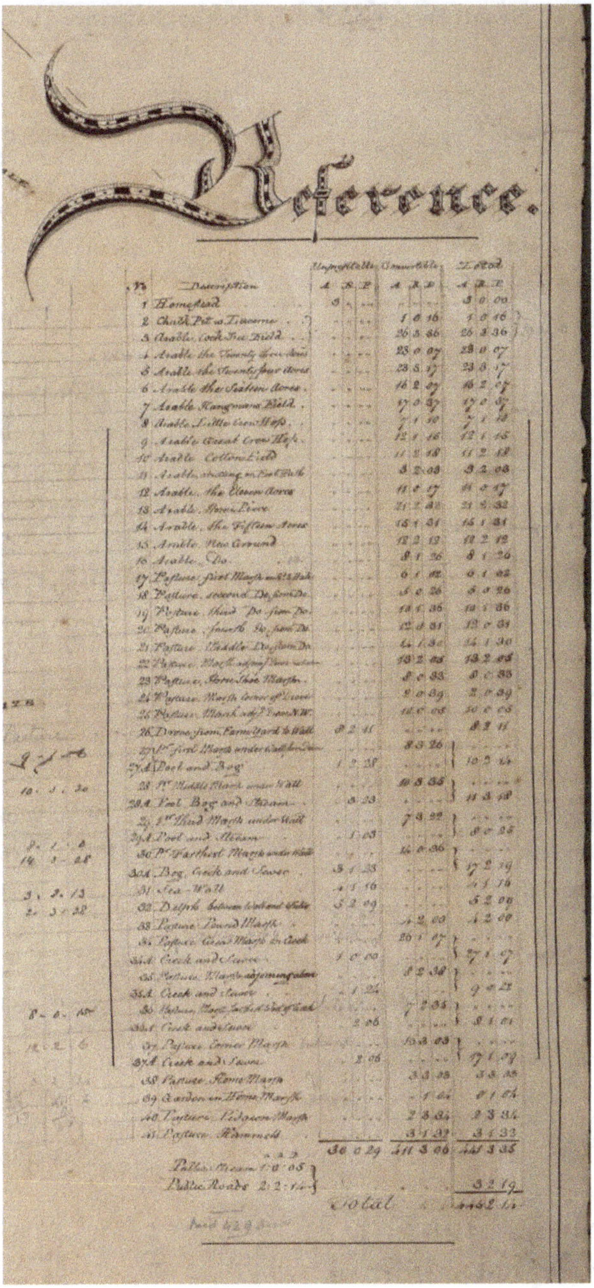

Fig. 57. **Reference list of fields**

Fig. 57 gives an idea of the reference list of fields, which has been transcribed in the table, Fig. 58. Columns headed A, R and P refer to the measurements of each parcel of land in acres, rods and perches:

[Shuart Farm Plots from 1826 Map] Reference									
No.	Description	Unprofitable			Convertible			Total		
		A	R	P	A	R	P	A	R	P
1	Homestead	3	"	" "	"	"	" "	3	0	00
2	Chalk Pit is Lucerne	"	"	" "	1	0	16	1	0	16
3	Arable, Cock Tree Field	"	"	" "	26	3	36	26	3	36
4	Arable the Twenty Three Acres	"	"	" "	23	0	07	23	0	07
5	Arable the Twenty four Acres	"	"	" "	23	3	17	23	3	17
6	Arable the Sixteen Acres	"	"	" "	16	2	07	16	2	07
7	Arable Hangmans Field	"	"	" "	17	0	37	17	0	37
8	Arable Little Crow Hop	"	"	" "	7	1	10	7	1	10
9	Arable Great Crow Hop	"	"	" "	12	1	15	12	1	15
10	Arable Cotton Field	"	"	" "	11	2	18	18	2	18
11	Arable, abutting on Foot Path	"	"	" "	3	2	03	3	2	03
12	Arable, the Eleven Acres	"	"	" "	11	0	17	11	0	17
13	Arable, Home Piece	"	"	" "	21	2	32	21	2	32
14	Arable, the Fifteen Acres	"	"	" "	15	1	31	15	1	31
15	Arable, New Ground	"	"	" "	12	2	12	12	2	12
16	Arable, Do.	"	"	" "	8	1	26	8	1	26
17	Pasture, first Marsh on Rd. to Hale	"	"	" "	6	1	02	6	1	02
18	Pasture, second Do. From Do.	"	"	" "	5	0	26	5	0	26
19	Pasture third Do. From Do.	"	"	" "	10	1	36	10	1	36
20	Pasture, fourth Do. From Do.	"	"	" "	12	0	31	12	0	31
21	Pasture, Middle Do. From Do.	"	"	" "	14	1	30	14	1	30
22	Pasture, Marsh adjoining Drove next above	"	"	" "	13	2	5	13	2	5
23	Pasture, Horse Shoe Marsh	"	"	" "	8	0	33	8	0	33
24	Pasture, Marsh Corner of Drove	"	"	" "	2	0	39	2	0	39
25	pasture, Marsh adjt. Drove N.W.	"	"	" "	10	0	5	10	0	5
26	Drove from Farm Yard to Wall	8	2	11	"	"	" "	8	2	11
27	pr. First Marsh under Wall from Drove	"	"	" "	8	3	36	"	"	" "
27A	A Pool and Bog	1	2	28	"	"	" "	10	2	14
28	pr. Middle Marsh under Wall	"	"	" "	10	3	35	"	"	" "
28A	Pool Bog and Stream	"	3	23	"	"	" "	11	3	18
29	pr. Third Marsh under Wall	"	"	" "	7	3	22	"	"	" "
29A	Pool and Stream	"	1	03	"	"	" "	8	0	25
30	pr. Farthest Marsh under Wall	"	"	" "	14	0	36	"	"	" "
30A	Bog, Creek and Sewer .	3	1	23	"	"	" "	17	2	19
31	Sea – Wall	4	1	16	"	"	" "	4	1	16

32	Detpb, between Wall and Fulls	5	2	09	"	"	" "	5	2	09
33	Pasture Pound Marsh	"	"	" "	4	2	00	4	2	00
34	Pasture, Great Marsh on Creek	"	"	" "	26	1	07	"	"	" "
34A	Creek and Sewer	1	0	0	"	"	" "	27	1	07
35	Pasture, Marsh adjoining above	"	"	" "	8	2	38	"	"	" "
35A	Creek and Sewer	"	1	24	"	"	" "	9	0	22
36	Pasture, Marsh farthest West of Creek	"	"	" "	7	2	35	"	"	" "
36A	Creek and Sewer	"	2	06	"	"	" "	8	0	4
37	Pasture, Corner Marsh	"	"	" "	16	3	03	"	"	" "
37A	Creek and Sewer	"	2	06	"	"	" "	17	1	09
38	Pasture, Home Marsh	"	"	" "	3	3	03	3	3	03
39	Garden in Home Marsh	"	"	" "	"	1	04	0	1	04
40	Pasture, Pidgeon Marsh	"	"	" "	2	3	34	2	3	34
41	Pasture Hammels.	"	"	" "	3	1	32	3	1	32
		30	0	29	411	3	6	441	3	35
	Public Stream 1:0:05									
	Public Roads 2:2:14							3	2	19
							Total	445	2	14

Fig. 58. **Transcription of the reference list of fields at Shuart Farm, 1826**

The 1826 map of Shuart Farm is large. Hailly gave it an elaborate title panel, executed with a large tree to the left, one of whose branches overhangs the panel protectively: see Fig. 59.

Fig. 59. **Title panel, Shuart Farm map**

The panel reads,

Plan of Shuart Farm in the Parish of St Nicholas, Isle of Thanet, County of Kent, Property of Eliab Harvey Breton Esq. and in the occupation of Mr. Henry Pett A.D. 1826.

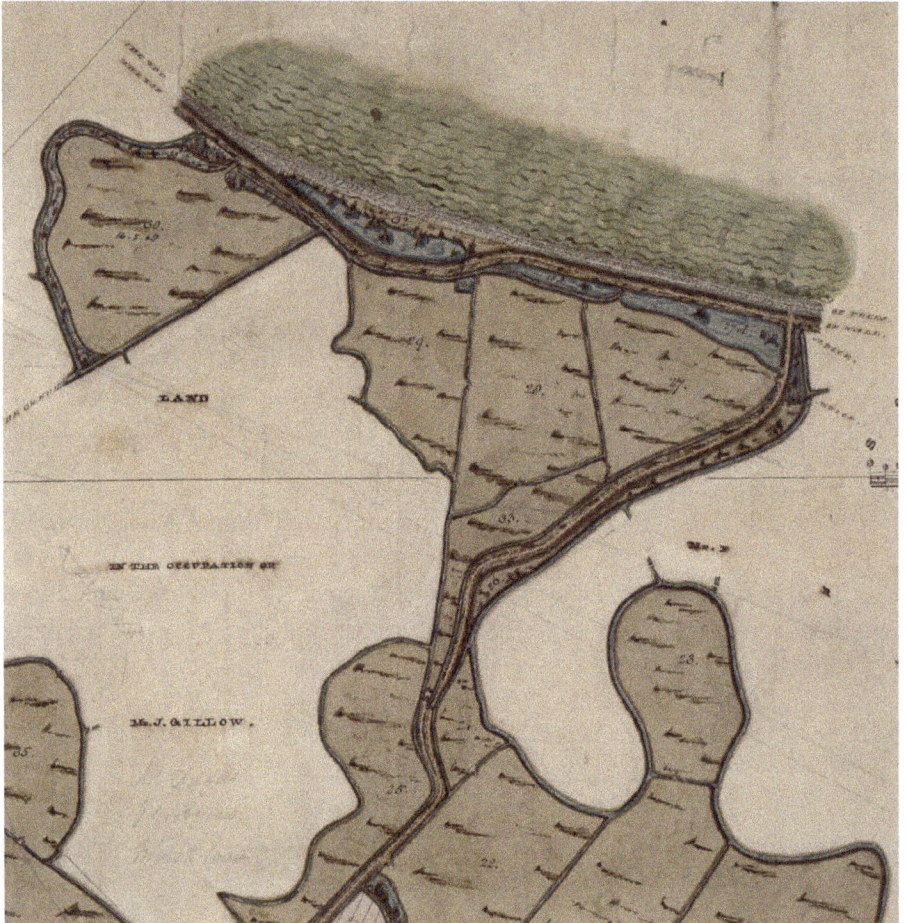

Fig. 60. **Map of Shuart Farm: close-up of seawall and Brooksend stream**

A series of pools indicated on the map reference as 27A, 28A and 29A, could almost be a stream. Together with the seawall and the wavy sea beyond, they form the northern boundary of Shuart Farm. The dull green and reed tufts in the fields indicate marshy land; comparatively few fields are not marshy.

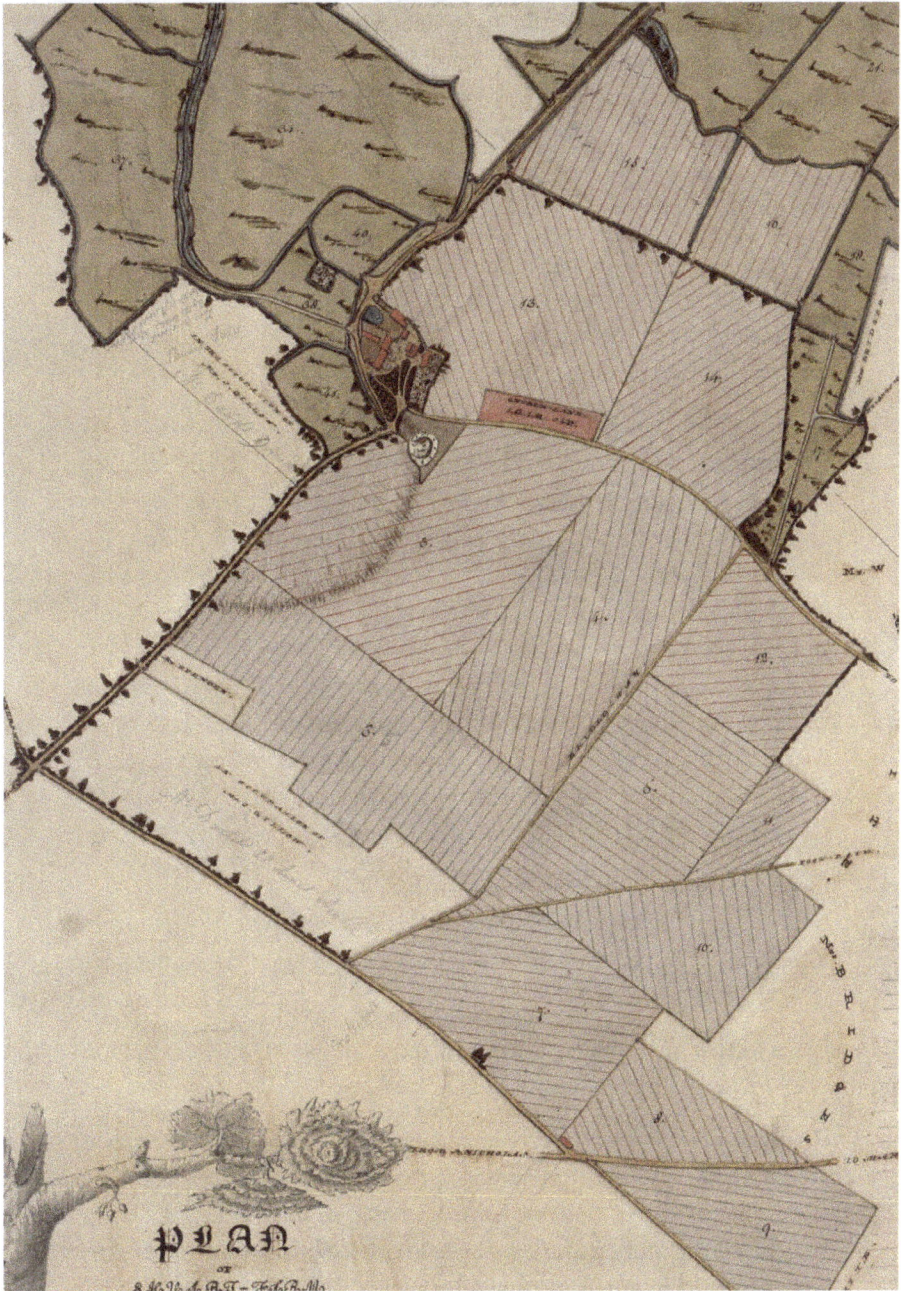

Fig. 61. **Shuart Farm enlargement showing cultivated fields (hatched)**

A rough calculation using the measurements in the reference list shows that about 150 acres were marshland. That would constitute a third of the farmland total. In addition, as the farm was bordered by the sea it was very exposed to the bitter, salt-laden north-easterlies, so it would have been difficult to make a decent profit, particularly in hard winters. Fields being cultivated in 1826 are shown as hatched on the map, see again Fig. 54. They are, without exception, well away from the seawall.

In recent correspondence with the present occupier, Martin Tapp, of Shuart Farm, I have learned that only two of the fields still have the same names. Martin wrote:

On average plots used to be much smaller, particularly where vegetables are grown on the upland as most farms grew many more crops than now. Also with a larger staff and no huge machines, field size did not matter much.

A number of major events have reshaped the area since the 1820s. The railway was built in the 1860s and plots 27 to 32 became separated. They were not part of the land I took over from St. John's College. The College also owned Crumps Farm by the Church. The Thanet Way was built in 1933 through both farms and there was some swapping done to square up. At a later stage the tenants at Crumps did not want any marshland and a few marsh fields were added to Shuart before my time. The Thanet way was [built] in the 1980s plus the new Potten Street Road. And a boundary simplified in the 1970s and straightened in the south east corner by the old dual carriageway. After all the comings and goings the acreage now stands at about 460. The only fields of the same name are Chalkpit (now nearly 30 acres) and Horseshoe, which is the field shape.

I would like to know the origin of: Hangmans, Crow Hop and Hammals. We are more up to date with Roundabout, Depotfield and Elmfield. All elms now dying.

In reply to a further query which I sent him about salt marsh on the property, Martin wrote

There is no salt marsh at Shuart now. This would have been both North of sea wall (still is) and possibly the blue area [on the map] just south of the wall. Most of this 'marsh' would be lost when the railway was installed and the farm shrunk. Other marshy areas have been drained by ditch maintenance, water level control (tidal flaps etc.) and some piped under drainage. The only really wet field is the one on extreme south west corner, currently in environmental set aside

Appendix 2f – Maps showing Shuart Farm on the Isle of Thanet

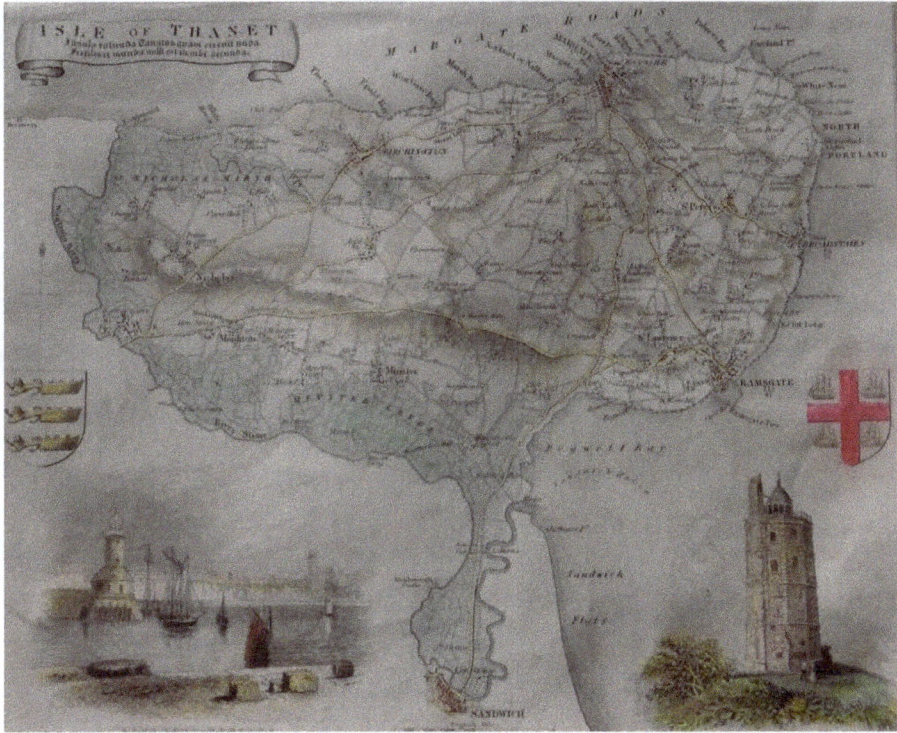

Fig. 62. **Map of the Isle of Thanet,**[347] **Thomas Moule, 1836**

As mentioned earlier, it is many centuries since the Isle of Thanet was an island, but in Roman times it was separated from the rest of England by the Wantsum Channel. Wikipedia tells us that

> [t]he Wantsum Channel was a strait separating the Isle of Thanet from the north-eastern extremity of the English county of Kent and connecting the English Channel and the Thames Estuary. It was a major shipping route when Britain was part of the Roman Empire, and continued in use until it was closed by silting in the late Middle Ages. Its course is now represented by the River Stour and the River Wantsum, which is little more than a drainage ditch lying between Reculver and St Nicholas-at-Wade and joins the Stour about 1.7 miles (2.7 km) south-east of Sarre.[348]

---

[347] Author's photograph of an early edition of Thomas Moule's etching from a period before the railway was built. It includes vignette views of Ramsgate Harbour and North Foreland Lighthouse.

[348] https://en.wikipedia.org/wiki/Wantsum_Channel

St Nicholas-at-Wade is just visible on Moule's map of the island (Fig. 62). North of the village, Moule identified what he called 'Suarts F.' (Fig. 63), tucked in on the edge of St Nicholas Marsh.

Fig. 63. **Close-up of Moule's map showing 'Suarts F.'**

This map corroborates the large-scale map of the farm commissioned by Eliab (Harvey) Breton II,[349] indicating that the terrain between the homestead and the sea was marshy. It should be noted that although Moule extends the map south to Sandwich, the town is not on the Isle of Thanet, as it is on the south bank of the Stour. The tongue of land on the north side is Stonar Spit. This can be seen more clearly on the 1886 map (Fig. 64) drawn by C M Hinds, a Ramsgate surveyor, who marked the farm 'Stuart's Far.':

---

[349] See **Appendix 2e – The map of Shuart Farm, 1826**, p. 147

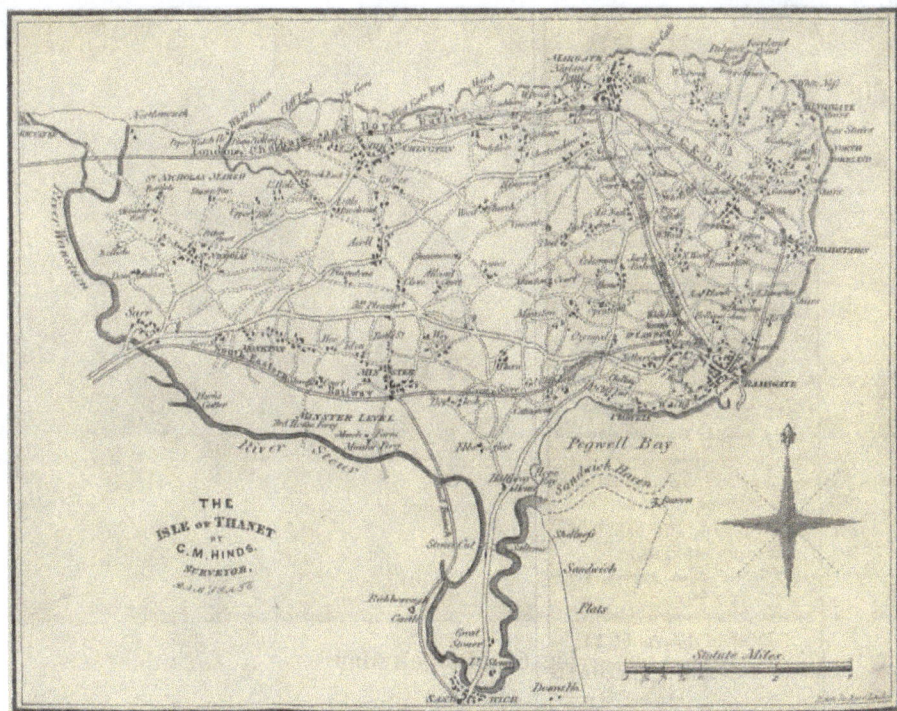

Fig. 64. **Map of the Isle of Thanet by C M Hinds, surveyor (1886)** [350]

Shuart Farm is most clearly seen in William Mudge's *An Entirely New & Accurate Survey of the County of Kent, With Part of the County of Essex* published in 1801 and now simply known as 'Mudge's Map', Fig. 65. This remarkable map was the first ever to be issued under the auspices of the Ordnance Survey, although published by William Faden.[351] It is a very large map, an extraordinarily detailed record of the county as it was in 1801 when the Curlings were living in Shuart. The map measures 122 cm × 170.5 cm, and yet another spelling of our farm appears on it: Fig. 66 and Fig. 67.

---

[350] *Map from the New Guide to Ramsgate, Margate, Broadstairs & St Peter's* 1886, from the British Library Flickr stream (public domain) via picryl.com: http://bit.ly/3t2fQNf

[351] Copyright Cartography Associates http://bit.ly/39pcgox. The full title of Mudge's work is *General Survey OF ENGLAND and WALES. An entirely new & accurate Survey OF THE COUNTY of KENT, WITH PART of the COUNTY of ESSEX, Done by the Surveying Draftsmen of His Majesty's Honourable Board of Ordnance, on the basis of the Trigonometrical Survey carried on by their Orders under the direction of CAPTN. W. MUDGE of the ROYAL ARTILLERY. F.R.S.*

Fig. 65. **Mudge's Map**

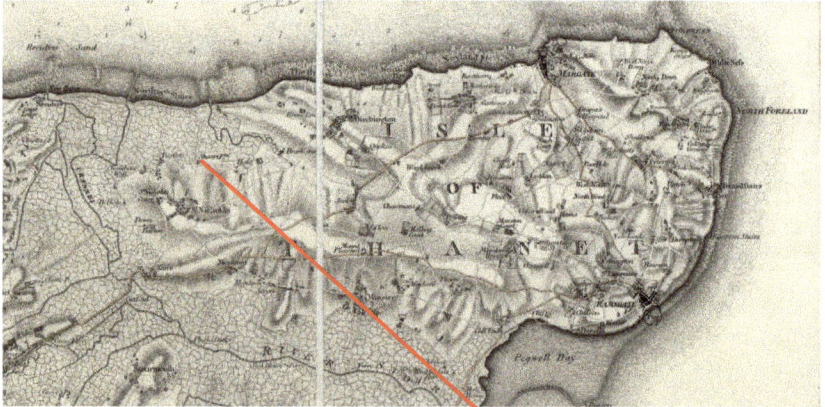
Fig. 66. **Mudge's Map, detail showing location of 'Shoart Fm'.**

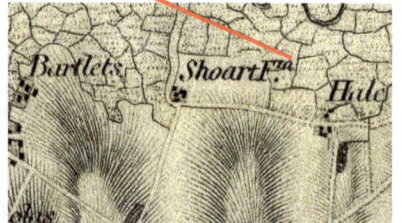
Fig. 67. **Further enlargement of Mudge's Map**

Appendix 3a – Francis John Kelly, a brief biographical note

Elizabeth Oakley's first husband, Francis John Kelly, was the second son of four, so he was not in direct line to inherit the family's Devon property.[352] Kelly family lore has it that he was disinclined to follow the family's directive that he should become a clergyman and inherit the house which went with the living in the village of Kelly. Between 1768 and 1771 he attended Oxford University's Wadham College[353] but does not appear to have graduated. Whether for this reason or another, he was disowned by his parents and purchased entry to the 18th (Royal Irish) Regiment of Foot as Ensign Kelly. In the *Scots Magazine* record of the appointment he is described as 'Gent', which will in due course have intimated to Thomas Oakley II that Elizabeth was marrying into a 'good family'. The most likely reason that Francis came to know the Oakley family is that, as mentioned earlier, there was at the time an enormous army presence on the south Kent coast, preparing for embarkation to fight in the Napoleonic wars and building defences in case of invasion. By the time of his marriage, according to the Kelly entry in Burke's *Genealogical and Heraldic Dictionary of the Landed Gentry*,[354] he had risen to the rank of captain. The 18th Regiment was on the move in February 1782.[355] However, after his marriage, although Kelly continued to be employed as a soldier in the 18th; from the pay and muster rolls for the regiment we learn that he was frequently sent on recruiting drives in Kent, so had not joined his colleagues who had been sent to Jersey.[356] In 1790 he sold his commission, which meant he left active service. There is a gap of fourteen years in his story before he became the barrackmaster at Hythe.[357] These were the years when his children were growing up, so providing for his family would have been a priority for him.

---

[352] Kelly House, Kelly, Devon http://kelly-house.co.uk/.
[353] *The Registers of Wadham College Oxford Part II*, p. 126. https://bit.ly/App3aFJKUni
[354] http://bit.ly/Ap3aKellyBurke *A Genealogical and Heraldic Dictionary of the Landed Gentry of Great Britain and Ireland*, p. 803 Bernard Burke, publisher Harrison, 1863.
[355] See *Historical Record of the 18th or Royal Irish Regiment of* compiled by Richard Cannon, pub 1848, for the relevant dates here: http://bit.ly/App3a18thRegHist.
[356] TNA WO 17/120.
[357] *Protecting the Empire's Frontiers*, Steven Baule, Ohio University Press 2014.

Appendix 3b – The Royal Staff Corps

The Royal Staff Corps [RSC] was a little-known precursor of the Royal Engineers. It had been founded at the behest of the army's commander-in-chief, Frederick Duke of York, and was initially known simply as the Staff Corps. Prior to this time, if an expeditionary force were going to war, the master general of the ordnance allocated a small detachment of Royal Engineers and Royal Military Artificers to the force. Here is some further information, which includes two Napier quotations, extracted from an article entitled 'The First British Combat Engineers' by Major J T Hancock RE in the *Royal Engineers Journal*, vol. 88, no. 4, December 1974.[358] The related footnotes are Hancock's:

> The Royal Military Artificers consisted of a number of static companies based on important fortifications in Britain and the Colonies. Their standards as Artificers were low and due to their static nature, their standards as soldiers were even lower. Engineer detachments supplied for expeditionary forces, therefore tended to consist of the worst of a poor selection and worked under Royal Engineer officers that they had probably never even seen before.[359]
>
> In 1799 the Commander-in-Chief, Frederick Duke of York, was forming a force for the expedition to the Helder and the Master General of the Ordnance proposed to supply the normal small, ad hoc, detachment from his Engineer Department. Since the start of the Napoleonic Wars, the role of Engineers in continental warfare had changed considerably and the Duke of York did not consider the size of the engineer force adequate for the expedition (one Sergeant, two Corporals and thirty five Artificers were allotted as support for a corps of 12,000 men).[360] The Quarter Master General, who came directly under the Commander-in-Chief, was responsible for hiring local civilians, as pioneers, on any expedition. To supplement the engineer force allotted, the Commander-in-Chief extended the powers of the Quarter Master General and formed a military Company of Pioneers for this expedition. The Company of Pioneers, working directly under the Quarter Master General, was successful in the Helder Campaign. As a result, on 15 January 1800, a warrant was issued raising a Corps of Pioneers which were to be known as the Staff Corps.[361]

---

[358] I am grateful to Colonel Gerald Napier RE (retd), for supplying me with a copy of the article.

[359] Pasley, C W, *A Course of Elementary Fortification* (London 1822, 2nd Edition), vol. 1, Notes to the Preface, pp. iii and iv. Connolly, T W J, *The History of the Corps of Royal Sappers and Miners* (London 1855, vol. 1, p. 118).

[360] Connolly, vol. 1, p. 127.

[361] PRO, WO 26/38 p. 63. [Now held at TNA. LAC]

The new Corps was commanded by a Major and consisted of a small Regimental Headquarters and four Companies. Each Company was commanded by a Captain ... [the] total strength of the Corps being twenty-two Officers and 423 Rank and File (for comparison, the establishment of the Royal Military Artificers was 975 all ranks but its recruited strength was only 743).[362] By the end of the year 1800, twenty of the Staff Corps' twenty-two Officers had been appointed and 366 of the 423 Rank and File had been recruited.

Unlike the Infantry and Cavalry, commissions in the new Corps were by appointment, not by purchase. The trades of the soldiers were very similar to those of the Royal Military Artificers. The Artificers at this period were not armed with muskets and required infantry protection when in contact with the enemy.[363] The soldiers of the new Corps were to be armed and trained as Infantry as well as being trained in Engineer duties.

When the Staff Corps was formed, Woolwich was the Headquarters of the Engineer Department ... The Headquarters and Depot of the new Corps was at Chatham Barracks (on the site of the present Kitchener Barracks) ...

At the end of 1800 the other three companies of the Corps moved to Chelmsford where a fortified camp was under construction as part of the defences against a possible invasion by Napoleon. It was here that they worked, for the first and last time, under the direction of a Royal Engineer Officer. Construction of the camp was under the supervision of an Engineer of the District. Work continued for some years, but in the later stages a Major of the Staff Corps took over entire supervision of the work.[364] ...

The [Royal Military] Canal was part of anti-invasion defences. When the civilian contractors failed, [Lieut-Colonel John Brown, commanding officer of the RSC at the time] was placed in virtual control of the construction and naturally used his Staff Corps to supervise much of the work. It was as a result of their work on the canal that their Headquarters and Depot moved to Hythe. There they built their own barracks which were later to become better known, after their disbandment, as the School of Musketry.[365]

... [I]t was pointed out that a system of instruction was required for the Staff Corps, if they were to be effective as engineers. It also recommended that a suitable area for training must be found ... :

No place can be more eligible than Chatham should [sic] His Royal Highness may think it proper to apply to the Master General of the Ordnance for the ground adjoining to the Barracks [Chatham Barracks] originally taken by the public for the purposes of defence for a plan since abandoned to which has occasioned the ground to be applied to private use.

---

[362] Connolly, vol. 1, p. 127.
[363] Connolly, vol. 1, pp. 227 and 228.
[364] Eleventh Report of the Commissioners of Military Enquiry, Appendix no. 17, pp. 108 and 109.
[365] Vine, p. 91.

There is no record as to whether or not the ground was allotted before the corps moved to Hythe in 1805, but on 20 April 1804 Charles Napier (at the time commanding a company of the Royal Staff Corps at Chatham) wrote to his mother and said that they were practising the construction of field works.[366] Field engineer training was therefore taking place at Chatham some eight years before the School of Military Engineering was established.

In the same memorandum a new rank and pay structure was proposed ... The officers were to receive the (higher) Cavalry rates of pay instead of those of Infantry.

There appears to be no record of the approval of the title Royal to the Staff Corps. In the yearly Army Lists, the first time that they were given the full title of Royal Staff Corps was in 1804. It can be assumed, that the title Royal was approved at roughly the same time as the other changes were made in their establishment and organization (ie June 1803).

It was unfortunate, though perhaps to be expected, that petty jealousies and antagonisms developed between the RSC and the engineer department of the Ordnance Board. As already stated, the Royal Military Artificers' role was mainly the construction and maintenance of permanent fortifications and the conduct of sieges in time of war. The RSC were formed specifically for war and the field engineer role. When not actively engaged on operations, it was only natural that they should be used on tasks which encroached upon the engineer department's provinces. The first indication of petty jealousies comes in a letter dated 1 May 1804; once again Charles Napier was the writer:

> However, two of our Companies go to Dover in a week to work under Engineers; so we are to be overseers not Engineers! [Major] Nicolay[367] swears he will resign' but when the Quarter Master General hears of his pets being so scurvily treated we shall be righted.[368]

The construction of the Royal Military Canal, by the RSC, did little to improve relationships. The Commander-in-Chief was authorised to spend money on temporary works only, leaving the permanent works to the Master General of the Ordnance and his Engineer Department. The ordnance Board had taken so long to approve the erection of Martello Towers, for the defence of the Southern Coast, that when the decision was made to construct the canal as a priority defence task, the Commander-in-Chief's funds were used in order that the work could start immediately. The consequent use of the RSC in building the canal was a blatant encroachment on the preserves of the Engineer Department. A proposal to use the RSC on the construction of the

---

[366] *Life & Opinions*, vol. 1, p. 43.

[367] Major William Nicolay was the officer appointed to lead the Royal Staff Corps when it was first set up. (Wikipedia).

[368] Napier, vol. 1 p. 45.

buildings for the Royal Military College at Sandhurst was a similar encroachment, although in the event they were never actually employed on this task. They did construct at least one bridge[369] and took a part in the lay-out of the plantations in the surrounding area.[370] At the end of 1803 a company was sent to Ireland, where it constructed Martello Towers and other permanent defence works. In 1806 a company was sent to Jersey and Guernsey for similar work and remained on those Islands until 1812. None of these tasks were likely to endear the RSC to the Engineer Department, even if they had accepted them in their war-time role of Field Engineers.

---

[369] Mockler-Ferryman, Major A F, *Annals of Sandhurst* (London, 1900), pp. 4 and 6.
[370] Tenth Report of the Commissioners of Military Enquiry, Appendix no. 24.

Appendix 4a – The Becker-Solley family of Kent

by Peter Wilkinson, descendant

The rest of this appendix, below this paragraph, consists of an extract from Peter Wilkinson's extensive paper entitled *A Story of Families: The Wilkinson-Becker and Kelleher-Hogan Families in Australia: 1822 to 2017* (2017). Peter has been the linchpin for a group of researchers focusing on the Becker and Solley families who were living in south-east Kent in the eighteenth and early nineteenth centuries. This extract gives much detail on the family background of our 3× great-grandmother Jane Becker (1757–1796); as she is named after her mother, I have called her Jane Becker II. There is also a junction with another branch of the Curling tree. Jane's parents were Michael Becker II and his third wife, Jane Belsey (1758–1825), grand-daughter of Ann Belsey née Curling, who was a great-aunt of our Thomas Curling I. This extract begins with Jane Becker II's father, Michael Becker II, the second generation of that name to live in Dover and one of our 4× great-grandfathers.

Michael Becker II (1757–1796)

Michael Becker II, the son of Michael I and Elizabeth (née Funnell), was baptized at St Mary the Virgin Parish Church in Dover on 13 March 1757. He probably received his education at Dover, and was indentured as an apprentice sailmaker, as was his brother, Peter (1766–?). In June 1787 Michael II was listed as a 'sailmaker', and in 1779 as a 'Master on his trade' taking on apprentices. In the later years of his parents' life, it would appear that the family moved to Hougham, a village not far from Dover, where Michael II, aged 21, married the 20-year-old spinster Jane Belsey (1758–1825), of Hougham Manor on 8 October 1778. Jane is thought to have been the daughter of George Belsey (1727–1795) and Jane (née Hudson) (1732–1805), and to have been born in 1758 at Capel-le-Ferne, a small town not far from Hougham.

In his early years in Dover, Michael II appears to have become a man of some means. While it is possible that the inheritance he received from his father's estate was substantial, he himself seems to have been a shrewd businessman. *The Dover and Deal Directory and Guide* for 1792 lists a 'Michael Becker, Gentleman', who is more than likely Michael Becker II. He may have had some share in the ownership and/or administration of the prominent business of Becker and Jell, Rope and Sail Makers, of which his brother Peter Becker and Richard Jell were the principal owners [cf. www.doverhistorian.com].

In 1790 the population of England is estimated to have been around 8 million. The first census of the population of England, Scotland and Wales was carried out on 10 March 1801 by a house-to-house enquiry, together with returns of baptisms and burials between 1700 and 1800, and marriages between 1754 and 1800 as supplied by the clergy.

St Mary the Virgin Parish Church, Dover, Kent

St Mary's, the ancient parish church of the town of Dover, has been a centre for Christian worship for over 1,000 years. It was built on the site of a Roman structure, and part of the existing building dates from the Norman period. The church of St Mary's is also the Civic Centre of Dover, its patrons being the Archbishop of Canterbury, the Lord Warden of the Cinque Ports and the Lord Lieutenant of Kent. Dover is the busiest passenger seaport in the world,[371] only 21 miles from the French port of Calais, and famous for its white chalk cliffs and Dover Castle. In 1966 Queen Elizabeth II bestowed on former Australian prime minister Robert Gordon Menzies the title of Lord Warden of the Cinque Ports and Constable of Dover Castle.

Fig. 68. **St Mary's Church and Dover Castle** [372]

Records for the Manor of Hougham Court (also known as Northcourt) in east Kent indicate that a 'moity' (half) of the manor was purchased by a Michael Becker of Dover in 1786 from Robert Cooper Jnr and Ann Barnes, and later, in 1792, on-sold by Mr Becker to Philip Leman of Dover Castle. There was no court held for the manor, but annexed to it was 'the right to wreck of the sea along the coast, from

---

[371] It was at the time of writing, but by 2021 it had lost its crown to Helsinki.

[372] St Mary's Church & Dover Castle, drawn and engraved by S Rawle, pub. *The European Magazine*, 1798. This copy is held in the archives of Dover Museum and Bronze Age Boat Gallery, reference number DOVRM 2005.16.81.

166

High Cliff to Archcliff Fort'.[373] It is almost certain that this Michael Becker was Michael II, as his wife Jane Belsey and her family were living at Hougham Manor when they met and married.

Michael II and Jane had six children ... all born at Dover, Kent. Their first son, Michael, died as an infant.

Original correspondence in the East Kent Archives at Whitfield[374] indicates that in 1795 or 1796 Michael Becker II – of supposed Prussian descent – leased Guilton Rectory and its attached lands at Overland, Goldstone (in the Parish of Ash-next-Sandwich), from the Messrs Cobb, brewers and bankers. Part of the correspondence between Michael Becker II and the lessors [Cobbs] related to the lease reads:

> *Gent^m I received yours but cannot think of giving any more than I offered (for Guilton Parsonage and apendages with the Marsh Land and Immediate Possession) which I think is as much as it is worth. If you think of taking the Money please let me know by Return of Post and I with Mr. Kennett will meet you on Tuesday next at Sandwich where if you will bring all the particulars and I approve of them we will bind the Bargin. I am your Humb Ser^t,*
> > *Mich Becker*

> > > *Dover 19th. June 1794*

> *Answer verb^y by Mr Austen – that we would not accept the offer.[375]*

There must have been other communication, following up Mr Austen's rebuff, because Michael Becker was not put off. Almost three weeks after his first letter, he wrote from Dover:

> *I with M^r. Kennett will meet you on Sunday next at the Bell Sandwich 10 or 11 Oclock in the morning where if you will bring a copy of your lease and other particulars of Guilton Parsonage & apendages and I like the Title and we can agree we will finally settle the business.*

> *I am your Most Humb Ser^t,*
> > *M Becker*

> > > *Dover July 9 1794*

---

[373] *The History and Topographical Survey of the County of Kent*, vol. 9, pp. 451–462, Edward Hasted, 1800, available online: http://bit.ly/App4aBelsey.

[374] Now in the Kent History and Library Centre, Maidstone.

[375] Letter of M. Becker, Dover, 18 June 1794, which was answered orally ['verb^y'] by Mr Austen. This and the following letters are held as a bundle entitled 'Michael Becker Guilton', KHLC EK/U1453/C18.

Later in the year 1794, Becker wrote two more letters to Cobbs. The first, written on 31 October, asked for clarification on how he should pay the lease on Guilton Rectory:

King's Tax	*91*	*19*	*4*	*5th Part*	*18*	*7*	*0*
Rent to the Bishop	*54*	*12*		*Do*	*10*	*18*	*43*
Do To the Parson	*50*			*Do*	*10*		
Do To Lord Radnor	*34*			*Do*		*6*	*16*

Gentm

I have Recd yours with a copy of a letter from Sir Chs Ratcliffs Attory, I'll thank you for the particulars of what you paid him last year for I do not know what to send him, you told me the Rent was 700 or 750 pounds a year. If it was 750 pounds a year the fifth part of that is 150 a year, 46.2.2¾. 103.17.9¼. Therefore I must send 101.17.9½ if it is 750 pounds a year, and if it is 700 pounds a year, I must send him 10 pounds less, but I hope you will send me the account of what you have paid him last year by Return of post, and I will Remit Mr. Desse the Money Immediately, I'll thank you who the other 20th. Part belongs to. I am Gents Your Humble Sert, M Becker

I have not yet got the Bills for Repears but I judge them to be about 10 pounds 10.

The final letter in the bundle was written by Michael Becker II from his new home at Guilton in November 1794:

Gentm

I have sent the Archbishop [of Canterbury] Money to Mr. Young his Receiver, and likewise Sr Charles Ratcliffe to Mr. Desse, and at the same time sent Mr. Shirley's to Geo. Burley Esq Lincoln Inn but was surprise'd to have the Money returned from Mr. Burley which was 32.5.5 with saying that he could not receive the money except he heard from Messrs Cobbs therefore I'll thank you to write to Mr. Burley. I am

> *your Humb Sert,*
> *Mich Becker*

> Guilton Nov 16 1794

Sent to Mr Desse	*129*	*1*	*7*
Do Mr G Burley	*32*	*5*	*5*
Do Mr Young	*74*	*12*	

Fig. 69. **Guilton Rectory** [376]

Guilton Rectory

The rectory at Guilton … was the family home of Michael Becker II, his wife, Jane (née Belsey) and their children from 1795 to 1825.

The lease of the Guilton Parsonage [Rectory] and 'apendages', situated on Durlock Road, only 900 metres west of Ash Village, was concluded in 1795. The money for the lease may have come from the 1792 sale proceeds of the moity of Hougham Manor. Guilton Rectory and most of its lands belonged to the Archbishop of Canterbury, but the lease was secured by Charles Delmar, a wealthy Canterbury man who in 1823 married Michael II's daughter, Mary Becker. The Upper Goldstone Farm, which was later tenanted by Michael Becker III and Hannah Solley, was owned by Charles Delmar who rented it to them.

Michael II with his wife Jane and their five [*sic*] children probably moved into Guilton Rectory in Ash in 1795, soon after the lease was finalized. Sarah, their eldest child would have been aged 15 at the time, Jane was eleven, Michael III –

---

[376] Image © Historic England, IOE01/13751/13. Information about the house is available on the Historic England website: http://bit.ly/Ch4HEGuiltonRectory.

169

named after an earlier sibling who had died as an infant – aged 9, and the youngest, Harriot, aged 6.

Sometime between 6 February and early March 1796, shortly after moving to Guilton and at the young age of 39 years, Michael Becker II died, and was buried at Hougham on 7 March 1796. He left his widow to raise their five young children alone. Jane did not remarry.

According to Michael II's will the principal beneficiary was his wife Jane, who thereafter became known as the 'Widow of Guilton'. She continued to live at Guilton Rectory for a further 30 years before dying on 16 February 1825 at Guilton Town, Ash, aged 67 years. Her passing was reported in the *Kentish Gazette*.

In Jane's Last will and Testament, proved on 11 June 1825, she bequeathed £1000 to her daughter, Jane (married to Thomas Oakley Curling (1781–1825) and then living in Van Diemen's Land, Australia); £3000 upon trust to her daughter, Mary (Mrs Charles Delmar); £100 to her niece, Anne Garnett (probably the daughter of Jane's sister); with the remainder of her estate to go to her son, Michael Becker III, upon her burial. Jane's other children, Michael (infant), Sarah, Mary and Harriot, had all predeceased her.

4.1.4. Michael Becker III (1786–1851)

Michael Becker II and his wife Jane's first son Michael, born in October 1782, survived less than three months, but they had a second son whom they also named Michael. Michael Becker III was born at Dover on 24 May 1786, and on 7 June 1786 was baptized, like his siblings, at St Mary the Virgin Parish Church at Dover. His first ten years were likely lived at Dover, until the family moved to Guilton Rectory at Ash-next-Sandwich in 1795. From that time his father had become a 'farmer' of the gentlemanly kind, and Michael III, as the only surviving son, probably saw his future as one day inheriting the family property and living out his life as a gentleman like his father. Michael III was 10 years old when his father died.

Fig. 70. **Map showing Ash, Dover, Canterbury, Faversham, Capel-le-Ferne** [377]

Dr Mary Abbot, in her scholarly work, *Family Ties: English Families 1540–1920*, notes that most well-to-do farmers in nineteenth-century England sent their children to boarding school for their education. So it may be assumed that, although there are no records to confirm it, Michael II and Jane Becker [I] followed this custom and ensured that all their children, both male and female, were well educated.

Following Michael II's death in 1796, Jane probably managed the farm herself, with help, until the children had received their education and were ready to take on their responsibilities. Perhaps around 1807, when Michael III was aged 21, Jane may have handed him partial or full administration of the family farm. But it was not until Jane's death and burial in February 1825, 30 years after her husband's death, that the property passed fully to Michael III.

A word portrait of the young Michael Becker III is given by the Reverend George Robert Gleig, the Curate of the Parish of Ash during the 1830s, who knew him well. In his 3 volume work, *The Chronicles of Waltham*, published in 1835, Gleig attempted to disguise Michael Becker III by giving him the fictitious name of 'Mr Thomas Amos, the overseer' – but everyone living in Ash at the time knew who Amos really was. In the chapter titled 'A Man of Authority' (vol. I), with real names in brackets [ ], Gleig wrote:

---

[377] © Dániel Fehér, https://www.freeworldmaps.net/

Mr Thomas Amos [Michael Becker III], at this time overseer. of the poor in Waltham [a blend of the real-world villages of Wingham and Ash], had inherited, when very young, a moity of the tithes of Appleby [Guilton]; the other moity being bequested to his sister [Mary Becker], then a girl, but who has since married the prosecutor [Mr Charles Delmar] in the late actions. For many years, that is to say, throughout the good times of the [Napoleonic] war [1803–1815], Mr Amos hired her portion from his sister, and, living in Appleby, collected the whole of the tithes of the parish in kind, and with a rigid hand. Holding the lease, moreover on very easy terms, as well with reference to the Archbishop [of Canterbury] as to his relative, he found himself in the enjoyment of a large income, which he spent among cock-fighters, card-players, boxers, and other flash people, with the utmost fairness and liberality. In his personal habits, likewise, he was the very beau ideal of a gay, jovial, thriving yeoman of Kent. Nobody throughout the surrounding districts rode such excellent horses, or dressed with greater taste than he; and among the women he was said to be irresistible; for, in addition to a striking exterior and an athletic form, he could boast of manners which, in his own sphere, were regarded as princely. And his accomplishments were in every respect in agreement with his exterior. Mr Amos was a dead shot, a fearless hunter, a skilful dancer, and an expert pugilist. He was likewise a man of courage as well as of gallantry; indeed, he was known to have fought at least one duel with a subaltern officer in a marching regiment, in vindication of his right to the smiles of a pretty servant girl whom the jealous soldier took it into his head to watch too closely. But the traits of character on which, above all others, Mr Amos piqued himself, were his unyielding resolution and his bold infidelity. Let him once pledge his word to anything, and there was no degree of trouble or expense that he would not undergo to redeem it. Let him once utter a threat, and no consideration of pity or remorse would hinder him from carrying it into execution. In like manner, his play, whether in the cock-pit, at the billiard-table, or elsewhere, was perfectly fair; and he paid his debts, as well to tradesmen as to sharpers, punctually. With respect again to religion, he held that as light as he held the restraints of moral obligation. Mr Amos believed nothing, feared nothing, hoped for nothing beyond the present state of existence; and he was a great deal too honest to act the hypocrite. On the contrary, Sunday was with him the busiest day in the week; and as if to mark the contempt in which he held the prejudices of others, Sunday was the day on which he made it a rule to go abroad in his shabbiest attire. When I add, that Mr Amos was from his boyhood a friend of the people, I have said enough to set his general character in its true light.

Michael III grew into manhood during the Napoleonic Wars. After the defeat of Napoleon at Waterloo in 1815 by the Anglo-Allied army under the command of the Duke of Wellington, the decade that followed, which was expected to be an age of peace and prosperity, turned into a period of economic recession and social turmoil. Commerce languished, manufacturing slowed, agriculture went into decay, and widespread unemployment and poverty followed. An economic recession had struck. So stunned were the English citizenry that few, especially the wealthy, adjusted their lifestyles, but continued to live as if the times were still prosperous. When ruin befell them, they blamed only the politicians. Farmers like Michael Becker III now found themselves with ruinously high rents, tithes grinding them into the dust, little profit from their crops, and growing pressure from the poor rates. For farm labourers, work became scarce and wages fell, especially if they were unmarried; and for the poor and unemployed the assistance provided by the parish shrank significantly.

It was when the recession was at its worst and when, at a personal level, he had hit a major hump, that Michael Becker III was appointed by the vestry of the Ash Parish to be Parish overseer. Gleig recounts his situation in the following account of Mr Thomas Amos:

> The arrival of bad times affected no one more distressingly than Mr. Amos [Michael Becker III]. It is true that his leasehold property was still valuable, and that a man of prudent habits might have lived very comfortably upon it; but Mr. Amos's habits had never been prudent. In his vices, on the contrary, he had always been extravagant; for, besides keeping himself constantly within water-mark by the strictness with which he discharged his debts of honour, more than one female had legal claims on him for a pension. When a reverse came, therefore, Mr. Amos had no fund laid up wherewith to meet it; and he was a great deal too high-spirited to sail, as he himself expressed it, under false colours. The consequence was, that after hanging on for a while in the groundless hope that times might mend, this singular man all at once changed his habits of living entirely. He had taken into keeping a woman of low origin [Hannah Solley], by whom he had a family. He now withdrew from society altogether, and confined himself to her. From the best dressed man in the parish he became the most perfect sloven. His game-cocks were sold, his hunters were disposed of, his groom dismissed. With his gay companions, among whom it was hinted that the celebrated Thurtell and Hunt[378] had been numbered, he broke off all connexion; and adopting the habits of a boor, he lived entirely in his kitchen. The character of the man, however, continued to be as fully exhibited in every action of his life as it had ever been. He was still a man of his word. In his debasement he was not less ostentatious than he had been in his elevation; and in politics and religion

---

[378] Thomas Thurtell and Richard Hunt were the defendants in one of England's most famous murder trials, in 1824. It was almost the last famous trial to take place under the old Tudor 'inquisitorial' procedure and the first trial 'by newspaper' in which there was a very serious collision between the Bench and the Press as to the duties of the latter in relation to the detection of crime and its investigation.

he became more and more liberal every day. One little statement more illustrative of the temper of his mind, and I resume my narrative.

Mr. Amos had continued to hire his sister's portion of their joint property, up to the period when difficulties began to arise in settling for their small tithes with farmers. When this befell, he became all at once tired of the business, and having himself taken a farm in Waltham, expressed great anxiety to remove thither. Accordingly his brother-in-law [Mr Charles Delmar] was persuaded to change positions with him. No sooner was this done, however, than Mr. Amos declared himself, in all companies, an enemy to the tithe system. It was a positive robbery of the occupier; and for his part he would, though depending on it mainly for his own subsistence, lend a willing hand to get rid of it altogether. Of course such language, coming from one who was known to be himself a lessee, but who was not generally known to have sub-let his portion for a term of years, was pronounced liberal in the extreme; and when party spirit began to run high, no man proved more active, or was more looked up to among the Blues, than Mr. Amos.

Of Amos's [Becker's] appearance, Gleig also gives the following description:

A tall stout man, dressed in a filthy fustian shooting-jacket, cord breeches clouted at the knees, grey worsted stockings, and huge hob-nailed shoes, with an old blue cap upon his head and a bludgeon in his hand... his costume as conspicuous as his habits were notorious. Mr. Amos, to be sure, was not one of those who delighted in receiving marks of obsequious attention. Unprincipled – that is to say, totally wanting in religious principle – he might be; but he was manly, and had therefore no desire to be fawned upon. But he, like all others of his order, had his own notions of what was due to himself.

Note from LAC: The author, the Reverend G R Gleig, knew Michael Becker III personally. His 'disguised' description of Michael Becker III as above is followed in Peter Wilkinson's document by brief biographical details of each of Michael Becker's III siblings. Of Jane, he wrote:

Jane was the first member of the Becker family to migrate to Australia, and through the stories she must have told of her Australian experiences, she probably sowed the seeds for many of the later migrations of her nephews and nieces to the antipodes. However, none of her own children, who had spent their early years in Tasmania, ever returned to Australia to settle there permanently, although one grandson, Henry Oakley Curling, the son of Thomas Jnr, did go to Australia and his direct descendants are still living there.[379]

---

[379] [added by LAC] Jane's son John moved from India to New Zealand in about 1851. He was a member of the Legislative Council there for about three years, then became a teacher and died in New Zealand in 1889.

Appendix 4b – History of hunting in East Kent

In January 2017, curious to know if the Isle of Thanet Hunt had survived to present times, I emailed Nicholas Onslow, historian and author. He kindly replied as follows:

The research for the recently published A History of the East Kent Foxhounds *(to mark the pack's 200th anniversary in 2014) revealed that over the centuries a number of packs hunted in East Kent. While the East Kent have always been a foxhound pack, as is often the case foxhound and harrier packs share country and this is the situation with the Thanet Hunt. The immediate predecessor of the East Kent was a trencher pack managed by Frank Pettit the landlord of The Bell in Hythe. They hunted the country from about 1795. Tantalising references were discovered to other packs in Kent but the records are very sketchy – in one case merely an accounts book entry from 1768 for the delivery of "hay for ye houndes" to Waldershare. ... The Thanet Harriers were established in about 1762 and were kennelled at Cleve Court, Minster – the pack being maintained and hunted by Mr J F Farrer. In 1775 the kennels were moved to Gore Street Monkton. The Victoria History of the County of Kent (1908) gives the following:*

As early as 1760 Mr Farrer of Cleve Court kept hounds in the Isle of Thanet. These were undoubtedly used for hare-hunting, though we find an account in the Kentish Gazette of 27 September 1769, of a hunt after a deer, which was run with Farrer's hounds. In 1761 an advertisement appeared in the Kentish Gazette for a huntsman, but no record of the appointment is extant. The Isle of Thanet hunt as it now exists was established on 2 April 1813, at a meeting held at the Mount Pleasant Inn near Minster, where Messrs. Ambrose Collard, John Swinford and Henry Collard were appointed stewards, and Thomas Oakley Curling secretary. The hunt has been carried on in the Isle of Thanet continuously from that date. In 1849 Mr John White took the country and built new kennels at Brooksend, moving the hounds thither from Hoo Corner, Monkton; and he hunted the country till 1873. The pack was known as the Brooksend and Isle of Thanet Harriers, and was made up of 20- to 21-inch harriers and dwarf foxhounds.

The pack went on to become the Thanet and Herne Harriers. It disappeared after the first war and the Herne Harriers were re-established in the 1950s before eventually being consumed by the West Street Harriers.

Nicholas Onslow

Appendix 5a – Thomas II's letter to the Board of Agriculture, 1816

Thomas O Curling. – The Farmers here being in an extensive line, have been enabled to keep from actual bankruptcy longer than men in small occupations could have done, by selling some stock on immediate pressure, there are many of them now in great distress, who at one time might have made from 5000l. to 10,000l, by the sale of their stock and crop; their friends obliged to call money from them by their own necessities, which the farmer finds impossible to replace in his business; consequently, his lands must go this summer half stocked, if grazing; all improvements stopped on arable, and every acre cropped, to produce something towards preventing total ruin. – The stack-yards empty, so that a rise in price before harvest, will be of no use to the man wanting support; his next crop must be thrashed with the greatest expedition, unless more dicided steps are taken to relieve him by the rise in price of corn, than any hitherto adopted; another such a year must bring many men, late of the property above-described, to complete ruin.

The expenditure of the poor rates is higher than in 1811, 1812, or any year during the distress of the poor, from high price of provisions, arising from the great number of labourers out of employment, who receive daily pay from their parish, and are sent to spend the day in what is called mending the roads, really earning no more pence than they are paid shillings, and contracting every bad habit attending on idleness, and associating with the worst of labourers, and broken down smugglers, who, of course are the first sent from the farm to the parish for relief. I can see no prospect, but an increase for some years, of this destructive system and I beg to state my reasons. The young are not deterred from marrying by the present want of employment (although I have seen men employed in hay season, on the roads, by the parish) knowing they must always receive sufficient for existence from the poor-rates. The farmer of Thanet must, from economy, come to use two-horse ploughs, instead of the old Kent ploughs requiring four horses, and a man and lad to each; the two-horse ploughs requiring only one man, must very shortly send all these young men to daily labour; while they are single, they can work cheaper than a married man; and many farmers will, in consequence, employ them, and the others must go to the parish.

Some benevolent characters, thinking these pressing times will not last, do now employ the labourers paid off by the farmers, who have laid aside all ideas of improving their land; but as it will be some time before speculative farming will again be in fashion, these men must tire at employing more than is necessary on their farms, and will send supernumeraries to the parish, as others have done before them.

To afford adequate relief, some strong measures must be resorted to, calculated to restore in the public that confidence in the agricultural interest which now appears lost, and to renew that credit, which heretofore enabled it to perform so much. It appears to me, that, among these measures, must be a direct prohibition of all importation of corn for two years; a high duty on imported wool, flax, hides, tallow, and on some seeds, particularly of clover; the money sent abroad for the payment of which must be considered as gone to improve the agriculture of your enemies, and consequent exaltation of their national strength, instead of keeping in good cultivation, at a small expence, and ready to grow corn when wanted, a proportion of that land, which the country may some day deplore having rendered its cultivation impossible, by allowing its occupier to be ruined, by a foreign supply of an article, the overflow of which can do no good, or the dearth any mischief immediately to the public.

An alteration in the poor-laws appears decidedly necessary; trade and property must be brought to pay in proportion with the land; in some parishes, the poor-rate amounts to nearly a rent of the land. St Bartholomews farm, in the vicinity of Sandwich, was charged, last year, with 1l. 2s. per acre. The unfortunate occupier could never calculate on such a sum, as he had not been the means of settling any poor; which on the contrary, was done by the rich commercial men, who settled numbers of sailors and ship-builders, and now pay, comparatively, nothing towards their support. If the poor were supported by the nation at large, manufactories of clothes, shoes, hats, and agricultural implements, might be established, under competent authority; and, if they lost by every article sold, it would not amount to the sum now squandered away to the encouragement of idleness, and in litigious disputes concerning settlements;[380] the sum paid in one year for disputes on settlements, would build nearly all the establishments.

A late decision in favour of the keep of a cow, gaining a settlement, has deprived many labourers of that comfort; has afforded a good harvest for the lawyers, and left the parishes with about the same number of poor they begun with, only having changed some faces.

---

[380] Settlement was the means by which paupers seeking to move, whether for work or personal reasons, could be allowed to settle in a new parish. 'The principle of settlement, established in 1662, meant that travelling paupers could be returned to their home parish, usually that of their birth for relief, unless they carried a certificate which promised that their parish would reimburse the parish where they became dependent.' BBC History web page: http://bit.ly/BBCSettlement 'The initial Act defining the meaning of a 'settlement' was passed in 1662, but was substantially revised in the 1690s. ... Any JP could hear appeals by paupers against a parish, and order relief as he saw fit, or refer the matter to Quarter Sessions.' https://www.londonlives.org/static/PoorLawOverview.jsp

Appendix 5b – The Curling family vault at St George's Church, Ham

Thomas Curling I must have been particularly attached to his childhood home, Ham Farmhouse, also known as Ham Manor, near Deal, Kent, because in 1799, following the deaths of his father and brother, he applied to Canterbury Cathedral Diocese to have a family vault in the little church of St George at Ham, where he and his eleven siblings had been baptized.[381] The vault is on the chancel step. The parish register indicates how small Ham was, for on just one double page the records stretch from January 1790 to March 1819. They include the burial records for the following Curlings, relatives of Thomas Curling I:

Relation	Baptismal name	Surname	Date	
mother	Jane, née Bunce	Curling	22 Jan	1790
infant niece	Elizabeth daughter of his sister	Osborn from Margate	24 Sep	1795
father	John	Curling I	11 Oct	1797
brother	John	Curling II	02 Apr	1798
sister-in-law	Mary, wife of his brother William Curling of Betteshanger	Curling	25 Jan	1803
daughter	Catherine	Curling, aged 23	16 May	1805
2nd infant niece	Elizabeth	Osborn	16 Sep	1808
sister-in-law	Elizabeth	née Jull, aged 62, widow of John Curling	18 Oct	1818
And the last entry on the page, Thomas himself:				
	Thomas	Curling, aged 62	01 Mar	1819

That is nine Curling records out of a total twenty-three in the hamlet between 1790 and 1819. Thomas's widow Catharine did not long outlive him, being buried in Ham on 9 November 1819, although her burial is not recorded on this page. It is remarkable that all the Curlings are gathered together in this vault, which Thomas had only requested in 1799, so he would have had to organize disinterments and reinterments for the bodies of both his parents and his brother John. It is significant

---

[381] KHLC DCb/EF/Ham St George/1 https://bit.ly/App5bCurlingVault

that the only other vault, situated next to the Curling one on the altar step, is that for the Bunce family, they being Thomas's maternal ancestors, Jane's parents Edward and Ann Bunce (née Rammel) and grandparents Thomas Bunce and Mary née Boys.

In 1977, when St George's Church, Ham, was about to be deconsecrated and sold as a habitation, one of the parishioners, William May, took on the task of making a handwritten record of as much as he could about the church. This has been transcribed by Andrew Parkinson of Northbourne. From this transcription, we find that William May wrote as follows:

THE PARTLY USED CURLING VAULT

During the year 1964 a small hole appeared in the floor of the sanctuary, between the altar and the south wall of the church. It was a small and simple job to pack it and level up the tiles. But several months later a larger hole appeared as the tiles sank down. A more thorough investigation revealed that the floor was resting on a wooden 'bridge' under which was a small empty chamber. This was the burial vault of the Curling family, partly used and with space left for other members of that family when they died. But the vault, left empty for them, was never used. It was filled in with concrete in June 1965.

Memorials elsewhere in the church include one on the south wall to John and Jane's son Bunce Curling, 'Doctor in Medicine from the Parish of St. Mary le bonne, London' (7/7/1826 aged 68), and Bunce's son James Bunce Curling, who died while 'staying at Ramsgate but visiting at Kensington' (6/1/1863 aged 62). James worked in the royal household for a time and published a book, *Some Account of the Ancient Corps of Gentlemen-At Arms*, a facsimile copy of which is available free on Google Books.[382] James was 'Clerk of the Cheque' to the Corps.

The original of William May's record, handwritten in a school exercise book, is in Sandwich Library.

---

[382] http://bit.ly/AncientCorpsJBC

Appendix 6a – The letters of Catharine and Thomas Curling

Stone House, near Great Marlow, Bucks

Sept 4th 1819

Master Curling
The Rev G Abbot's
Ramsgate
Kent

My dear Grandson,

Since the commencement of our correspondence, your letters have been at all times welcome, and pleasurable to me, but your last of 19th inst proved more particularly so, from the distance by which I am at present separated from you all; and accept my best thanks for the length of your epistle, account of the Harvest, anecdotes of your new acquaintance at the seaside, his faithful and sagacious dog Neptune, of your birds, your Stud, in which I include the Dandy Charger with the Poney, and Donkey; and of other matters; which as they had interested you, could not fail to be acceptable to me, as was more especially the assurance that yourself and Edward were in good health. I have been likewise favored with a comfortable long letter from your Mother, date 16th inst, at which period your younger Brother's were still at home, but as the favorable opinion of Mr Freeman, or his brother in law Mr Smith, of the complaint in their heads, is further corroborated by that of Mr Elwyn, I trust Mrs Morris will no longer object to receive them, as the testimony of three surgeons, I should suppose, must justify her to the parents of her other pupils, in so doing.

I have great satisfaction in offering the most affectionate congratulations on the approaching return of your birth day, on Tuesday next you will be 14, and I will endeavour so to dispatch this, that it may be put into your hands on 7th Septr but we are inconveniently situated here with respect to the post, so that if it be a day before, or after. I flatter myself it will prove equally acceptable, as conveying my heart felt wishes for your health, & happiness, and that your conduct may be such, that your Parents and friends, may have pride, & pleasure in you, I would prompt you to repeat the following prayer, from Young.

"Father of Light and Life, Thou God Supreme,
O, Teach me what is good; teach me thyself,
Save me from folly, vanity and vice,
From every low Pursuit, and feed my soul
With knowledge, conscious peace, and virtue pure;
Sacred, substantial never fading bliss —"

*in "what is good" is comprised first, duty to God, then duty &
affection to your parents, Brother's and Sister; and a steady
application to your studies, under Mr Abbot, to fit yourself for the
profession or employment you may be placed in; to endeavour to
advance yourself in it, by industry & attention, which cannot fail to
render you respectable in life, and a good example to your younger
brother's.*

*I was much pleased to find that you had called on Miss Stewart
when at Sandwich as she is a very kind and good friend of mine, as
well as a relation; and I consider any mark of respect to her as a
favor done to myself, by any of my family, and I know she is much
gratified by it. I was indeed as she told you, much pleased with the
situation of Mr Kelly's family at Albr'o Hatch, the house was called
Hainault Cottage, we removed from thence on 17th ins^t to this place,
where we are settled in a very pretty convenient house; the river
Thames runs at the bottom of a small garden or lawn in front, which
we cross over in a flat bottom boat belonging to the house, to Great
& Little Marlow, we were last Sunday at Church at the latter, and I
have been to the former, which is a mile & ½ distant; you will no
doubt recollect hearing of the Military College there, to educate, and
prepare boys for the Army, but which was transferred to Sandhurst in
Sussex about 8 years ago, where there is a suitable building for the
purpose, which was not the case at Marlow, where the Masters,
professors and pupils were obliged to be lodged at several different
houses, but all, of course repaired to one called the College, at the
hours of Study, and where as many were lodged as the house, or
houses would accommodate.*

*Stone House, our present residence, stands in Berkshire, which
the Thames divides from Buckingham-shire, in which County Great
Marlow our best town is; therefore if you cast your eye on the map of
England, you will see the spot of our residence; the front of the house
commands a prospect of a very beautiful country, but at the back part
of it, is a high hill, which by a bad road, we descend from the main*

road, to get to the house. Barges pass frequently on the Thames which go to Oxford etc etc – since I have been writing this, an elegant one with a party of pleasure on board, sailed by; decorated with flags, and had a band of music; opposite the parlour windows is an Island of six acres, on the river, from which, since I have been here, they conveyed the Hay off in a boat: our parish is Cookam 2 miles distant. Maidenhead is 5 miles [and Lond]on 31. When at Hainault Cottage we spent [a] day in the [rel]ated forrest of that name, which the hou[se is] on the borders of; it was while Miss Stewart was on a visit to your Aunt Kelly, we took cold Lamb etc for our dinner, which we sat down under a tree to eat, and made a little fire to boil the potatoes, quite in the Gypsey style; your cousin Henry Kelly who is very cheerful & droll affecting to scream at the Wasps which beset our provision.

Fig. 71. **Fairlop Oak & Fairlop Fair, Samuel Hieronymus Grimm, 1774** [383]

We saw the famous Fairlop Oak, considered the largest tree in the Kingdom, but I must confess I was disappointed in the expectation I had formed of its dimensions, but it now appears to great disadvantage, as from old age it has not a leaf on it – Tradition gives its age, as half the Christian era – therefore being (if that is correct)

[383] V&A, Prints Drawings and Paintings Collection, accession number P65-1921.

of course 910 years old, we can only look for a kind of monument of its former state. There is a Fair held under it, on July 2nd, the origin of which was from a Citizen of London, John Day, going annually there, with a party of friends to eat Beans & Bacon.

Fig. 72. **Fairlop Oak, 1820** [384]

The road thro the Forrest is very bad at places, but I should have been sorry not to have rode thro it, as there is an air of grandeur, and solemnity in such an assemblage of lofty Oaks, and other trees which is striking to a mind that has been only accustomed to behold common plantations, or now & then a park. It was in the time of vacation, and I saw two boys there who looked so like you & Edward, that I could scarce believe they were any other than yourselves. I was glad to hear that you had begun to learn French as I think you will find it both useful and pleasant, and you will both no doubt acquire it with facility at your age, and previous course of education. I am likewise pleased

---

[384] The Fairlop Oak, 'Drawn & published by G. Remington Chadwell Heath'. Vestry House Museum, London Borough of Waltham Forest.

that you have resumed the game of Cricket, as it is a healthy and gentlemanly sport. I read your letter to the family here, who were much pleased with it, and desire I will give their united love to yourself & Edward, who I hope will let me hear from him before I leave this part. God bless you my dear Boys is the prayer of your affectionate Grandmother

C Curling -

Three weeks after Catharine had written her letter, Thomas III sat down at the Reverend Abbot's boarding school to reply:

Ramsgate 25th Sept, 1819

Mrs Curling
Stone House
Near Great Marlow
Buckinghamshire

My Dear Grandmother,

As you said in Edward's letter that you wished me to write to you, to give you some account of the Isle of Thanet Races, I take great pleasure in complying with your wish. My Father was so kind as to send for us on Wednesday, and we walked to Dandelion, and got there just as the Horses were going to start; which was better than getting there early, as we should only have had to wait. They were excellent Races and were well attended; there were no less than twenty three thousand people, a number which Mr Friend said he never recollected seeing, at Canterbury or any other races; the carriages were seven deep a great way round the course, and the people on horseback ... exceeded all description. Mr Palmer won the first plate, beating Mr Page, Mr John Curling, and Mr Duihampton. Mr Curling must have beat, if his mare had been properly trained previously, as she was

Fig. 73. **A vignette of 'Dandylion' races** [385]

*rather in too good condition; he had a jockey from the Prince
Regent's own stables, on purpose that his horse might be properly
trained; but the man was quite ignorant of the manner of training a
horse and consequently ... lost. Mr Duihampton rode his own horse,
and got a very bad fall whilst riding the first heat; he was sent home
to Mr Gillow's where he was staying; but he was a great deal better
the next morning; as Captain Clowes who was staying at our house,
and myself, went up to St Nicholas, to enquire how he did, he fell on
his head, consequently he was much hurt about that part; his fall was
occasioned by his turning the corner rather too swift by which his
horse was flung down; it was an excellent race between Mr Palmer's
and Mr Page's. The next heat there were several horses ran but the
two best were the horses belonging to the two Mr Neames, but after
two obstinate and well contested races M^r R Neame was the victor.
Mr Garner won the next easy. He also won the next day, beating the
same horses. Mr Pullen won the plate for the losing horses; he had
entered into a plate on Wednesday on purpose to get beat that he*

---

[385] *A Trip to Margate*, Plate 6, Paul Pry, pub. Thomas McLean, undated, but plates
watermarked 1827. Paul Pry was a pseudonym of the artist William Heath
(information from NMM website). Digital image supplied by SPL Rare Books, a
wonderful treasure trove to browse. Its income supports the British Asian
Trust: https://www.britishasiantrust.org/.

might be entitled to run in the losing horses plate however he had a hard struggle for it. All the race Horses looked exceeding well; there were two boys rode, one so very small that I do not think he was higher than my brother Robert's shoulder. My Father had a party after the races on Wednesday. Mr Ashenden, Mr Friend, Captain Clowes and two or three others ca ... the party. I dare say you have heard of the death of Sir Edward Knatchbull ... last Saturday; his two sons are gone home; he has left eighteen children, the youngest only four months old; he is much lamented here, as he always took the part of Ramsgate in Parliament. Mr Diggs has left the Watch House, and is going back to Ireland soon, the reason why he left was because they ordered him not to depart from the Watch House at any time, nor to visit any person in the neighbourhood without first writing to Margate, to ask the permission of the Lieutenant; a Mr Drake has taken his place. I like the French language very much as does Edward likewise. Mrs Curling said she should ask us up to Ozengell next Sunday at the races; but she has sent word down that she will ask us out next Sunday week instead; they were at the Races both days, they came and stood by us the whole time in their chaise. Julia Clowes was also there as she was staying at Ozengell during the races. Mrs Curling was so kind as to say she would ask us out next Sunday, but she sent down to tell us that it would be the Sunday after that we might not be disappointed. Edward received your letter on the 21st ins^t; and returns thanks for it. His bird is dead and the servant was [so] *careless as to let one of my gold finches go when she opened the door to put fresh water in, she forgot to shut it and the bird flew away; but Edward is going to buy another when he goes home for the Christmas Holydays. We are to have my Uncle Becker's poney in the next Holydays, to go hunting; I am very glad of it as it is a very nice one and the little poney gets too old and too small for me and Edward. You said in the letter ... me ... at there ... er Thames I should like to see it ver ... as I have never seen anything of the ... large a river as the Thames; the river ... the only one I have ever seen; but I am ... is not near as large as the river Thames, ... island, as large as that you speak of, can ... Stour. I should like to Walk in such large ... you speak of; but there were very large ones at Nye, and we used to go nutting in them, always on half holydays, two or three boys generally went ... partey with one another in the profits of the day.*

Fig. 74. **Children Nutting** [386]

We have not done bathing yet, but I do not think that we shall keep it on longer than next month or the end of this; as I think the weather gets a great deal colder. There are a great many people here this summer but of very inferior quality, than the preceding years. Sir John Honywood's and Sir Henry Ahenden's sons are coming very soon; we have got thirty boys this half year. John Bridges came home to the Races but I did not see him. We saw my Uncle Becker[387] at the Races both days. He staid at Margate during the Races; he gave us a half crown between us.

My Mother told me she had received two letters from you; and that you were coming to Sandwich on the 13th or 14th of October. I

---

[386] *Children Nutting*, etching, 1788, William Ward and Edward Dayes after George Morland, image with thanks to Donald A Heald Rare Books and Prints, https://www.donaldheald.com/. Nutting (i.e. gathering nuts) was a traditional activity amongst rural children of the period. The children in this illustration are snacking close to home as evening draws in.

[387] Michael Becker III, see **Appendix 4a – The Becker-Solley family of Kent** (p. 170).

hope you will write when you get to sandwich to tell me whether you have got down safe and with the most sincere love; I am,

    My Dear Grandmother

    Your affectionate grandson

        Thomas Curling

Sunday afternoon 26th Sept I have mentioned one thing over twice in my letter

The final letter in this set came from Catharine, a full month after Thomas III had written to her.

                    Sandwich Oct 26th 1819

My dear Grandson

    I felt very much gratified by your affectionate solicitude respecting my journey from Berkshire, and safe return to Sandwich; and for the request that I would inform you of my arrival at this place; which it was my intention to have done before, but I was unwell for several days after I came here, being much fatigued with travelling so far, which to me is rather unusual; and I have had many of my relations and particular friends to call on me almost every day. I took leave of my dear sister's family at Stone House on Monday 18th inst, which is 32 miles from London and met your Father that evening in the Strand; we left Town next morning at eight oclock, and I reached Sandwich at seven in the evening, having parted from your Father at Canterbury, who proceeded to Sarr in a Margate Coach. It was a great satisfaction to me to have his protection and assistance on my journey, as he kindly prevented my having the least trouble or inconvenience. I conclude you know he was then returning from Brentwood Fair which was held on 15th & 16th inst.

    Accept my best thanks for your entertaining letter of 25th inst, your account of the Races was perfectly clear, and well expressed, and afforded much pleasure to myself, your Uncle, Aunt, and Cousins. I was glad to find the sport had been so good, and so much company present, indeed I never remember to have heard of such an assemblage of spectators at Margate Races before ---

Fig. 75. **The Cambridge Telegraph Coach at the White Horse Tavern** [388]

I was much obliged to you for informing me of the death of M^r
Edward Knatchbull; for although it was a very melancholy
occurrence, yet one does not like to remain ignorant of such an event
having taken place; I did not at that time see a newspaper and no one
of my correspondents mentioned his death but yourself; a respectable
public character, and the father of eighteen children, must be
considered a great domestic and general loss; and I was pleased with
the observations you made on the services he had rendered to
Ramsgate in Parliament, and of the regret felt by its inhabitants for

---

[388] ©National Trust Images. Image number 985660. Full title: 'The Cambridge Telegraph
Coach at the "White Horse Tavern & Family Hotel", Fetter Lane, London 1857', by
James Pollard. Greg Roberts, who has been researching nineteenth-century coaching,
sent me a quotation from the timetable for 1819: 'Canterbury, Kent [56 miles] Coach –
White Horse, Fetter Lane – daily and hourly, and Sunday afternoon at 6pm.' So this
painting shows the very inn from which Catharine and her son Thomas would have left
on 19 October 1819. The coach in the picture is going to Cambridge, but although this
picture of it was painted thirty-eight years after their journey it gives a very good
impression of what their departure would have been like.

their loss; as they assured me you did not suffer important events to pass "unheeded by" or without making suitable reflection on them.

Your Aunt Kelly being informed by your letter, that you were pleased with learning the French language, felt a desire to address you in it, and gave me a letter to convey to you, which I will take the opportunity of sending in a cover with this of mine; I am going tomorrow (Thursday) to dine at Shuart that I may see your Mother for a few hours; I shall take the letters to her as I know she will have the goodness to get them sent to Ramsgate on Saturday by some of the marketing people. As I have never acquired any knowledge of French, I must be content to write to you in English, but I should be pleased, if I was competent to correspond with you in that fashionable and useful language which you are now commencing the study of, to endeavour to promote your improvement in it, by inducing you to write, and converse in French as soon as you are able, without waiting till you can do so with that facility which requires time and practice to effect; your Aunt Kelly tho I am sure she will be happy to receive a letter from you, will not expect an answer to hers till you may feel it pleasant to address her. she frequently said how happy she should feel to see yourself and Edward at Stone House, that you might go on the Thames, and stroll in the finer young woods in that neighbourhood, there are no Forrests near to their present residence, as there was in Essex but many ... beautiful views over a fine country. I was pleased that my ... description of it amused you at all, as I had not much ... epistolary intercourse, seeing very few persons, and those strangers to you. ---- You must regret the removal of your friend Mr Diggs, as I understood you passed many hours in his society during the summer vacation, and will miss your favourite Neptune. I was sorry to hear of the loss of yours, and Edwards birds, and have no doubt but the poor maid servant was concerned that she had been so remiss, in her care of yours as to let it escape from the cage at Xmas when you have supplied the loss, you will be able for some weeks to take them under your own immediate care, which will be a pleasant employment; there is one bad thing attending to nursing these little protégées, that when, in spite of every possible attention, any disaster befalls them; it occasions a sensation of painful regret for a day or two, longer than that you would not allow yourselves to grieve for a bird.

I am at present with my friends Miss Stewart, & Miss Kirkwood, who send their kind remembrance to you both.

God bless you my dear boys, and believe me
Your Affectionate Grandmother
                              C. Curling

Oct 27th I go tomorrow to Shuart in a post chaise with Miss Stewart, and we return to Sandwich in the evening.

Appendix 6b – Mary Ann and Matthew Curling Friend

Matthew Curling Friend

The Friend and Curling families had been united by the marriage in 1771 of John Friend and Mary Curling. They were the parents of Matthew Curling Friend, born 1792, whose period in the navy during the Napoleonic Wars included serving on HMS Bucephalus, which then escorted Napoleon to exile on the island of St Helena.

After the Napoleonic wars Matthew turned to scientific interests, and in 1817 constructed a meridian line in the Clock House of Ramsgate Harbour. On 16 March 1820, certified as 'a gentleman of great acquirements, particularly in nautical and practical astronomy', he was elected Fellow of the Royal Society. In 1822 he entered Sydney Sussex College, Cambridge; in 1827 he received the gold medal of the Medico-Botanical Society of London, and later, a diploma from the Royal Statistical Society of France.[389]

It is quite likely that Matthew was the 'Mr Friend' in Thomas's letter. Matthew later settled in Van Diemen's Land, where he was for many years a prominent member of the community. His first wife Mary Ann kept a journal, which included many illustrations, during their first journey to Hobart. Matthew returned to England, setting in Clevedon, Somerset, for the final years of his life.

Mary Ann made a name for herself as an artist. The National Library of Australia has the following biographical note for her:

> **Mary Ann Friend, née Ford,**
>
> **b. c.1800, d. George Town, Tasmania 1838**
>
> Mary Ann Friend captured early impressions of her new homeland, Australia, often depicting dry landscapes which highlighted the struggles of the early pioneers.
>
> A sketcher and lithographer, Friend [was] born in London, daughter of John Ford of Hampstead. In 1826 she married Matthew Curling Friend (1792–1871), a retired naval officer, inventor and nautical scientist. Three years later they left Portsmouth on board the *Wanstead*, a merchant ship of which her husband was master, transporting settlers to the new Swan River settlement in Western Australia. They arrived on 30 January 1830 ... In March, Mary Ann made a drawing of the camp at Fremantle on the banks of the Swan River where she, her husband and her husband's brothers, Daniel,

---

[389] Phillip K. Cowie, 'Friend, Matthew Curling (1792–1871)', ADB, National Centre of Biography, Australian National University, http://bit.ly/App6aMCFriend, published first in hardcopy 1966, accessed online 11 August 2019.
This article was first published in hardcopy in *Australian Dictionary of Biography*, vol. 1, (MUP), 1966.

Charles and George, were living. (Two of the brothers, her husband and the artist herself can be seen in the image.) Later published as a lithograph, her 'View at Swan River.[390] Sketch of the Encampment of Mattw Curling Friend, Esqr. R.N. Taken on the Spot & Drawn on Stone by Mrs M.C.F. March 1830 (Mitchell Library)' shows the unusual core structure of her temporary home and studio (supplemented by tents and tarpaulins) – a 'horse house' from the ship converted into what she herself called a 'cottage orné'.[391]

---

[390] See p. 109.

[391] Extract from an online biography of Mary Ann Friend on the website of Design and Art Australia Online: http://bit.ly/App6MAFriendbiog

Appendix 8a – T H Scott

It is probable that this T H Scott was Thomas Hobbe Scott, secretary to John Thomas Bigge, the commissioner of enquiry mentioned in a letter from Macquarie, governor of New South Wales, to Earl Bathurst, written on 21 March 1821:

> *My last General Dispatch to your Lordship was dated the 7th February of the present Year, and was entrusted to the care of Thos. H. Scott, Esqr., Secretary to the Commissioner of Enquiry; and I have now to report to your Lordship that Commissioner Bigge and his Secretary, Mr. Scott, sailed from hence in His Majesty's Storeship Dromedary on the 14th of last Month both in perfectly good Health.*

Macquarie's next letter, four months later, gives clarification

> *My Lord, I had the honor of addressing Your Lordship last, under date the 21st March, per Ship Shipley, commanded by Captn. Moncrief, to whom I gave charge of My Dispatches of that date, including the Duplicates of those forwarded by H. M. Store Ship Dromedary, which Sailed for England on the 14th of February, and on which Ship Commissioner Bigge and his Secretary, Mr Scott, went home Passengers*

When Thomas Oakley Curling was making his applications to emigrate and using Scott as a point of reference, a possible reason for Scott's confusing signals to Thomas II was that Scott himself may have been preoccupied with his own plans. Towards the end of the same letter, Macquarie also wrote:

> *I beg leave to report to Your Lordship that I have deemed it expedient for the good of the public Service to make the following Colonial Appointments and Promotions, until his Majesty's Pleasure shall be known thereon ...*
>
> *Mr. Thomas Scott to be Assistant Surveyor of Lands in Van Diemen's Land, with a Salary of 5s per Diem.*

Scott himself was in the throes of preparing to emigrate to Van Diemen's Land.

Appendix 8b – A testimonial

Testimonial on behalf of Thomas Oakley Curling from those who knew him

September 1821

We whose names are subscribed below, do affirm that we have known Mr. T. O. Curling of Shuart Farm in the Parish of St Nicholas in Thanet, for many years past. That his family and connections are highly respectable – That he has been regularly brought up, from his earliest years, to the business of Farming and Grazing, and for seventeen years past has occupied and managed a Farm of upwards of [five] hundred Acres of ploughing and pasture land that his habits of business have been those of an industrious [re]gular and active man – That he has been for twenty three years past a member of the Thanet Troop of Yeomanry (Coast) and upon all occasions has evinced his loyalty and attachment to the government. – That his conduct as a Neighbour has also entitled him to the approbation and good will of all those who have known him, having been uniformly hospitable, friendly and conciliatory. – And, that we as most sincerely regret the necessity he is under of leaving his native country [as] would earnestly recommend him to the notice and good offices of those who may have it in their power to serve him.

Henry Oxenden,
  Broome Kent
Deane I^r: Parker,
  Banker Canterbury
Henry Stewart, a Magistrate
  for the County of Kent
Chas. Emmerson
  Banker, Sandwich
John Garrett, Capt of Isle of
  Thanet Troop of Yeom^ry
Robert Garrett, Capt. 90th Reg^t
George Hannam
  Magistrate for ye Liberties
  of ye Cinque Ports
Latham Osborn
Edward Thompson of Dover

W Frederick Bayley Vicar of
  Margate, a Magistrate for the
  County of Kent
T Staines Captn. R.N.
  K.C.B. K.S.F &c
J^no. Bridges. St Nicholas.
Edw. Boys Magistrate for the
  County of Kent
R Halford Senr. & Junr
  Bankers Canterbury
Mantell Magistrate of Dover
Thos. Garrett. L^t. Col^l.
  East Kent Reg^t. Yeom^y
Henr. Latham Mayor of Dover
Danl. Jarvis of Margate Surgeon

Appendix 10a – Letter from Van Diemen's Land

Thomas Oakley Curling's letter was written almost a year after he and his family had arrived in Van Diemen's Land. This letter is often quoted in published texts on the lives of early settlers in Australia, and particularly Van Diemen's Land. It was written to Sir Thomas Mantell, who had signed Thomas II's petition for assisted passage. The only currently available text is the contemporaneous copy held in the Liverpool Papers at the British Library,[392] which I have presumed is faithful to Thomas II's original. The item immediately preceding this copy in the Napier Papers folder of originals is Mantell's cover letter to Lord Liverpool, dated 21 August 1824[393] which confirms that the original of the copy letter he is sending was written by Thomas Oakley Curling. The complete text of Thomas II's letter follows. There is virtually no paragraphing, so it takes a little time to get into the swing of his writing style; but it is worth persevering to the end for the insight it offers into the way of life and the thinking of a settler of the time.

Guilton on the Lake River, Van Diemen's Land 14ᵗʰ Nov 1823

My Dear Sir

> *Among the many friends I had in England and whom I wish to convince that change of climate does not always make a change of feeling, stands your name and I trust a letter written under these feelings from the Land of Speculation and hope to so many of the English Nation will prove acceptable to you; independent of the account it may contain of the situation of the family of one who has been so long known to yourself and your Relations.*

> *Whether or not it proceeds from the English expecting more than they ought from an uncultivated country it is almost an universal feeling that disappointment should take place on the first view of this Colony and a wish arise that the voyage had never been undertaken particularly in those who were not fit at first to leave home not having a sufficient stimulus caused by misfortune or a strong wish to mend their condition to make them bear up against every unfavourable prospect all such had better stop in England as there is a great deal of trouble required to procure a little comfort in the first stages of a settlers condition, to those who like myself were impelled by necessity or some other motive equally strong to proceed forward without*

---

[392] BL Add MS 38299 ff 67–75.
[393] BL Add MS 38299 ff 65–66, given in full in **Appendix 10b – Commentary on the letter from Van Diemen's Land** p, 202.

looking to right or left for a better Country to fix themselves in, the first strange appearance of the Land gradually wears off and a more just estimate begins to be formed of the value of the place very different from the first impressions, the climate is found to be something changeable like England but much less in extremes as to changes from day to day as well as in the difference between Winter and Summer, Winter here resembles a fine English November; there was no ice thicker than a sixpence, no snow except on the high tiers of mountains, or any cold weather during the whole Winter to make us shut our door more than two or three times in the day time; there were many hoar Frosts which made it cold in the mornings and evenings and towards the Spring cut our forward potatoes and in the Spring the Turkey Beans; this part of the year is very pleasant but further in the Summer it is hotter than the generality of English Summers but the heat is more mild and soft and in my opinion not so oppressive as I have known the weather in July at home; the soil is very variable, at parts very rich but rich and bad are intermixed in small patches much more than in England the poorer parts will produce more than would at first be thought on account of the fineness of the Climate; Wheat weighs from 60 to 70 lb per bushel and all corn would grow very fine if the land which is fit for the plough was at all well farmed, there is not more than one tenth of the inhabited part of the Island fit to grow corn from being wet, covered with timber or unequal on the surface; great part of the Country resembles the waves of the Sea, not the short waves near the shore but the long swells of the great Ocean which are 200 yards and more apart. The land is not thickly timbered about here all the underwood being burnt away as the Grass is fired in Summer therefore as soon as the Timber is drawn off the plough goes without waiting for the stumps being grubbed the tops of the Trees forming the first fence – the Pasture is not good and in my opinion injured by the long succession of burning when dry in Summer it does not keep at present more than one Sheep on three Acres but it would keep three on one acre in Summer if the land was fenced and fed down to prevent the necessity of firing the long Grass, sown with English Grass after ploughing the land would keep five the year round on an average; Sheep grazing pays 100 per cent per annum at the present price 5d per lb for mutton as you are sure that each Ewe will produce two Lambs in 15 months as lambing and shearing goes on all the year round; my ewes began lamb about the 20th of April and there are near *a score of them which have already turned off their first lamb and got a second, one ewe had two in May both now well and had two last night both well this is the most profitable way of employing capital and there is no drawback except the loss by sheep stealers to insure against whom it would be worth 8 per cent as they take 200 at a time, cattle are not so hazardous but they do not pay so good a return but even Cattle grazing is better than farming which does not pay at any distance from the Towns, Wheat can be grown at 4*s*/- the bushel it now sells at 5 *s*/- but 2 *s*/- will not pay the carriage and keep the Farmers the greatest part of whom are in a State of Insolvency I mean the second rate settlers who have no Flocks and generally speaking are idle extravagant drunkards – as to myself my farm is beautifully situated for grazing; the Country round my hut beautiful in prospect and tolerably good in general tho I have not more than 100 acres out of 1000 that will plough to any profit; I do not intend to work more than enough for my own consumption as I am 30 miles from Launceston I have 20 acres sown with wheat 2 with potatoes and peas and ½ an acre of old Stockyard for a Garden now producing finer Vegetables than ever I saw in England and in which young apple trees, Currants, Strawberries, Raspberries, Melons and all sorts of herbs are looking very promising. I shall make 20 acres of Fallow for next years Crop, I have got 365 sheep, 6 working Bullocks some Pigs but no Cows at present; Cows with calves by their sides are worth from £12 to £20, Sheep about 20*s*/- each, a Mare and foal £150 – my family all work at farming and sheepkeeping – I have three convict men who behave very well and I have very little fear but that I shall do well but am very short of money which is a very general complaint in the Colony, it requires £2000 in Cash or Property to come from England and establish a family like mine in the Country as many things are very expensive it cost me £150 after leaving the ship before I reached my farm; an industrious Single man could get on with £500, a person who has not that sum on landing has no business here, unless he is a Carpenter, Blacksmith or Shoemaker as those trades must answer if the Man will keep sober I like the Country very much and am very glad I came, Land is getting very scarce in this Island but there is plenty at Sydney untaken beyond the Blue Mountains people who come here must not expect much comfort but ought to look well out against Villainy no easy John's will thrive here there is plenty of intellect in all classes but little honesty – A Gentleman of your profession of respectability who had landed when I did might by this* time be in the receipt of £600 a year by his Profession (my own calculation) and he would have got his grant of land according to his Property which he might either sell or let, and employ what capital he might have at liberty in grazing Sheep on thirds, that is by giving a Grazier one third of the increase at the end of the years for feeding and taking care of them, this system pays both parties well as 100 ewes in three years will increase to about 1100 sheep; a Person came out in the Regalia as a steerage passenger and is now in partnership with Mr Cartwright a brother of Tom Cartright who was at Pettmans and they are doing a great deal of Business also Mr Dawes has lately began Practice, has married (Miss Lord) and is doing well – ... – nevertheless there is still an opportunity of doing well expenses of House rent are high in Hobart Town but a man might buy or build a house for £250 good enough to reside in. I wish my cousin William Curling had come out, he might have settled himself well as there must be a great run of business for the profession from the number of Executions and Transfers of Property which are now and will for some time arise from the distress for money many men with good property in Land Cattle and Sheep cannot raise £100 for the life of them therefore on a pinch something comes to the hammer at a low price for hard cash I bought 120 sheep by Auction for Dollars at 14/6 each and would not now take 30/- each for them and their increase, they were very cheap as I gave 26/6 for some a week after not so forward in lamb – a Man must not expect to return home from here with a fortune in a few years but must be content to grow rich in land and Cattle; if he forces a Sale of these to return it will be at half their value; it is the Country for me to establish my family of boys; those who come out and for short periods had better content themselves with the sale of Merchandise and take Wool back to England; all Articles of Merchandize are low in price nearly or quite as cheap as the retail price in England – provided they are bought here by the dozen or in that proportion but the Cape of Good Hope is the best place for a Merchant there as well as in Hobart Town Auctions daily take place and goods are sold frequently at half the prime Cost in England, it is very difficult to name articles that would pay well here Brandy Rum and Salt Pork perhaps as well as anything I have given my friend Champion a list of what a settler should bring, therefore I refer you to him in case you have a friend coming and I have given him a long account of the Country and leave people to judge for themselves; all I say is I have no wish to return unless to see my old friends once more and then come to this Country again to end my days, I wish my steps had been directed here when I had property; I should have been well off indeed ere this time. There is a M*r* Leith about 15 miles from me who came from Chatham and says he is related to you and mentioned the circumstances of your Uncle's being robbed; he is coming to see me to talk over Kent and buy some of the breed of Pigs I brought out from England; he is very industrious, makes shoes for his family and does much within himself. I believe he has been in the Commissariat the bush rangers robbed him some time back and now he and his men go armed to Plough and he is contriving Traphatches in his house to catch them like rats and mice and good luck to his traps I say for he is in the worst neighbourhood for those Gentry – Now my dear Sir you were so good as to say you would once more try to get a word in for me with those able to serve me, the case stands thus, every person coming here gets his grant of land according to the Amount of Property he makes Oath to having brought with him thus a Jew Matchmaker gets as much as I did by the regulations of the Colony; you recollect I was disappointed about a free passage after some encouragement being held out to me in that way. Baron Bubra a German has arrived here with a large family and I believe he gets a grant of land for himself and in addition ones for his son 13 years old on hearing this I sent my letters of introduction to Sir Thomas Brisbane to ask the favour of Grants for two of my sons of the ages of 17 and 16 years this was in June last and I have as yet received no answer therefore I conclude my application has not been successful; can you therefore get a word from the Earl of Liverpool to the Colonial Office for my six Sons out here to have grants allowed them at the earliest age it can be allowed it is of material consequence to me as I may otherwise lose the opportunity of fixing them near me in places which would be valuable – joined to my farm but of little value to Settlers of respectability and I shall have for neighbours the emancipated convicts who get Grants of a few Acres and are by no means desirable near a Sheep run – the readiest way to accomplish this object would be a recommendation in my favour to Colonel MacArthur who is to succeed Colonel Sorrel in him every Settler will lose a friend he has been very kind to me in everything and his departure will be much lamented but it strikes me he will remain in the Island as he is rich in flocks and herds.

Nov 20*th* I am on the point of going to Hobart Town to bring home my Merino Rams left there on landing I shall endeavour to get the

Captain of a Ship to take this in which case I will enclose a few Newspapers which I beg the favour of you to forward afterwards to my friend Champion at Sarr together with a short Postscript to a Letter I sent which you may read before you send – I beg you to remember me to your Uncle Messrs White and Francis and particularly to my old friend Miss Oakley also to Master John, to whom I wish every success in life mention my remembrance also to Messrs Hulkes, John Iggulden, Miss Knocker and Miss Betsey Oakley and all Deal friends who care anything about me.

Hobart Town Decr 7th 1823 The stagnation in all business till the new Bank opens is beyond precedent great Dollars have been caught up to make payments on the Bank shares to such a degree that £10 cannot be raised on Goods worth £200 nearly all the parties who have issued notes are insolvent I suppose there is £10,000 worth of bad notes about this place the issuers may be able to pay in a few Months but at present no Dollars are seen in circulation; they would be worth 6^s/- in discounting good Bills – things are certainly in a bad state here – but wheat is worth 10^s/- per bushel in the interior – washed Wool 8^d pence p lb – I shall be much obliged to you to put the enclosed in the post

I am Dear Sir

Most sincerely yours

T O C [394]

[394] BL Add MS.38299 ff.67-75, There is no signature in the British Library copy, but it is initialled as above, and catalogue details give Thomas Oakley Curling as the author.

Appendix 10b – Commentary on the letter from Van Diemen's Land

Sir Thomas Mantell,[395] the recipient of the 1823 letter, was, as already mentioned, one of the signatories on the testimonial[396] signed by Thomas Oakley Curling's friends when he was making his preliminary applications to be allowed passage to Van Diemen's Land. The letter arrived at Mantell's home in Dover in August 1824. Forwarding a copy of the letter to Lord Liverpool Mantell wrote in his cover note

> *My Lord,*
>
> *We beg leave to transmit for your Lordships perusal the accompanying Copy of a Letter from Mr Thomas Oakley Curling, dated from Van Diemens Land the 14 Nov. 1823 Conceiving so detailed a Statement of the Colony from a practical Kentish Farmer may be interesting to Your Lordship ~*
>
> *And we avail ourselves of this Opportunity to recommend to Your Lordships Attention his Application to Sir Thomas Brisbane for Grants of Land to his Sons, And to solicit your Lordships Interference with the Colonial Office that the Grants may be made as near to the Land occupied by Mr Thomas Oakley Curling as may be found convenient.*

We have the honor to be,
My Lord, Your much obliged
faithful Servants~
T Mantell
Geo. J. P. Leith[397]

Sr T. Mantell
desired I would
sign also
  G.J.P.L.

Mantell was an important figure in Dover society, mayor of Dover in 1809, 1812, 1819 and 1824 and a relative by marriage of Thomas II. The obituary for Sir Thomas published in the *Gentleman's Magazine* (January 1832) records that he married Anne Oakley, daughter of William Oakley, mariner, of Dover, who was an uncle of Thomas Oakley Curling's mother Catharine. Thomas II's request to be remembered to two Oakley women supports this. Sir Thomas Mantell was a

---

[395] For biographical details of Sir Thomas Mantell, see his obituary in *The Gentleman's Magazine*, vol. 151, pp. 88–89 and 651. https://bit.ly/App10bMantell.

[396] **Appendix 8b – A testimonial** (p. 195).

[397] BL MS Add 38299 ff 65–66. The George Leith whom Mantell asked to be co-signatory may have belonged to the family of the Mr Leith whom Thomas II mentions in his letter as being related to Mantell and who is in Van Diemen's Land with him.

surgeon practising in Dover with a keen interest in history, and a Fellow of the Society of Antiquaries, having published several books on historical topics. His wife Anne had apparently been an actress prior to her marriage.[398]

As well as being Prime Minister, Lord Liverpool was also Lord Warden of the Cinque Ports, and until taking up the premiership had been Secretary for War and the Colonies, all reasons why Thomas II's letter might have been of interest to him.

Prior to starting family history research it had not occurred to me that in earlier centuries, before the era of photocopiers and scanners, handwritten copies of interesting letters might be made by recipients in order to share them with colleagues, family or friends. But as my research progressed I discovered that this was in fact common practice both between family members and at an official level. Examples are mentioned in the Napier Papers correspondence in the British Library in which from time to time members of the Napier family copied relatives' letters to pass on to each other, and in the Royal Navy archives at the Caird Library in the National Maritime Museum, where copy books of all outbound letters are held. Thomas II's letter had been written to Sir Thomas Mantell, who had a copy made and sent to Lord Liverpool, with a covering letter requesting any available help for Thomas II's appeal that he should have his formal grant of land.

Thomas II's letter is full of practical information to be relayed to prospective settlers, demonstrating to his recipient the seriousness of his intention to succeed in the grand project which so many people had helped him undertake.

He gave his address at the head of the letter as Guilton on the Lake River. Guilton is the name of an area in the parish of Ash-next-Sandwich, Kent, where his wife Jane had been brought up by her parents Michael and Jane (I) Becker from the age of eleven – prior to that her family had lived in Dover.[399] Thomas II had named his new property Guilton, probably to please Jane, but the name of the farm had changed to Rockthorpe by 1825, when his grant of land was noted in John Helder Wedge's diary, and Rockthorpe is still its name today. The farm is now a prominent sheep stud.[400]

At the outset of the letter Thomas hinted at the arduous nature of the undertaking, citing a universal feeling of disappointment when new settlers saw the colony. He said that he felt this had happened because the uncultivated land did not meet their expectations, and that this was particularly true of those whose motivation for the enterprise was insufficiently strong. When the disappointment wore off, a more

---

[398] See Lorraine Sencicle's blog 'The Dover Historian': http://bit.ly/App10bAnneOakley.
[399] Ash-next-Sandwich Parish Family Reconstitution Form [FRF], courtesy of David Cave, former parish archivist.
[400] https://bit.ly/App10bPolwarthSheep This is the most up-to-date information in which Rockthorpe is mentioned. There are other online database references. The owner of Rockthorpe sheep stud is named as R E Lawrence.

balanced view began to form. The climate was found to be generally milder than England's, with fewer extremes both day to day and between seasons. He found the quality of the soil patchy, varying between rich and poor – but it turned out that even the poorer soil would produce a decent crop because the climate was so good. Grass was 'fired' in summer, by which he may have meant stubble-burning after harvest. Whatever his meaning, Thomas II deplored the practice as he thought it injured the soil.

The crops he began growing included early potatoes, Turkey beans, wheat and peas, and in his garden, vegetables, apple trees, currants, strawberries, raspberries, melons and herbs. His principal stock was sheep, of which he had 365; he felt they were the best investment, being the most profitable use of capital. He outlined the farming methods employed and warned of the hazards of sheep stealers, insurance against the problem being expensive. Cattle were not so easy to steal but they did not provide as solid a profit as sheep. If the farm was not near a town (and his farm was 30 miles from Launceston) even cattle were better than 'farming', by which he must have meant arable crops. He had six working bullocks (probably for ploughing and drawing carts) but no cows at the time of writing and was already in a position to sell some of the pigs which he had brought with him from England. What with the sheep and the pigs, the hold of the ship *Cumberland* must have been unbearable both for the livestock and their owners, and it must have been extremely challenging to keep the animals healthy throughout the five-month journey.

Thomas eulogized the beautiful setting of his farm, both for its location regarding grazing and for its aesthetics. However, he decided to cultivate only enough land to feed the family because they were so far from the town; the implication was that it would not be cost-efficient to grow crops for sale.

The whole family worked 'at farming and sheep-keeping' – although I presume baby Arthur was not required to do time in the fields. There is a warning that the cost of coming from England and settling as a farmer is high. Thomas was optimistic about his prospects but at the time of writing was 'very short of money', adding that this was a general complaint in the colony, with the implication that it was not through any imprudence on his part. He detailed the low price which sheep were fetching, although, having bought some at bargain prices he would not now part with them for double the money. He told Mantell that certain trades and professions were in sufficient demand to support their practitioners adequately and even in some cases would make sufficient to build a house. He also mentioned products which might sell well for the prospective retailer – brandy, rum and salt pork. There were daily auctions in Hobart, presumably goods which settlers had found they didn't need, or which they were selling having decided to return to England, and bargains were to be found.

Thomas implied that he was planning to stay in Van Diemen's Land for the long term, because it would take time to grow rich in land and cattle, but he felt 'this is the country for me to establish my family of boys'.

Thomas twice mentioned his friend (Mr) Champion[401] who lived at 'Sarr', now spelt Sarre, a village less than 2 miles from St Nicholas-at-Wade. Thomas A(shenden) Champion had been one of the signatories on the supporting documents for Thomas's application for a grant of land. Thomas sent him 'a list of what a settler should bring', no doubt hoping that his friend would join him in Van Diemen's Land. Towards the end of the letter Thomas said he was going to enclose some newspapers which he asked Sir Thomas Mantell to forward to Mr Champion when he had finished with them, with a further note for Champion. Thomas's father had shared the Churchwardenship of St Nicholas-at-Wade with William Champion, T A Champion's father, in 1815.

Other new neighbours were mentioned, the first being Mr Leith, who knew Mantell and whose visit Thomas was looking forward to, so they could reminisce about Kent.

There are disparaging comments on the farming practices already in use by earlier settlers. Both he, and later his second son Edward, were passionate about the highest standards in farming and could not bear to see slovenly methods which led to uneconomical land use. It is strange therefore to see him criticized by surveyor John Helder Wedge for apparently slovenly practice 'a crop of corn entirely spoilt by cattle from the want of a fence'.[402] However, I suspect that the root problem in that instance was money. Thomas II's letter indicates that he was struggling financially, as were many in the colony at the time, and creating a boundary fence would have cost a considerable sum.

Coupled with this passion for farming processes was the keen business acumen on which Thomas, and later Edward, would draw to ensure a solid income for their families. The figures mattered to them, and they wanted those with whom they communicated to understand the reasons for their actions in the light of balanced financial accounts. Thomas was at pains to explain to Mantell that the hardship he was experiencing was not for want of careful money management.

It is somewhat disconcerting to a twenty-first-century mind, in the knowledge that Thomas II and Jane had not only seven sons but also two daughters – Jane and Catherine, both born before the family emigrated – to see that neither his daughters nor his wife are mentioned at all in his letter. It is a telling indication of women's place in society. When Thomas mentions making financial provision for his children, it is just his sons that he refers to. He probably assumes that his daughters

---

[401] Probably Thomas Ashenden Champion 1782–1849 (FindMyPast records).
[402] *The Diaries of John Helder Wedge 1824–1835*. See footnote 279 (p. 113) and its context.

will be somebody else's responsibility once they are married, and their place will be in their new marital home.

The significance of one point which seems to have escaped all who have, over the two centuries since it was written, quoted Thomas II's letter, is that towards the end is a plea for further practical assistance, as he appears not to have received a grant of land.

Thomas's grand project for long-term financial security for his sons via immediate hardship, adventure and endurance, looked as though it was foundering because the state of financial affairs in the antipodes turned out to be as precarious, albeit for different reasons, as it was in the old country. The value of goods had plummeted and 'nearly all the parties who have issued [promissory] notes are insolvent'. However, despite financial stagnation, and indeed serious depreciation of the dollar, Thomas was hopeful that the new bank which was to open would bring improvements.

It seems odd that Thomas should have had to wait so long to have his request for land reviewed, particularly as we know that James Ross, who arrived on the ship *Regalia* with the Curlings, had received his grant of land quite quickly after arrival. It seems from Thomas's letter that others, too, were taking precedence over him, whether because of a difference in social status, his inadequate knowledge of the system or lack of sufficient support by people of influence. Sharon Morgan has written:

> Those who had lived on or had cultivated their land were more likely to receive extra grants than those who had ignored their duty as landowners, although it was alleged that corruption and patronage played a part in such decisions. Patronage was admitted (privately, at least) by some of its beneficiaries. John Leake doubted that his additional 2000-acre grant of 1825 would have been so large had he not been under Arthur's 'frequent notice'.[403] Other factors were also considered: help in capturing bushrangers, especial endeavour in particular areas of farming, the plight of large families; all influenced officials.[404,405]

In the closing lines of his letter, Thomas II asked to be remembered to various named friends, all of whom seem to be inhabitants of Deal; they included two of his Oakley relatives, and Messrs Hulke and John Iggulden, who were shipping agents in the town, like his Oakley grandfather. The Oakleys, Hulkes and Igguldens

---

[403] Morgan's reference: West, *History of Tasmania*, p. 113.

[404] Morgan's reference: W H Hudspeth, 'Experiences of a settler in the early days of Van Diemen's Land'. Papers & Proceedings for the Royal Society of Tasmania for the year 1935, p. 151.

[405] *Land Settlement in Early Tasmania: creating an antipodean England*, p. 8, Sharon Morgan, Selwyn College, Cambridge, CUP, 1992.

provided mayors for the town many times in the seventeenth, eighteenth and nineteenth centuries.

Newspapers of the era provide excellent articles on the development in colonial virgin territories. **Appendix 10c – A newspaper review** (p. 208) had a transcript of one such article about Van Diemen's Land published only a month before Thomas II wrote his letter.

Appendix 10c – A newspaper review

A review of Van Diemen's Land in the *London Courier and Evening Gazette,* 'Tuesday evening October 5 1824'

The following article gives a vivid account of early progress in agriculture and market gardening in Van Diemen's Land. Written in the middle of the Curlings' residence in the country, the article provides a second perspective with which to compare Thomas II's views on the benefits of the climate and terrain.

VAN DIEMEN'S LAND

A series of Gazettes from Hobart-town, Van Diemen's Land, from January 30 to the 2d of April inclusive, were received yesterday at the New England Coffee-house. This Colony continues to make rapid advances in improvement. Owing to the fineness of the climate, all the fruits and plants of Europe are gradually bringing into cultivation there. Grapes, in particular, had succeeded beyond expectation, and the produce in that fruit was expected to be greater than in any section since the formation of the Colony, Other fruits, of which the crops had been extremely productive, were the green gage and all sorts of plums in great abundance; cherries, apples, raspberries, and walnuts. This latter fruit, it was supposed, would not come to perfection in this climate, but the experience of the present season, in which the walnut trees have borne for the first time, has proved the contrary, All the different species of clover answered perfectly in the soil of Van Diemen's Land; and it is remarked, that clover sown in the latter end of September had seeded in the beginning of February – a rapidity of growth extremely uncommon. The agriculturists in the neighbourhood of Hobart-town had succeeded in rearing the indigo plant. The common hollyhock, or rose-mallow, which has lately been discovered to yield a blue dye, equal in beauty and permanence to the best indigo, was also growing in several parts of the island in the greatest luxuriance. In the rearing of live stock, and in the improvement of the existing breeds of cattle and of sheep, the settlers are also proceeding prosperously. In the last accounts from this colony it was stated, that several cargoes of Merino sheep, through want of proper care and attention, had died on the voyage out, to the great disappointment of those to whom they were consigned. This evil had, however, been remedied. By the *William Shand,* which arrived at Hobart-town early in February, the colony had been again benefitted by an importation of no less than 128 fine ewes and rams of the pure Merino breed, most of them shipped from the flock of Sir John Sebright, whose attention to this subject is well known to English agriculturists. There had also been imported by another vessel, 80 full grown pure Merino sheep. Out of the whole number brought by both these vessels, only ten died on the passage.

The natives of Van Diemen's Land continued, unfortunately, to annoy the settlers. Two instances had occurred within a short period, of persons appointed to watch the flocks and herds in distant places, having been murdered by them.

Several expeditions had been planned, or were actually in progress, for exploring the interior of Van Diemen's Land, for the purpose of ascertaining the course of the rivers, or of discovering the different natural productions of the country. Capt. Rolland of the Buffs, who were stationed at Port Dalrymple, and Mr. Hardwicke, of Norfolk Plains, had recently returned from excursions – the former by land, and the latter by Bass's Straits – to examine the north-west extremity of the island. Mr. Hobbs, of Coal River, was engaged in another voyage, with two well-equipped boats, to circumnavigate the island, with instructions to examine carefully the whole coast, proceeding by the south and west, and to penetrate wherever a favourable prospect appeared. These expeditions, it was believed, would lead to the discovery of a considerable portion of valuable country to the north-west, by which the capability of grazing, and probably of future settlement, would be enlarged. The *Triton*, the first ship sent out by the Australasian Company, which has been incorporated in England, arrived at Hobart town in the latter end of January; and during its stay there, Mr. Bushby, who had come out in that vessel as mineral surveyor, was employed in examining the country in the neighbourhood of Coal River. He ascertained that that valuable article, coal, was produced there in very large quantities, and being near the surface, that mines could be formed and worked at a very moderate expense. Some of the specimens produced were deficient in bituminous matter, and therefore burnt with difficulty, but that was supposed to be incidental only to the strain of coal that lay nearest to the surface, and that the defect in quality would not be found to exist on penetrating deeper.

Her Majesty's ship *Tees* sailed from Hobart-town early in Feb. on a cruise to New Zealand; during her stay in the harbour, Mr Fielder, the purser of that ship, unfortunately fell overboard and was drowned. The first and third Lieutenants immediately after the accident leaped into the water, but their attempts to save him were without success.

The charter of incorporation of a bank at Hobart town, an accommodation long wanted by the inhabitants, had arrived, and its notes were put into circulation on the 15th March.

In the latter end of February, a new township was laid out, in the district of Coal River, advantageously situated on the bank of that stream, and the Lieut.-Governor, who presided on the occasion, had given it the name of Richmond.

The Royal Charter appointing a separate Court of Justice, and granting other privileges to Van Diemen's Land, arrived from England, in the *Hibernia* transport in the middle of March. Mr Justice Pedder, who had been appointed Judge of the Supreme Court of Van Diemen's Land, had arrived out in that vessel. On the 31st March, the Royal Charter above alluded to, was read at Government-house by the Provost Marshal, in the presence of the Lieutenant-Governor, and the principal officers and inhabitants of the colony; and a salute of 21 guns was fired on the occasion. Mr. Forbes, the new Chief Justice of New South Wales, arrived at Sydney in the beginning of March.

Appendix 11 – Did First Nations people use guerrilla tactics?

The British invasion of Australian territories was a grave threat to the way of life of the First Nations people who had inhabited them for countless centuries previously. Dealing with the acquisitive and dominating nature of the British, together with their superior weaponry and implements of every kind, was a long-drawn-out trauma for them. The worst of it was that, in common with indigenous peoples of other nations, for instance the First Nations people of North America, taken by the British, 'The Aborigines seem to have been prepared in the first years (in the eighteenth century) of European settlement to share their land with the new-comers'.[406]

Fig. 76. **Group of Natives of Tasmania** [407]

In 2002 Keith Windschuttle's book *The Fabrication of Aboriginal History*, was published, and proved controversial among Australian historians. In writing a rebuff to one of five critical articles published in the Australian magazine *Labour History* no. 85, Windschuttle said:

> Apart from that of genocide, the question of whether the Aborigines responded to British colonisation with guerrilla warfare or wars of resistance is the most important and contentious issue in this debate. Naomi Parry's paper has the virtue of addressing this question directly by focusing on the

---

[406] *Land Settlement in Early Tasmania, Creating an Antipodean England*, p. 3, Sharon Morgan, Cambridge University Press, 1992. For full quotation see **Chapter 10 – Land of Speculation and Hope**, p. 112.

[407] Artist Robert Dowling (1827–1886), National Gallery of Australia.

Sydney Aborigine named Musquito, who she describes as a 'resistance fighter' and an Aboriginal 'nationalist' [408]

This rebuttal goes on to present evidence to support his theory that there was no organized resistance which could be termed guerrilla warfare, and that the many murders committed at this time were criminal acts without political motive. His description of Musquito's activities is as follows:

> Musquito first surfaces in the historical record in the pages of the *Sydney Gazette* in 1803 and 1804. He was a well-known Aborigine on the streets of Sydney. By 1805 he was named in government orders as the main person responsible for assaults and killings of settlers in the lower Hawkesbury River district in April that year. He was captured and transported to Norfolk Island where he remained until 1813. He was sent to Van Diemen's Land where for most of the next decade he was employed on pastoral stations and as a black tracker. From November 1823 to August 1824 he led a group of Aborigines in a number of assaults on Van Diemen's Land settlers. He was captured, put on trial and executed in February 1825. His career as outlaw thus had two distinct phases, one in Sydney and the other in Van Diemen's Land.

Windschuttle quoted Naomi Parry as saying:

> [Musquito] was actually a formidable resistance fighter — someone with a very strong sense of 'nationalism', if that word is useful in this context. A Gai-Mariagal man, by 1805 Musquito had become notorious for leading 'outrages' against settlers in the lower Hawkesbury River area, and was named in Government Orders. After he and another man, Bulldog, were apprehended, Governor King pondered what to do with them. Noting the conflict had taken more Aboriginal than white lives, and believing that he could not charge them under British law, King decided to set an example and exiled them, without conviction, to Norfolk Island.[409]

Windschuttle used an argument of particular interest in this present history to counter Parry's criticisms of his theory:

> The only reason Parry gives for discounting what amounts to a solid body of evidence is that she disbelieves a report by the Bothwell Magistrate Charles Rowcroft, who identified Musquito's gang as responsible for five of the incidents in his local area. Parry claims Rowcroft's account was not reliable

---

[408] *Guerrilla Warrior and Resistance Fighter? The Career of Musquito* Keith Windschuttle, Contested Histories Forum – Responses http://bit.ly/App11Windschuttle *Labour History* 87 (2004).

[409] Naomi Parry, quoted by Keith Windschuttle in the above article. Her full article, *Many Deeds of Terror; Windschuttle and Musquito,* is in the Australian journal *Labour History*, no. 85 (November 2003) pp. 207–212, available to read online via JSTOR.

because of his description of the injuries received in one incident by one woman, Mrs Osborne, who was assaulted at the same time her husband was killed by Black Tom. Parry claims Rowcroft was unfamiliar with this particular incident. But the only evidence she offers is that he initially reported Mrs Osborne's life was 'despaired of', whereas she actually recovered from her wounds. This is hardly a compelling reason to discard Rowcroft's account of this murder, let alone his report about Musquito's other assaults in his district. In any case, Parry's doubt is misplaced. Osborne's neighbour, Robert Jones, who questioned the injured woman, confirmed that Osborne was killed by the 'tame mob, a mob of half-civilised blacks, such as have had much intercourse with white men ... The mob consisted of the blacks who were in the habit of visiting Hobarton and getting provisions and other things there'. The only Aboriginal band fitting that description in June 1824 was the tame mob led by Musquito. Parry does not comment on the four other assaults attributed to Musquito by Rowcroft, so offers nothing to question their authenticity.[410]

Rowcroft's report was not the only one. James Scott, the Bothwell surgeon, and Thomas Salmon, the chief constable at Oatlands, both of whom were in the colony in 1824 and who knew the two affected districts at first hand, gave evidence to the 1830 Broughton Committee on Aboriginal Affairs set up by Governor Arthur. They said that Musquito was responsible for 'many murders' and 'depredations' that year. The Hobart chaplain, the Reverend Robert Knopwood, agreed. He wrote in his diary in August 1824: 'Musquito the Sydney black, who has speared and killed so many stockkeepers has at last been taken and lodged in gaol.'

Parry said that the newspaper editor Henry Melville had tempered such reports by observing: 'Many deeds of terror are laid to Musquito's charge, which it is impossible for him to have committed.'[411] Parry, however, on quoting Melville's sentence, omitted the following telling clause: 'but doubtlessly, several lives were sacrificed by him'.

Rowcroft introduced Musquito in *Tales of the Colonies*, Chapter XIII, and the biographical details for Musquito are accurate. This gives added weight to Rowcroft's story, although Naomi Parry wrote:

[A] letter from the Magistrate Charles Rowcroft, which Windschuttle quotes, should be viewed sceptically. Rowcroft wrote to Lieutenant Governor Arthur on 16 July 1824 pleading for armed assistance and alleging Musquito had committed six attacks, including four murders. Many of these attacks

[410] *Guerrilla Warrior and Resistance Fighter? The Career of Musquito*, Keith Windschuttle, as above.
[411] Parry's reference: Henry Melville (ed. G. Mackarness), *The History of Van Diemen's Land from the year 1824 to 1835 Inclusive, During the Administration of Lieutenant-Governor George Arthur*, Horwitz-Grahame, Sydney 1836 (1965), p. 32.

occurred in the neighbouring territories of the Big River people, yet Windschuttle lays them at the feet of the 'detribalised black bush-rangers'.[16][412] He takes at face value Rowcroft's allegation that Musquito was involved in Matthew Osborne's murder, and that his widow's life was 'despaired of'. Yet Rowcroft did not know the Osbornes and was exaggerating. On the very day of Rowcroft's letter the Gazette reported that Widow Osborne had recovered from her injuries and published her account of the ordeal, in which she incriminated Black Tom but never mentioned Musquito.[413]

First Nations history is overwhelmingly loaded with tragedy as the people attempted to protect their homelands and heritage whether in organized guerrilla warfare or unco-ordinated individual attacks. Violent deaths occurred on both sides, and the root reason for each individual killing was clouded by partisan interest. Parry wrote:

> The only attack in which Musquito was definitely involved in 1824 was a non-fatal spearing at Pitt Water in August.[17][414] This means Musquito and Black Tom committed only one each of the eleven-recorded attacks in that year … Given that Windschuttle demands a very high standard of proof for killings of Aborigines, it is bizarre that he so readily apportions blame for attacks on settlers to just two people. Clearly, other Aborigines were launching attacks independently.[415]

Six years after the Curling family had left Van Diemen's Land, their surname and former home appear in print in an article which illustrates the danger that isolated farming families were in, and demonstrates that Thomas Oakley Curling might have been the victim of a previous attack. On p. 3 of the *Van Diemen's Land News* of 19 April 1831, the following report appeared, which includes gruesome details:

> The blacks, we regret to learn, have made their appearance at Norfolk Plains, and committed some dreadful outrages, in a quarter too which hitherto had escaped their ravages. … They first visited, (says our correspondent) about 7 o'clock on Sunday morning, a stock run of Mr. Lawrence's, where three men are stationed. Two were absent going round their sheep, the other unfortunate man was found, on the return of the shepherds, a frightful corpse, being beaten literally to pieces in the yard where he was in the act of milking, the pail being found standing by his side, and the hut plundered of its contents. No tidings of their appearance in the neighbourhood had yet got abroad; and after the murder of Mr. Lawrence's man, they were seen crawling in the long grass, and attempting to come on the hut of the late Mr. Curling, in which

---

[412] Parry's reference: Windschuttle, *The Fabrication of Aboriginal History*, p. 85.
[413] *'Many deeds of terror': Windschuttle and Musquito*, Parry, as above.
[414] Parry's reference: *Hobart Town Gazette*, 16 July 1824 and 6 August 1824.
[415] *'Many deeds of terror': Windschuttle and Musquito*, Parry, as above.

were two men, a woman and child. At this moment two of Mr. Fletcher's servants were fortunately going thither on an errand, one armed with a double barrelled gun, and it is supposed their appearance induced the savages to take the scrub [*sic*], and abandon their attempt on the hut, where their slaughter would no doubt have extended to all the inmates, as the arms they had were of course unloaded, and had to be looked up and put in order. They then stole up the scrub about 3-4ths of a mile, and attacked Mr. O'Conner's hut (formerly Abel's): here there was only one man at home, and he had been put on his guard by a man from Curling's hut, who started to give the alarm on the arrival of the men, and told him to be on his guard, as the blacks were in the scrub. Notwithstanding this caution however, the natives contrived to steal on him and deliver a spear which wounded him in the back at the moment he was leaning on a log and absolutely looking out for them. He took to his heels and got away, his wound not being dangerous, and the hut they most effectually plundered of all its contents.

Two other men belonging to Mr. Parker were not so fortunate. They fell in with some of the tribe while taking a Sunday's walk, about a mile from their master's house, and the first notice of the natives being near was, as usual the receipt of two spears from them, which wounded each of them. They contrived however to reach their master's house, after a sort of running fight with the blacks, of whom they only saw two, although spears, waddies, sticks and stones, were flying in every direction. However, they managed to keep them off, having disarmed them of their spears. One poor fellow has three spear wounds; one hit the point of his nose, which was pinned to his cheek, and two in his body. It is thought he cannot possibly recover. The other has received two spear and other wounds, but is not considered in danger.

Their numbers are variously stated, not more than six being seen together; but it appears, from comparing the time of attack at each place, that they were very widely dispersed in small parties, and their total number must have been considerable. As soon as a party could be mustered together, search was of course made after them, but they returned at 9 o'clock without any trace of them. I hear some of Mr. Lawrence's men were sent by the overseer to endeavour to come up with them in the night. The result of course remains unknown.

Increasing concern amongst the white population arose from the number of attacks on them and the premises which they regarded as theirs. In 1830, Governor Arthur set up an inquiry to look into 'the origin of the black hostility and recommend measures to stop the violence and destruction of property', and appointed Archdeacon William Broughton to chair it.[416]

In England concern was growing separately about the treatment of indigenous people in British settlements round the globe. This led in 1836 to a separate inquiry

---

[416] See Wikipedia page 'Black War' https://en.wikipedia.org/wiki/Black_War.

whose *Report of the Parliamentary Select Committee on Aboriginal Tribes (British Settlements)* was reprinted in 1837 'with comments by the Aborigines Protection Society'.[417] The full extent of the history of oppression of First Nations people in Tasmania by the British, as in their treatment of indigenous people in the territories which they seized across the empire, is still being uncovered, and the repercussions of the myriad injustices are still expanding in the twenty-first century, like the seismic ripples of an earthquake. Issue XX (2000) of *The Canadian Journal of Native Studies* carried Michael D Blackstock's article *The Aborigines Report (1837): A Case Study in the Slow Change of Colonial Social Relations*.[418] It opens thus:

> This paper is a case study in British colonial social relations as they are expressed in the Aborigines Report (Anon., 1838). The report was commissioned by the British government, and it is a valuable snapshot of the negative effects of colonialism on Aboriginal people. The author argues that these negative effects still persist because the key colonial players are still motivated by the interests of their predecessors of a century ago. Additionally, the author examines how 'good intentions' by the colonizer can fail to deliver social justice.

Ever-expanding financial acquisitiveness – greed – was the principal driver of the European empire building which had its roots in the seventeenth century, and Britain was a leader in the field. Social conscience was slow to emerge, and in the meantime layers of depredation, deprivation and abuse were laid down, and these continue to be excavated. From their next-door neighbours within the British Isles to their farthest-flung conquests like Tasmania, the British, and the many pioneers from other aggressively acquisitive nations, committed many appalling atrocities in the name of their monarch. However, the picture is necessarily complex, and there were also well-intentioned people, both British and of other nationalities, who tried to redress the balance, each in their own era.

We will probably never know whether Thomas Oakley Curling was murdered or died in another way. He had all but attained his goal of setting up his sons with an inheritance, and died just as he was about to settle down to the real work of developing his land.

---

[417] An online copy of the report is available here: http://bit.ly/ATReport1837.
[418] Available online: http://www3.brandonu.ca/cjns/20.1/cjnsv20no1_pg67-94.pdf.

Appendix 12 – Robert Gregory

Robert Gregory made only the briefest appearance in the Curling story, but his own tale is interesting, and his boarding of the *Cumberland* with Charles Rowcroft, just prior to departure, may be significant. His name appears in the Convict Records of Australia website. The researcher was Margaret Wilson.[419] She wrote that Robert Gregory

> married Jane née Millar 19/6/1822 had two boys one being Thomas Mamby Gregory and disappeared around 17/9/1825 supposedly on the *Cumberwand* or *Cumberland* and was never heard from as far as Jane (wife) was concerned, she remarried and became Jane Patterson.

The other data on the page are

Date of Birth	21st October 1801
Convicted at	Surrey Assizes
Sentence term	14 years
Ship	Malabar
Departure date	21st October 1821
Sailing to	Van Diemen's Land
Passengers	Travelled with 170 other convicts.[420]

Convict records are now viewable online, and from Robert Gregory's we have the details that he was indeed transported on the *Malabar*, departing 29 March 1821, for fourteen years for the crime of 'Uttering Forged Notes'.[421] The initial record, written in red pencil at 90 degrees to the page layout, continues

> *Gaol Report – character unknown*
> *Hulk Report – quiet & orderly*
> *Stated wife relations in London.*

This sounds as though Gregory was already married when he was convicted, that he was detained aboard one of the convict hulks to await deportation, and that his wife had relations in London. The following note was added to his record. It was

---

[419] See https://convictrecords.com.au/convicts/gregory/robert/97158.

[420] Primary Source: Australian Joint Copying Project. Microfilm Roll 88, Class and Piece Number HO11/4, p. 48. This record is one of the entries in the British Convict Transportation Registers 1787–1867 database compiled by the State Library of Queensland from British Home Office (HO) records, which are available on microfilm as part of the Australian Joint Copying Project.

[421] Gregory's convict record is viewable here: http://bit.ly/App12ConvictRecord.

written in black ink, all in the same handwriting, and ran across the normal page view at right angles to the arrival record above, which had been written in red:

September 28 1824 Neglect of Duty 25 Lashes (P.A.M.) May 4 1824
Neglect of Duty 50 Lashes, I recom^d. To be kept in the Penit^y. (P.A.M.).

This I interpret to mean that Gregory was sentenced while in prison to fifty lashes in May 1824 and twenty-five further lashes in September 1824, for 'neglect of duty'. It is odd that the September record was written before the May one, but it may simply have been that the punishments were not recorded until some time after the events, and the writer made an error while transferring them together from some other record. The initials P.A.M. are probably those of the officer who ordered the punishments. The abbreviations he wrote would seem to indicate that he recommended that Robert Gregory be kept in the penitentiary. These two punishments occurred sixteen months and twelve months prior to Robert Gregory's name appearing in the *Cumberland*'s departure list.

It is strange that Gregory made no attempt to conceal his true identity when boarding the *Cumberland*. The hasty scrawl of the boarding record and his appearance with Rowcroft throw up many questions for which we are unlikely to find answers. For example:

- Why did the boarding officer not question Gregory's authority to leave?
- Had his absence been noticed at the prison?
- Were passports required?
- Did Rowcroft, a former magistrate, and Gregory, with self-preservation skills in deception, collude, passing themselves off as master and manservant? Did they bribe the officer who added them to the ship's manifest?
- Did Rowcroft avail himself of Gregory's skills as a forger?

It would have been difficult for Gregory to complete the voyage to England, as he might well have been apprehended at the dock, so he probably left the ship in Rio de Janeiro to make a new life somewhere in South America.

Main Index

Locations Index

A

B

C

X

Names Index

A

Abbot, George (Rev.), 64–66, 69, 180, 181, 184
Abbot, William (Proctor at Canterbury), 58
Ahenden, Henry, 73, 187
Amos, Thomas (fictional character), 171–74
Anastasia, 6
Archbishop of Canterbury, 16, 58, 63, 123, 166–72
Ashenden, Mr, 71, 186
Austen, Jane, 14, 20
Austen, Mr, 167

B

Baldock, William, 51
Barnes, Ann, 166
Bathurst, Earl of, 88, 90, 92, 194
Bayliss, Carey, 6, 64
Becker, Jane I. *see* Belsey, Jane
Becker, Jane II, 6, 48–50, 65, 68, 83, 84, 87, 95, 96, 98, 109, 111, 113, 115, 116, 121–23, 165, 169, 170, 174, 203
Becker, Mary, 169, 170, 172
Becker, Michael I, 165
Becker, Michael II, 48, 49, 64, 65, 165–71
Becker, Michael III, 73, 92, 93, 122, 169–74
Becker, Peter, 165
Becker, Sarah, 169
Belsey, George, 165
Belsey, Jane, 49, 64, 65, 96, 165–71
Benbow & Alban, Messrs, 82
Bigge, John Thomas, 194
Bolívar, Simón, 120
Bootle-Wilbraham, Edward, 91–93
Bowring, Emily Stuart, 110, 116, 117
Boys, Edw, 195
Boys, John, 27, 28
Boys, Mary, 179
Bradley, Widow, 24
Bray, Gabriel, 12, 13
Brazier (artist), 55
Breton, Eliab Harvey (Eliab II), 26, 133, 140, 142, 143, 144, 153, 157
Breton, Eliab I, 20, 133, 140, 141
Breton, Lavinia, 142

D

Dowling, Robert (artist), 211
Drake, Mr, 72
Duihampton, Mr, 71

E

Edward III (monarch), 98
Elmham, Thomas, 131, 132
Elwyn, Mr, 180
Evans, Mr (Surveyor General, VDL), 104
Evernden, Mr aka Evenden, 27, 146, 148

F

Fielder, Mr, 209
Fletcher, Thomas, 110
Forster, Francis, 55
Frederick, Prince, Duke of York, 29, 32, 34, 161
Freeman, Mr, 180
Friend, Jacob, 128
Friend, Mary Ann, 109
Friend, Matthew Curling, 70, 109, 192
Friend, Mr, 70
Frost, Mrs, 47
Fuller, Thomas, 10
Funnell, Elizabeth, 165

G

Garnett, Anne, 170
George III (monarch), 37, 58, 81
Gillow, Thomas II, 24, 50, 71, 146, 148, 185
Gleig, George Robert (Rev.), 171, 173, 174
Gouger, John, 146
Gregory, Robert, 116, 119, 121, 217, 218

H

Hailly, C A, 148
Hardwicke, Mr (VDL), 209
Harvey, Michael, 143
Hasted, Edward, 133
Hattoon, Mr, 24
Hayter, Priscilla, 8, 34, 44
Hedges, Lucy. *see* Curling, Lucy Dorothy (Tooty)
Hobbs, Mr (VDL), 209
Holland, Anne, 126
Holmes, Mr, 26, 61, 62, 82

Sources Index

A

B

C

E

F

G

H

I

Other publications from Ōzaru Books

Ōzaru Books is a boutique publisher based in the Thanet village of St Nicholas-at-Wade. Our primary focus is on books with a local connection, ranging from creative writing by East Kent authors to (occasionally niche) scholarly tomes about Kentish history, but we have a secondary interest in works in translation, particularly from Eastern languages, and also tales from East Prussia. Some of our profits go to support gorilla charities, which is the origin of the name Ōzaru ('Great Ape') and our logo.

Discordant Comicals – The Hooden Horse of East Kent

George Frampton

Hoodening is an ancient calendar custom unique to East Kent, involving a wooden horse's head on a pole, carried by a man concealed by a sack. The earliest reliable record is from 1735, but other than Percy Maylam's seminal work "The Hooden Horse", published in 1909 (republished in an annotated edition in 2021: see below), little serious research has gone into the tradition.

George Frampton has rectified this, by cross-referencing dozens of newspaper reports, census records and other accounts to build a comprehensive picture of who the Hooded Horse were, why (and where) they did it, and how it related to other folk traditions.

He then goes beyond Maylam to look at the 'demise' of Hoodening in around 1921, its widely heralded 'revival' in 1966, and discovers that this narrative is in fact quite misleading, as several Hooden Horses were still active throughout that period. He includes descriptions of the current teams, and supplies plentiful appendices detailing past participants, places visited, songs performed, events on Hoodening's timeline, and the horses themselves.

Full indices make it easy for modern Men and Maids of Kent to check whether their ancestors might have been involved, and detailed references make this an invaluable resource for social historians too.

The book features over 70 full colour illustrations.

"a good read for the interested layman as well as a valuable resource for anyone interested in the custom" (The Morris Dancer)

"very readable research [...] backed up with generous quotations [...] reveals a tale of rich cultural heritage." (The Living Tradition)

"thoroughly researched [...] well presented [...] full of previously un-published interviews [...] in depth analysis [...] extremely interesting" (Around Kent Folk)

"provides a sense of the scope and history of the rarely studied practice of hoodening [...] offers the most up-to-date and comprehensive starting point for any scholar interested in the practice" (The Journal of Folklore Research)

"attractively published in hardback with numerous colour illustrations [...] A lot of admirable spadework and academic endeavour [...] copious references are given throughout" (Master Mummers)

"Frampton has left no stone unturned in his research [...] there is a very useful index, which helps make this a book to dip into profitably" (Archæologia Cantiana)

"profusely illustrated and printed in colour, it's a treat for the eyes [...] meticulous and detailed [...] a compelling and intriguing volume" (Tykes' News)

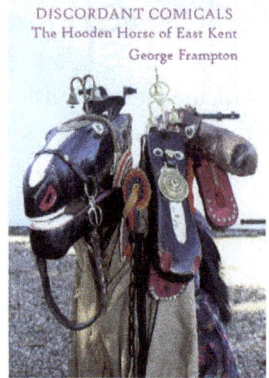

ISBN: 978-0-9559219-7-3

The Hooden Horse of East Kent – Annotated Edition

Percy Maylam

Percy Maylam's "The Hooden Horse: an East Kent Christmas Custom" was long the definitive work on Hoodening – indeed, the only full-scale study of the custom. It covered the current practice in Thanet at the start of the 20th century, past printed records, theories about its possible demise, similar customs in other parts of England and Germany, and speculation about its ancient, possibly pagan origins.

Although Frampton has arguably superseded Maylam as the authority on Hoodeners and their activities, his book still takes Maylam as a basis to explore what happened since his time. Maylam's original work is indispensable even now, but the first format is very rare, as only 303 copies were printed, and only a reduced edition appeared later.

This new eBook includes the whole of Maylam's text, with numerous features to help those wanting to push the research further – even those lucky enough to have a copy of the 1909 hardback. There are copious annotations, internal hyperlinks, images of and external links to original sources, and appendices with contemporary reviews. The eBook naturally allows readers to search the whole text, yet the page numbers are still present to enable cross-referencing to Frampton and others (N.B. some of the functionality may vary, depending on the device used to read the book). The list of subscribers (which was omitted from another edition) is present, along with brief biographical notes on many of them, to show who was reading Maylam and what impact he would have had at the time.

The book is therefore a vital source of information for anyone interested in folk drama, including mumming. It is rigorously academic by the standards of the day, but also remains readable for general fans of the genre. This edition also contains updated versions of the early 20C photographs.

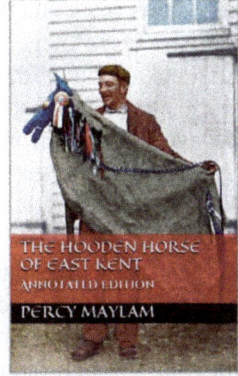

Available on Kindle

The Margate Tales

Stephen Channing

Chaucer's Canterbury Tales is without doubt one of the best ways of getting a feel for what the people of England in the Middle Ages were like. In the modern world, one might instead try to learn how different people behave and think from television or the internet.

However, to get a feel for what it was like to be in Margate as it gradually changed from a small fishing village into one of Britain's most popular holiday resorts, one needs to investigate contemporary sources such as newspaper reports and journals.

Stephen Channing has saved us this work, by trawling through thousands of such documents to select the most illuminating and entertaining accounts of Thanet in the 18th and early to mid 19th centuries. With content ranging from furious battles in the letters pages, to hilarious pastiches, witty poems and astonishing factual reports, illustrated with over 70 drawings from the time, The Margate Tales brings the society of the time to life, and as with Chaucer, demonstrates how in many areas, surprisingly little has changed.

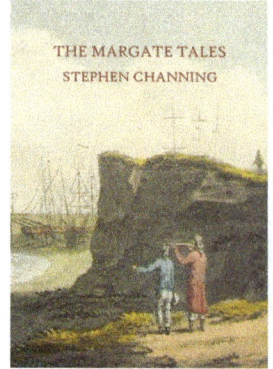

"substantial and fascinating volume…meticulously researched…an absorbing read"
(Margate Civic Society)

ISBN: 978-0-9559219-5-7

Turner's Margate Through Contemporary Eyes

– The Viney Letters –

Stephen Channing

Margate in the early 19th century was an exciting town, where smugglers and 'preventive men' fought to outwit each other, while artists such as JMW Turner came to paint the glorious sunsets over the sea. One of the young men growing up in this environment decided to set out for Australia to make his fortune in the Bendigo gold rush.

Half a century later, having become a pillar of the community, he began writing a series of letters and articles for Keble's Gazette, a publication based in his home town. In these, he described Margate with great familiarity (and tremendous powers of recall), while at the same time introducing his English readers to the "latitudinarian democracy" of a new, "young Britain".

Viney's interests covered a huge range of topics, from Thanet folk customs such as Hoodening, through diatribes on the perils of assigning intelligence to dogs, to geological theories including suggestions for the removal of sandbanks off the English coast "in obedience to the sovereign will and intelligence of man".

His writing is clearly that of a well-educated man, albeit with certain Victorian prejudices about the colonies that may make those with modern sensibilities wince a little. Yet above all, it is interesting because of the light it throws on life in a British seaside town some 180 years ago.

This book also contains numerous contemporary illustrations.

"profusely illustrated...draws together a series of interesting articles and letters...recommended" (Margate Civic Society)

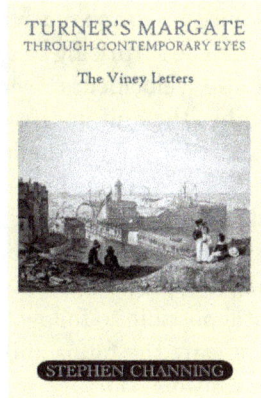

ISBN: 978-0-9559219-2-6

A Victorian Cyclist

– Rambling through Kent in 1886 –

Stephen & Shirley Channing

Bicycles are so much a part of everyday life nowadays, it can be surprising to realize that for the late Victorians these "velocipedes" were a novelty disparaged as being unhealthy and unsafe – and that indeed tricycles were for a time seen as the format more likely to succeed.

Some people however adopted the new-fangled devices with alacrity, embarking on adventurous tours throughout the countryside. One of them documented his 'rambles' around East Kent in such detail that it is still possible to follow his routes on modern cycles, and compare the fauna and flora (and pubs!) with those he vividly described.

In addition to providing today's cyclists with new historical routes to explore, and both naturalists and social historians with plenty of material for research, this fascinating book contains a special chapter on Lady Cyclists in the era before female emancipation, and an unintentionally humorous section instructing young gentlemen how to make their cycle and then ride it.

A Victorian Cyclist features over 200 illustrations, and is complemented by a fully updated website.

"Lovely…wonderfully written…terrific" (Everything Bicycles)
"Rare and insightful" (Kent on Sunday)
"Interesting…informative…detailed historical insights" (BikeBiz)
"Unique and fascinating book…quality is very good…of considerable interest" (Veteran-Cycle Club)
"Superb…illuminating…well detailed…The easy flowing prose, which has a cadence like cycling itself, carries the reader along as if freewheeling with a hind wind" (Forty Plus Cycling Club)
"a fascinating book with both vivid descriptions and a number of hitherto-unseen photos of the area" ('Pedalling Pensioner', amazon.co.uk)

ISBN: 978-0-9559219-7-1
Also available on Kindle

Bicycle Beginnings

The Advent of the Bicycle or Velocipede… and what people of the 19th century were really saying about it

Stephen Channing

Cycling is such a natural activity for millions of people around the globe now, it is difficult to imagine that a little over a century ago many regarded it as reprehensible, revolting, or indeed revolutionary. The best way to get a feel for what early 'velocipedists' encountered is to read the words of the times, and this book gathers into one volume the most enlightening, entertaining and extraordinary insights from contemporary sources.

The mammoth work (over 190,000 words, covering the period 1779 to 1912) contains race reports, legal developments, technical innovations and inventions, records, advertisements, acrobatics, clothing, poems, arguments for and against the new-fangled vehicles, debates over women cyclists, and a long travelogue, " Berlin to Budapest on a Bicycle" capturing the excitement of a forgotten age of adventure on two wheels.

Not all the inventions were two-wheeled, however. This book also reveals the numerous variations that came into being before makers standardized on the shapes we commonly see nowadays: tricycles, ice velocipedes, water-paddle hobby-horses... These are explained with the aid of numerous illustrations, covering the gamut from cartoons to technical drawings and photographs. Even the race reports demonstrate far more variety than we are accustomed to seeing: 'ordinaries' (penny farthings) versus 'safety' bicycles versus tandems, monocycles, dwarf cycles, tricycles, double tricycles, four-wheel velocipedes, horses, ice skaters, steamships...

Rather than a single narrative to be read in one go, it is an anthology of fascinating glimpses into cycling's 'golden age', providing a new understanding of a bygone age of experimentation and much amusement, whenever the reader dips into it.

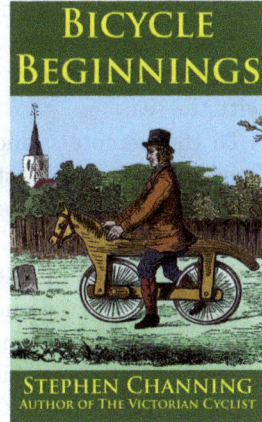

ISBN: 978-1-5210-8632-2
Also available on Kindle

The Call of Cairnmor

Book One of the Cairnmor Trilogy

Sally Aviss

The Scottish Isle of Cairnmor is a place of great beauty and undisturbed wilderness, a haven for wildlife, a land of white sandy beaches and inland fertile plains, a land where awe-inspiring mountains connect precipitously with the sea.

To this remote island comes a stranger, Alexander Stewart, on a quest to solve the mysterious disappearance of two people and their unborn child; a missing family who are now heirs to a vast fortune. He enlists the help of local schoolteacher, Katherine MacDonald, and together they seek the answers to this enigma: a deeply personal journey that takes them from Cairnmor to the historic splendour of London and the industrial heartland of Glasgow.

Covering the years 1936-1937 and infused with period colour and detail, The Call of Cairnmor is about unexpected discovery and profound attachment which, from its gentle opening, gradually gathers momentum and complexity until all the strands come together to give life-changing revelations.

"really enjoyed reading this – loved the plot…Read it in just two sittings as I couldn't stop reading." (P. Green – amazon.co.uk)

"exciting plot, not a book you want to put down, although I tried not to rush it so as to fully enjoy escaping to the world skilfully created by the author. A most enjoyable read." (Liz Green – amazon.co.uk)

"an excellent read. I cannot wait for the next part of the trilogy from this talented author. You will not want to put it down" (B. Burchell – amazon.co.uk)

ISBN: 978-0-9559219-9-5
Also available on Kindle

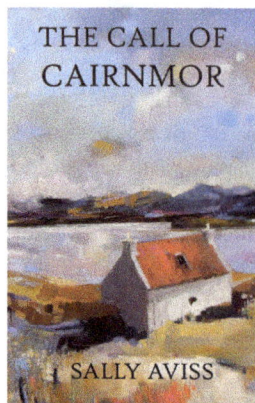

Changing Tides, Changing Times

Book Two of the Cairnmor Trilogy

Sally Aviss

In the dense jungle of Malaya in 1942, Doctor Rachel Curtis stumbles across a mysterious, unidentifiable stranger, badly injured and close to death.

Four years earlier in 1938 in London, Katherine Stewart and her husband Alex come into conflict with their differing needs while Alex's father, Alastair, knows he must keep his deeper feelings hidden from the woman he loves; a woman to whom he must never reveal the full extent of that love.

Covering a broad canvas and meticulously researched, Changing Times, Changing Tides follows the interwoven journey of well-loved characters from The Call of Cairnmor, as well as introducing new personalities, in a unique combination of novel and history that tells a story of love, loss, friendship and heroism; absorbing the reader in the characters' lives as they are shaped and changed by the ebb and flow of events before, during and after the Second World War.

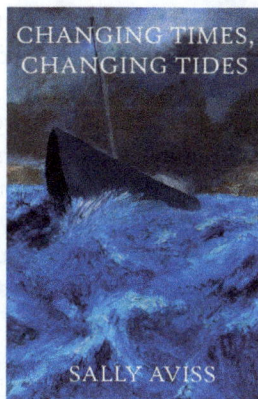

"I enjoyed the twists and turns of this book...particularly liked the gutsy Dr Rachel who is a reminder to the reader that these are dark days for the world. Love triumphs but not in the way we thought it would and our heroine, Katherine, learns that the path to true love is certainly not a smooth one." (MDW – amazon.co.uk)

"Even better than the first book! A moving and touching story well told." (P. Green – amazon.co.uk)

"One of the best reads this year...can't wait for the next one." (Mr C. Brownett – amazon.co.uk)

"One of my favourite books – and I have shelves of them in the house! Sally Aviss is a masterful storyteller [...She] has obviously done a tremendous amount of research, judging by all the fascinating and in-depth historical detail woven into the storyline." ('Inverneill' – amazon.co.uk)

ISBN: 978-0-9931587-0-4
Also available on Kindle

Where Gloom and Brightness Meet

Book Three of the Cairnmor Trilogy

Sally Aviss

When Anna Stewart begins a relationship with journalist Marcus Kendrick, the ramifications are felt from New York all the way across the Atlantic to the remote and beautiful Scottish island of Cairnmor, where her family live. Yet even as she and Marcus draw closer, Anna cannot forget her estranged husband whom she has not seen for many years.

When tragedy strikes, for some, Cairnmor becomes a refuge, a place of solace to ease the troubled spirit and an escape from painful reality; for others, it becomes a place of enterprise and adventure – a place in which to dream of an unfettered future.

This third book in the *Cairnmor Trilogy*, takes the action forward into the late nineteen-sixties as well as recalling familiar characters' lives from the intervening years. *Where Gloom and Brightness Meet* is a story of heartbreak and redemptive love; of long-dead passion remembered and retained in isolation; of unfaltering loyalty and steadfast devotion. It is a story that juxtaposes the old and the new; a story that reflects the conflicting attitudes, problems and joys of a liberating era.

"the last book in Sally Aviss's trilogy and it did not disappoint...what a wonderful journey this has been...cleverly written with an enormous amount of research" (B. Burchell – amazon.co.uk)

"I loved this third book in the series...the characters were believable and events unfolded in a beguiling way...not too happy ending for everyone but a satisfying conclusion to the saga" (P. Green – amazon.co.uk)

ISBN: 978-0-9931587-1-1
Also available on Kindle

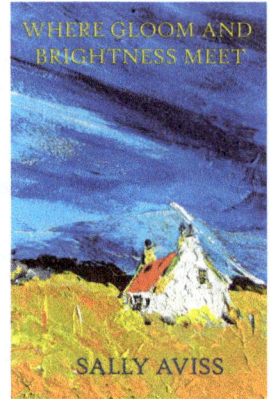

Message from Captivity

Sally Aviss

When diplomat's daughter Sophie Langley is sent on an errand of mercy to the Channel Island of St Nicolas in order to care for her two elderly aunts, she finds herself trapped in an unenviable position following the German invasion.

In the Battle for France, linguist and poet Robert Anderson, a lieutenant in the Royal Welch Fusiliers, finds himself embroiled in an impossible military situation from which there seems to be no escape.

From the beautiful Channel Islands to the very heart of Nazi-occupied Europe, Message From Captivity weaves factual authenticity into the fabric of a narrative where the twists and turns of captivity, freedom and dangerous pursuit have unforeseen consequences; where Robert's integrity is tested to the limit and Sophie needs all her inner strength to cope with the decisions and challenges she faces.

"The structure of the book takes you between the main protagonists and weaves their lives together as the story unfolds, add to that authentic research on the events of the period and you have a great story which keeps you guessing to the end." (P. Green – amazon.co.uk)

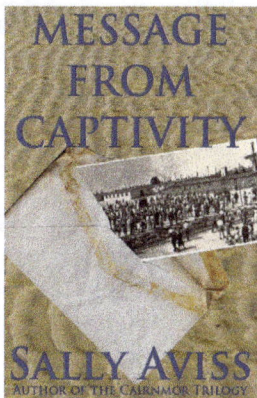

ISBN: 978-0-9931587-5-9
Also available on Kindle

The Girl in Jack's Portrait

Sally Aviss

When struggling barrister Callie Martin encounters soldier Jamie Rutherford on ceremonial duty near Horse Guards Parade, her life is changed forever. When Edie Paignton's ex-husband deprives her of alimony, she puts her lovingly restored Victorian house up for sale and finds her life transformed by a chance meeting with architect Ben Rutherford, Jamie's father. When successful businessman Erik van der Waals discovers an unknown name and telephone number on a piece of paper, he determines to meet the owner. And when mental health nurse, Sarah Adhabi, embarks on a dangerous new relationship, she discovers she is more than a match for the new man in her life.

Six people seeking an escape from their pasts; six people seeking redemption in the present; six people who find their lives interwoven and their secrets revealed.

But just who is the Girl in Jack's Portrait?

ISBN: 978-0-9931587-6-6
Also available on Kindle

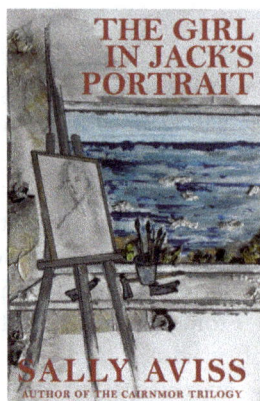

Reflections in an Oval Mirror

Memories of East Prussia, 1923–45

Anneli Jones

8 May 1945 – VE Day – was Anneliese Wiemer's twenty-second birthday. Although she did not know it then, it marked the end of her flight to the West, and the start of a new life in England.

These illustrated memoirs, based on a diary kept during the Third Reich and letters rediscovered many decades later, depict the momentous changes occurring in Europe against a backcloth of everyday farm life in East Prussia (now the north-western corner of Russia, sandwiched between Lithuania and Poland).

The political developments of the 1930s (including the Hitler Youth, 'Kristallnacht', political education, labour service, war service, and interrogation) are all the more poignant for being told from the viewpoint of a romantic young girl. In lighter moments she also describes student life in Vienna and Prague, and her friendship with Belgian and Soviet prisoners of war. Finally, however, the approach of the Red Army forces her to abandon her home and flee across the frozen countryside, encountering en route a cross-section of society ranging from a 'lady of the manor', worried about her family silver, to some concentration camp inmates

"couldn't put it down...delightful...very detailed descriptions of the farm and the arrival of war...interesting history and personal account" ('Rosie', amazon.co.uk)

"Anneli did not fully conform but she still survived, and how this happened is the real gem...There is optimism, humour, great affection and a tremendous sense of adventure in a period when this society was hurtling towards disaster." ('Singapore Relic', amazon.co.uk)

ISBN: 978-0-9559219-0-2

Also available on Kindle

German translation (with colourized photographs) available as ISBN 978-1-915174-00-0

Skating at the Edge of the Wood

Memories of East Prussia, 1931–1945…1993

Marlene Yeo

In 1944, the twelve-year old East Prussian girl Marlene Wiemer embarked on a horrific trek to the West, to escape the advancing Red Army. Her cousin Jutta was left behind the Iron Curtain, which severed the family bonds that had made the two so close.

This book contains dramatic depictions of Marlene's flight, recreated from her letters to Jutta during the last year of the war, and contrasted with joyful memories of the innocence that preceded them.

Nearly fifty years later, the advent of perestroika meant that Marlene and Jutta were finally able to revisit their childhood home, after a lifetime of growing up under diametrically opposed societies, and the book closes with a final chapter revealing what they find.

Despite depicting the same time and circumstances as "Reflections in an Oval Mirror", an account written by Marlene's elder sister, Anneli, and its sequel "Carpe Diem", this work stands in stark contrast partly owing to the age gap between the two girls, but above all because of their dramatically different characters.

"Marlene Yeo's account of living on a well to do farm is very engaging and her description of some of the small details of picking mushrooms in the woods, baking rye bread and skating in winter all brought the great political tragedy of the region down to an understandably human level for the non German reader … the description of desolation at the end of the book was heart breaking. " (Jonathon M Stenner, amazon.co.uk)

"Fantastic autobiography – beautifully written! Gives real insight into life and times in rural East Prussia in 1930s and 1940s. One of the best of several autobiographies of this period that I have read." (Mrs C.J. Pedley, amazon.co.uk)

" Fascinating look at a brutally ethnically cleansed province … This book was so interesting, I read it very quickly … The author does a great job of describing farm life in East Prussia as well as the chaos and insanity in that province in the waning days of the war. Gripping and highly recommended." (R. Miller, amazon.com)

ISBN: 978-0-9931587-2-8

Also available on Kindle

German translation (with colourized photographs) available as ISBN 978-1-915174-01-7

Ichigensan

– The Newcomer –

David Zoppetti
Translated from the Japanese by Takuma Sminkey

Ichigensan is a novel which can be enjoyed on many levels – as a delicate, sensual love story, as a depiction of the refined society in Japan's cultural capital Kyoto, and as an exploration of the themes of alienation and prejudice common to many environments, regardless of the boundaries of time and place.

Unusually, it shows Japan from the eyes of both an outsider and an 'internal' outcast, and even more unusually, it originally achieved this through sensuous prose carefully crafted by a non-native speaker of Japanese. The fact that this best-selling novella then won the Subaru Prize, one of Japan's top literary awards, and was also nominated for the Akutagawa Prize is a testament to its unique narrative power.

The story is by no means chained to Japan, however, and this new translation by Takuma Sminkey will allow readers world-wide to enjoy the multitude of sensations engendered by life and love in an alien culture.

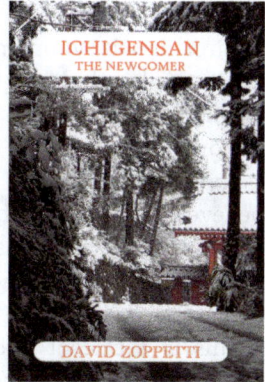

"A beautiful love story" (Japan Times)

"Sophisticated...subtle...sensuous...delicate...memorable...vivid depictions" (Asahi Evening News)

"Striking...fascinating..." (Japan PEN Club)

"Refined and sensual" (Kyoto Shimbun)

"quiet, yet very compelling...subtle mixture of humour and sensuality...the insights that the novel gives about Japanese society are both intriguing and exotic" (Nicholas Greenman, amazon.com)

ISBN: 978-0-9559219-4-0
Also available on Kindle

Sunflowers

– Le Soleil –

Shimako Murai
A play in one act
Translated from the Japanese by Ben Jones

Hiroshima is synonymous with the first hostile use of an atomic bomb. Many people think of this occurrence as one terrible event in the past, which is studied from history books.

Shimako Murai and other 'Women of Hiroshima' believe otherwise: for them, the bomb had after-effects which affected countless people for decades, effects that were all the more menacing for their unpredictability – and often, invisibility.

This is a tale of two such people: on the surface successful modern women, yet each bearing underneath hidden scars as horrific as the keloids that disfigured Hibakusha on the days following the bomb.

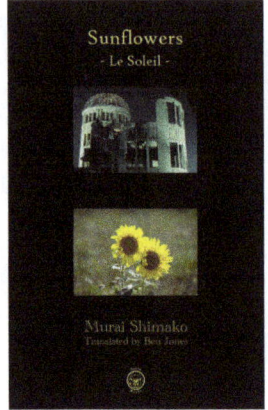

"a great story and a glimpse into the lives of the people who lived during the time of the war and how the bomb affected their lives, even after all these years" (Wendy Pierce, goodreads.com)

ISBN: 978-0-9559219-3-3
Also available on Kindle and Google Books

The Body as a Vessel

Approaching the Methodology of Hijikata Tatsumi's Ankoku Butō

Mikami Kayo
An analysis of the modern dance form
Translated from the Japanese by Rosa van Hensbergen

When Hijikata Tatsumi's "Butō" appeared in 1959, it revolutionized not only Japanese dance but also the concept of performance art worldwide. It has however proved notoriously difficult to define or tie down. Mikami was a disciple of Hijikata for three years, and in this book, partly based on her graduate and doctoral theses, she combines insights from these years with earlier notes from other dancers to decode the ideas and processes behind butō.

ISBN: 978-0-9931587-4-2

Courtly Feasts to Kremlin Banquets

A History of Celebration and Hospitality: Echoes of Russia's cuisine

Mikami Oksana Zakharova and Sergey Pushkaryov
Translated & adapted by Marina George

This is a book not only for lovers of food but also for those with an appetite for adventure and a thirst for the discovery of exciting gastronomic delights.

Russian history presents us with a rich tapestry of extravagant ceremony, characterized not only by the magnificent grandeur of individual courtly feasts but also by successive generations of nobility actively vying with each other to surpass the splendour created by their predecessors. Russian hospitality has always exuded a special vitality and sense of warm-hearted sociability. In Old Russia there was also a significant link between hospitality and the teachings of the Orthodox Church.

The political and social history of Russia has seen some very violent changes. The more shocking the political events of a country, the more brutal the cultural changes can be. At times, the differences between the past and the present are so extreme that one is faced with completely different worlds. Despite dramatic and often heart-breaking upheavals, we do surely have a duty to remember those distant roots that helped to nourish the present.

"Modern society contemptuously dismisses and sneers at the former way of life and deliberately breaks any connection with the past, which would always have been held to be so dear at the time." These words of writer, historian and theatre critic Yevgeny Opochinint were published in 1909 before the full horror of the revolutionary upheaval. The relevance of such remarks is surely as valid now as then.

Throughout history, special events have been an important way of imparting tradition from one generation to another, and symbolic meanings can still be found, if one knows the stories from the past. One just has to know where to look.

So, it is time to raise a toast in memory of bygone custom and tradition and to celebrate that great warm-hearted generosity of the Russian people.

ISBN: 978-0-9931587-8-0

Watch and Ward

A History of Margate Borough Police 1858 to 1943

Nigel Cruttenden

A comprehensive history of Margate Borough Police from its inception in 1858 until its amalgamation into Kent County Constabulary in 1943. It covers the origins of the modern police force, detailing the influence of local councillors, JPs, solicitors and freemasons, as well as central government and world events such as the Boer War and two subsequent world wars.

Alongside its new prosperity, the up-and-coming Victorian seaside resort also had an underbelly watched over by the boys in blue. The borough's residents and visitors encountered issues similar to those of today, ranging from nuisance dogs and speeding vehicles through to mental health, alcohol abuse, domestic violence and assault – even the occasional murder. This book therefore also serves as a social history of East Kent, offering local, social and police historians copious material for research. Whenever an incident occurred in Margate, a policeman would be lurking nearby: a police man, indeed, as there were no warranted female police officers until after amalgamation. Women did however also play an important role within Margate Police, as the book shows.

This is also an invaluable reference work for genealogists or other enthusiasts researching family history in and around Thanet. Family Trees are all very well, but they do not put the flesh on the bones, and even internet searches are quite limited. Full indices make it easy for modern Margatonians and Thanetians to check whether their ancestors might have been 'involved' with the police – on whichever side!

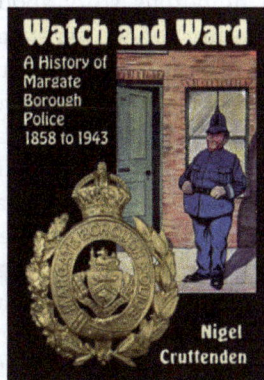

ISBN: 978-1-915174-03-1

Misadventures at Margate – A Legend of Jarvis's Jetty

Thomas Ingoldsby
illustrated by Ernest Jessop

This lavishly illustrated facsimile edition comprises a humorous story about the adventures of a 19th century London gentleman visiting the seaside resort of Margate. There he naively befriends a poor 'vulgar boy', only to have his trust betrayed... A quaint fable from the Victorian era, or a cautionary tale for modern-day DFLs coming 'down from London' to explore Thanet's nooks and crannies (and crooks and nannies)? Some of the faces depicted in Jessop's wonderful cartoons can still be found in the side streets around Margate Pier and the Turner Contemporary art gallery! The verse – in rhyming couplets throughout – forms part of the ever popular Ingoldsby Legends. An appendix also explains the witty references that pepper the poem, and some terms that may be unfamiliar to modern readers.

ISBN: 978-0-9931587-9-7

.